Northern Naval Superiority and the Economics of the American Civil War

Studies in Maritime History

William N. Still, Jr., Series Editor

Northern Naval Superiority
and the Economics of
the American Civil War

David G. Surdam

University of South Carolina Press

UNIVERSITY OF SOUTH CAROLINA *BICENTENNIAL*

© 2001 University of South Carolina

Published in Columbia, South Carolina, by the
University of South Carolina Press

Manufactured in the United States of America

05 04 03 02 01   5 4 3 2 1

Library of Congress Cataloging-in-Publication Data

Surdam, David George.
   Northern naval superiority and the economics of the American Civil War / David
George Surdam.
      p. cm.
Includes bibliographical references and index.
   ISBN 1-57003-407-9 (alk. paper)
   1. United States—History—Civil War, 1861–1865—Blockades 2. United States—
History—Civil War, 1861–1865—Economic aspects. 3. Confederate States of
America—Commerce. 4. Confederate States of America—Economic conditions.
I. Title.
E600 .S87 2001
973.7'57—dc21   2001000743

Permission to use the maps of "The Railroads of the Confederate States as of
June 1, 1861" is granted by the University of North Carolina Press.

Contents

Maps and Illustrations

Figures

Tables

ACKNOWLEDGMENTS

Many people have helped me in preparing this book. I thank the members of my thesis committee, Professors Robert Fogel, David Galenson, and D. Gale Johnson, for their many helpful comments and suggestions. Many other people contributed valuable comments, and I thank them for their help: Professors Timothy Fuerst, Joseph Ferrie, Mark Thornton, Richard Lindholm, Louis Cain, Lance Davis, Robert Gallman, Winifred Rothenberg, and Stanley Engerman. Participants at the following workshops also made useful comments: University of Chicago Economic History Workshop, Northwestern University Economic History Workshop, Loyola University of Chicago, Bowling Green State University, Villanova University, Auburn University, University of Oregon, DePaul University, Eli Whitney Cotton Gin Symposium, and the Institute for Humane Studies Current Research Workshop. Several anonymous referees also made valuable comments. I gratefully acknowledge financial help from the following sources: CIC Minority Fellowship, Division of the Social Sciences of the University of Chicago—PEW Fellowship, Claude R. Lambe Fellowship, Hayek Fund, Center for Population Economics, and the Charles Walgreen Foundation. Chuck Haberlein of the Naval Historical Center was very helpful in locating the photographs, and the Naval Historical Foundation quickly reproduced them for use in the book. Professors Lance Davis, Robert Gallman, and Albert Fishlow generously supplied me with some of their data. Dora Costa, Tyler Shumway, and Chulhee Lee helped with running the regressions. I also thank Marilyn Coopersmith, Carol Bridgeman, Cynthia Cook, and Peggy Rampersad for their many acts of kindness during my graduate years. Professor Max Hartwell provided encouragement and advice during the early years of my graduate experience. Al DiFranco generously donated his professional photography skills for the author photo on the jacket. The University of North Carolina Press graciously permitted me to use the map from one of their publications.

Amanda Kross helped in veryifying bibliographic entries. I enjoyed working with the members of the University of South Carolia Press. Fred Kameny and Alexander Moore gave me encouragement as my book wended its way towards acceptance. Catherine McGrady and Barbara Brannon were also a joy to work with. Arnold Friedman did a good job with the copyediting, as did Sarah Statz in compiling the index. I hope other first-time book authors are as fortunate as I was to have worked with and had the pleasure of knowing such professionals. Of my friends who have provided encouragement throughout my graduate years, I especially thank Diane Holliman for her support. Finally, I thank my parents for their help and encouragement all these years, but particularly my father for instilling a love of history in me.

Several journals granted me permission to quote from my articles. I thank the following:

"Cotton's Potential as an Economic Weapon: The Antebellum and Wartime Markets for Cotton Textiles." Reprinted from *Agricultural History* 68, no. 2, by permission (copyright spring 1994 by *Agricultural History Society*).

"Northern Naval Superiority and the Economics of the American Civil War." *Journal of Economic History.* 56, no. 2 (June 1996).

"Union Military Superiority and New Orleans's Economic Value to the Confederacy." *Louisiana History* 38, no. 4 (fall 1997).

"The Antebellum Texas Cattle Trade Across the Gulf of Mexico." *Southwestern Historical Quarterly* 100, no. 4 (April 1997).

"King Cotton: Monarch or Pretender? The State of the Market for Raw Cotton on the Eve of the American Civil War." *Economic History Review* 51, no. 1 (February 1998).

"The Union Navy's Blockade Reconsidered," *Naval War College Review* 51, no. 4 (autumn 1998).

"Traders or Traitors: Northern Cotton Trading During the Civil War." *Business and Economic History* 28, no. 2 (winter 1999).

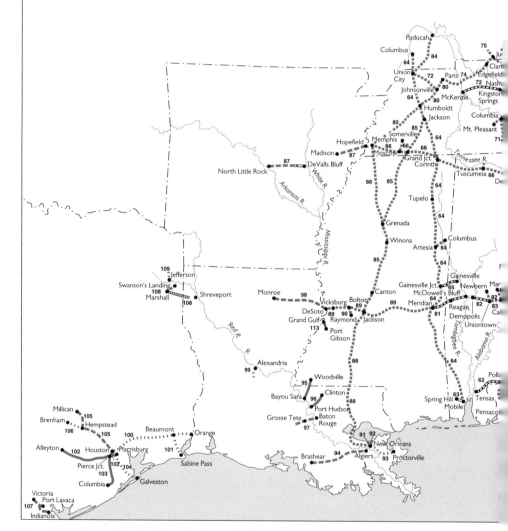

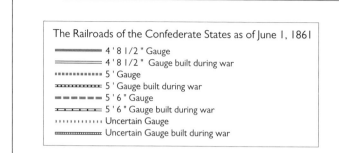

The Railroads of the Confederate States as of June 1, 1861

▬▬▬▬ 4' 8 1/2 " Gauge
═══════ 4' 8 1/2 " Gauge built during war
▪▪▪▪▪▪▪▪ 5 ' Gauge
▭▭▭▭▭ 5 ' Gauge built during war
▬ ▬ ▬ ▬ 5 ' 6 " Gauge
▭▭▭▭▭ 5 ' 6 " Gauge built during war
·············· Uncertain Gauge
▭▭▭▭▭ Uncertain Gauge built during war

From *The Railroads of the Confederacy* by Robert C. Black, III. Copyright ©1952 by the University of North Carolina Press; renewed by Robert C. Black, III. Used by permission of the publisher.

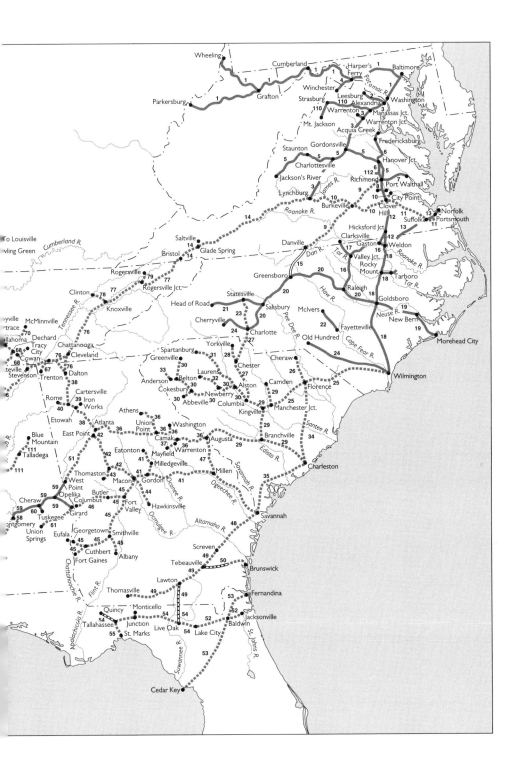

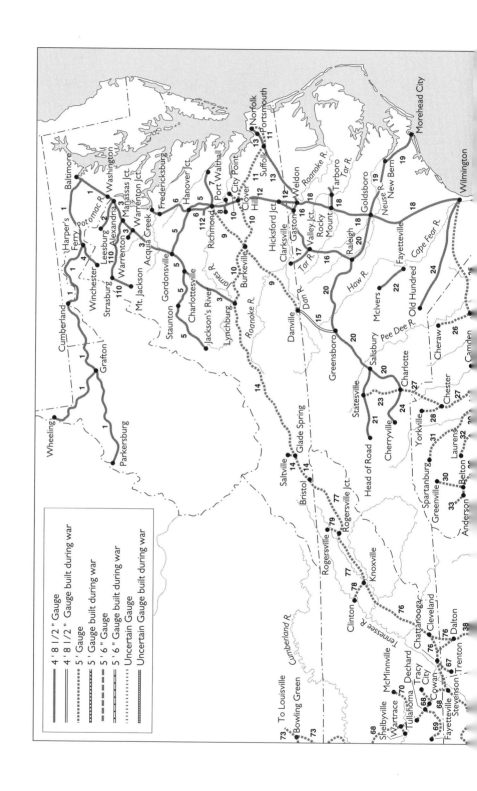

Legend

- 4' 8 1/2" Gauge
- 4' 8 1/2" Gauge built during war
- 5' Gauge
- 5' Gauge built during war
- 5' 6" Gauge
- 5' 6" Gauge built during war
- Uncertain Gauge
- Uncertain Gauge built during war

Wheeling

Parkersburg

To Louisville

Bowling Green 73

Cumberland R.

Clinton 78

Knoxville

Rogersville 79
Rogersville Jct. 77

Bristol 14
Saltville 14

Glade Spring

Head of Road

Chattanooga 76
Cleveland 76
Dalton 38
Trenton 67
Stevenson
Cowan 68
Tracy City
Tullahoma 68
Dechard 68
Fayetteville 69
Wartrace 70
Shelbyville
McMinnville
68

Baltimore 1
Harper's Ferry 1
Cumberland 1
Grafton 1
Winchester 4
Potomac R.
Washington 1
Alexandria 110
Leesburg 2
Strasburg 110
Manassas Jct. 3
Warrenton 3
Warrenton Jct. 3
Mt. Jackson 110
Acquia Creek 3
Fredericksburg 6
Hanover Jct. 5
Gordonsville 5
Charlottesville 5
Staunton 5
Jackson's River 3
Lynchburg 3
James R.
Richmond 112
Port Walthall 8
City Point 10
Clover Hill 10
Burkeville 5
Roanoke R.
Danville 15
Greensboro 20
Salisbury 20
Statesville 21
Cherryville 24
Charlotte 27
Yorkville 28
Chester 27
Spartanburg 31
Greenville 30
Anderson 33
Belton 32
Laurens
McIvers 22
Old Hundred 24
Cape Fear R.
Fayetteville 18
Pee Dee R.
Cheraw 26
Camden

Norfolk 13
Portsmouth 11
Suffolk 13
Weldon 18
Gaston 16
Valley Jct. 17
Rocky Mount 18
Roanoke R.
Tarboro 19
Goldsboro 18
New Bern 18
Morehead City 19
Wilmington
Raleigh 20
Haw R.
Tar R. 16
Clarksville 17
Hicksford Jct. 9
Dan R.
Haw R.
Neuse R. 19

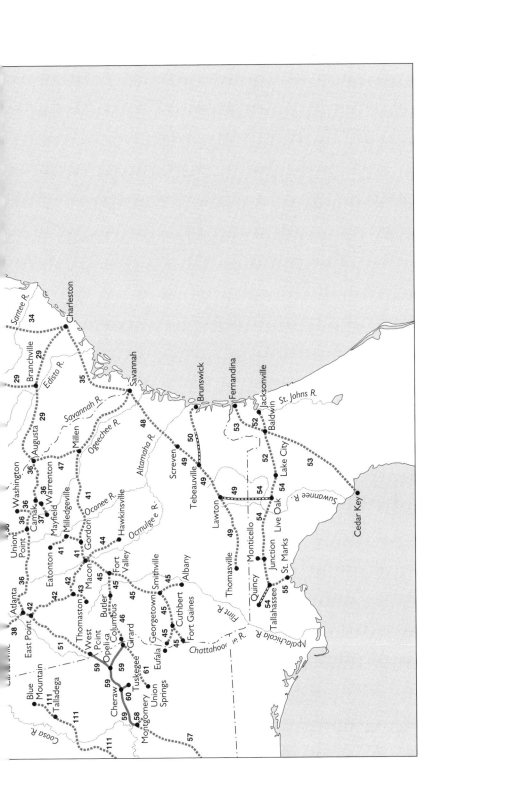

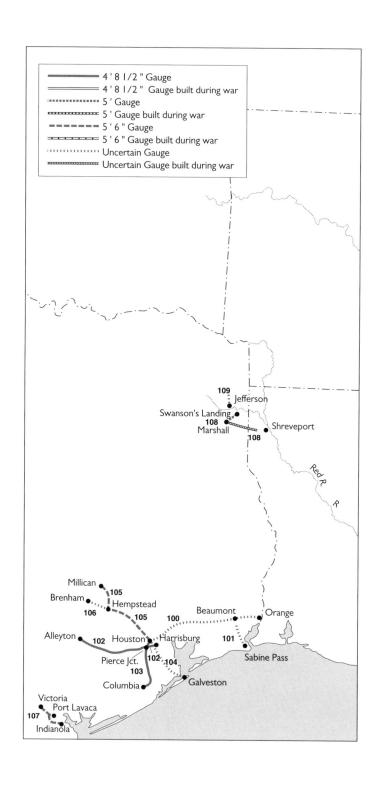

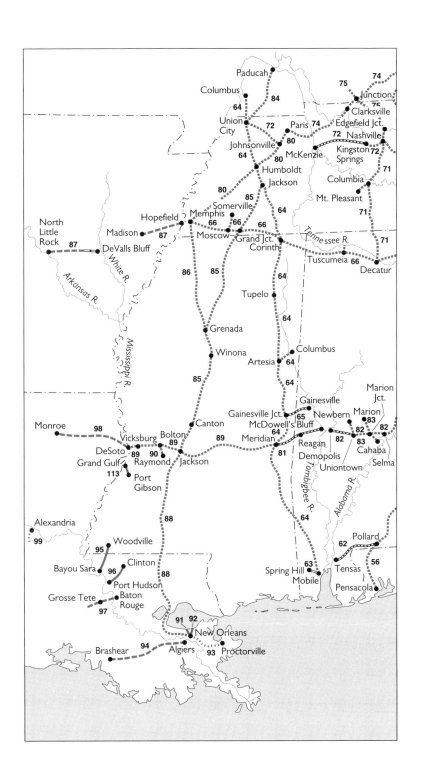

Northern Naval Superiority and the Economics of the American Civil War

Introduction

At the start of the Civil War, the Confederate states possessed three major war-making economic assets: raw cotton, cattle, and corn. Their raw cotton promised to be a formidable financial resource, while Texans boasted that their vast herds of cattle could feed the world. The Southern states produced sufficient quantities of corn and other grains, but they also imported grain primarily because Northern-produced grain was cheaper or more convenient. However, these assets proved disappointing. King Cotton failed to elicit European intervention, nor did revenue from its exports sustain the Southern economy. At the end of the war, a Texas cattleman's poverty could be "estimated by the number of cattle he possessed."[1] General Lee's troops went hungry and were beaten as much by their stomachs as by the Federal troops. Why did these assets fail the Confederacy? What role did the Union navy's blockade have in denying the Confederacy full use of these assets?

Given the South's relative paucity of manufacturing output, the Confederate government needed to import arms, munitions, iron plating for armored ships, ship engines and machinery, rail iron, railroad locomotives and cars, boots, cloth, niter, and other manufactured commodities. Given access to British, Canadian, and Northern producers, such deficiencies could easily have been remedied, assuming adequate financial resources (which the Confederacy potentially possessed, given its raw cotton asset). In addition, shipping such bulky materiel by water promised to keep the Southern railroads from being overloaded. How did the blockade affect the Confederacy's ability to obtain these supplies?

The Union navy's blockade has long evoked controversy and a wide range of opinions regarding its efficacy. Among the detractors are Richard Beringer, et al., Raimondo Luraghi, Frank Owsley, and Stephen Wise. Luraghi disputes the primacy of the blockade in defeating the South economically and, instead, attributes the defeat to the collapse of the Southern rail system: "The Confederacy was being defeated, and not, as the legend still maintains, because of the blockade. Simplifying the issue, one might surmise that the basic cause of defeat was, rather, the breakdown of the Confederate railway system."[2]

Beringer et al. believe that a collapse in morale, triggered by religious guilt, caused the South's defeat and that an "effective" blockade could, "not have equaled the task of crippling quickly so large and nearly self-sufficient a country as the Confederacy." However, they do not believe that the Union navy's blockade was effective. At best they view it as a sieve with varying-sized holes. In addition, the Union's failure to knock out or capture a few key Southern ports reduced the effectiveness of the blockade. Further, the authors conclude that even with these ports rendered useless: "in view of the Confederate ability to improvise, the quantity of consumer goods brought in throughout the war, and the relative Confederate independence of imports in the latter part of the war, it seems unlikely that a more effective blockade would have broken the military stalemate or seriously affected the capabilities of the Confederate armies."[3]

A third critic of the blockade, Frank Owsley, claimed that the blockade was easily penetrated, so Southern leaders were largely unconcerned about its economic effects. Instead, he discusses these leaders' self-righteous anger that England was allowing the North to perpetrate a "paper blockade."[4]

The most recent and most thorough student of the blockade, Stephen Wise, also criticizes the blockade. He asserts that the blockade was not a key contributor to the Confederate defeat, as it did not prevent sufficient munitions and supplies from reaching the Confederacy.

The blockade has its defenders. Edwin Coddington disputes the alleged ineffectiveness of the blockade: "Such analyses are unconvincing because they tend to divorce a study of the blockade and its effects from a consideration of Southern wartime economy in its entirety. It is hard to imagine a conquest of the South without the establishment of a blockade, defective as it may have been." Coddington agrees with Luraghi that the deplorable state of the Confederate railroads was a major reason for the Southern defeat, but he credits the blockade for starving the South of needed replacement rails, locomotives, and rolling stock. He concludes that "even an imperfect blockade was an important element in weakening Southern economy under the stress of war," and that the blockade running could only meet "the immediate, but not the basic requirements of Southern war economy."[5] He also believed that the Union chose to "loosen" the blockade when doing so would serve Northern interests (i.e. procuring cotton for Northern industry and perhaps to help the British cotton industry).

Naval historian Bern Anderson is a more enthusiastic believer in the blockade's effectiveness. He starts by crediting the blockade with disrupting the normal channels of trade to the extent that smuggling could never rectify. While he admits that other factors beside the blockade created the chaos in the Southern economy, he still gives it top billing: "Yet it should be recognized that it was the chief instrument for bringing about that condition [Southern economic chaos] directly or indirectly." Anderson continues by claiming "the Confederacy was drained of essential goods to the point that it could not continue the war," and that "the Union Army's major victories did not occur until the South was suffering from shortages imposed by the Union blockade."[6] Indeed, Secretary of State William Seward may have had the best gauge of the blockade's effectiveness: "the true test of the efficiency of the blockade will be found in its results. Cotton commands a price in Manchester and Rouen, and Lowell, four times greater than in New Orleans. . . . Judged by this test of results, I am satisfied that there was never a more effective blockade."[7] Economic historian Stanley Lebergott, too, commented on the burgeoning differential between the price of raw cotton in Southern port cities and New York. In 1864, cotton sold for six cents per pound at Houston and fifty-six cents in New York.[8]

The detractors of the blockade have relied largely upon the capture rates of blockade runners and the amount of materiel smuggled into the Confederacy. Marcus Price's work on the percentage of successful runs made by smugglers reveals that throughout the war the majority, even a vast majority, of attempts to run the blockade were successful (see Table I.1). However, Price himself touches upon some facets of these rates that demand caution in their interpretation. The successful blockade runner increasingly had to rely upon steam power instead of sail. By the end of 1862, blockade runners used *specialized* ships, so the supply of ships that could attempt a run became constricted. These ships were designed to elude the Federal fleet both by speed and design (light draft and special silhouette), but they required expensive "smokeless" coal. Price also cites the uncounted ships that turned back when sighted by Federal patrol boats and, of course, ships that didn't even bother to try to smuggle goods. Thus the capture rates are as liable to mislead as to illuminate, and a key argument in the detractors' arsenal becomes suspect.

Moreover, these historians may be asking the wrong questions. The effectiveness of the blockade cannot be measured solely by how much materiel was smuggled through it or by the success rate of blockade runners in piercing it. After all, for a high enough price, some people will always be willing to smuggle goods. Indeed, the claim that "a lot" of materiel

Table I.1. Number and Percentage of Successful Runs through the Blockade, 1861–65

Steam Vessels

Year	Attempts	Successful Attempts	Unsuccessful Attempts	Percent Successful
1861	1,411	1,407	4	99.7
1862	205	155	50	75.6
1863	545	472	73	86.6
1864	474	401	73	84.6
1865	108	90	18	83.3
Total	2,743	2,525	218	92.1
1862–65	1,332	1,118	214	83.9

Sailing Vessels

Year	Attempts	Successful Attempts	Unsuccessful Attempts	Percent Successful
1861	2,168*	2,058	108	94.9
1862	653	413	240	63.2
1863	458	259	199	56.6
1864	249	121	128	48.6
1865	45	13	32	28.9
Total	3,573*	2,864	707	80.2
1862–65	1,405	806	599	57.4

All Vessels

Year	Attempts	Successful Attempts	Unsuccessful Attempts	Percent Successful
1861	3,579*	3,465	112	96.8
1862	858	568	290	66.2
1863	1,003	731	272	72.9
1864	723	522	201	72.2
1865	153	103	50	67.3
Total	6,316*	5,389	925	85.3
1862–65	2,737	1,924	813	70.3

Note: Price counted as a "successful attempt" any run through the blockade, including packet stops along the coast. Many of the 1861 "attempts" were by coastal packets making stops at several small ports.

*Price's figures are off by 2.

Source: Price 1948, 1951–52, 1955.

Table I.2. Number of Successful Runs through the Blockade, 1861–65

| Year | Atlantic Ports | | Gulf Ports | | |
	Steam	Sail	Steam	Sail	Total
1861	1,036	765	371	1,293	3,465
1862	79	184	45	229	537
1863	347	66	78	193	684
1864	414	30	84	91	619
1865*	22	2	50	11	85
Total	1,898	1,047	628	1,817	5,390

* Through end of the war.
Sources: Wise 1988, various appendices and Price 1948, 1951–52, 1955.
Note: There were slight discrepancies between Price and Wise's number of successful runs by steamers (Price listed 1,118 versus 1,119 by Wise).

was brought through the blockade is inconclusive. We can also use the same evidence to make the blockade look effective. The fact that almost 5,400 successful runs (roughly 2,700 round trips) occurred during the blockade looks impressive until we realize that in a typical year, New Orleans alone had more than 1,900 vessels *enter* from the Gulf annually (see Table I.2). The number of runs is even less impressive, since Marcus Price employed a liberal definition of a "successful attempt." His definition includes packet-steamers that made stops at several coastal ports, with each stop counting as a "successful attempt." Thus, two coastwise packet steamers that made up to ten stops per trip made almost 800 of the runs made in 1861. Conversely, some of the captures counted as "unsuccessful attempts" included extremely small river vessels. Clearly, using such data gives an ambiguous picture of the blockade's effectiveness. Since the definition of successful attempts is liberal, using Price's figures gives a downward-biased estimate of the blockade that will be used throughout this discussion. Wise concluded his study by emphasizing the amount of military supplies imported through the blockade: "In terms of basic military necessities, the South imported at least 400,000 rifles, or more than 60 percent of the nation's modern arms. About 3 million pounds of lead came through the blockade . . . [amounting] to one-third of the Army's requirements. Besides these items, more than 2.25 million pounds of saltpeter, or two-thirds of this vital ingredient for powder, came from overseas. Without blockade running, the nation's military would have been without proper supplies of arms, bullets, and powder."[9] However, emphasizing the volume of military imports is an incomplete analysis of the blockade's effects upon the Confederacy's imports. Since the Confederate government's shortage of purchasing power has frequently been cited, finding that the blockade triggered a significant decrease in purchasing power would help redeem the blockade's reputation. The blockade raised the cost of shipping such materiel and eroded the Confederacy's ability to purchase war materiel. Second, the blockade raised transportation costs to high enough levels to *preclude* the shipment of many bulky products, especially railroad iron and machinery. Third, the blockade forced Southerners to import goods through less convenient ports; the goods imported via the Rio Grande at Matamoros (formerly spelled Matamoras)/Brownsville required a lengthy, expensive wagon haul back to central Texas. Fourth, the blockade combined with non-intercourse edicts to severely reduce the imports of Northern and European-produced civilian goods. The reduced flows led to shortages and higher prices and contributed to civilian discontent. Thus, although the blockade failed to "starve" the Confederacy of all necessary war materiel, it may have severely constricted the supply and therefore impeded the Confederacy's war-making efforts.

The focus upon imports has been almost myopic and also misses what may have been two of the blockade's most important achievements: disrupting intraregional trade and denying the Confederacy badly needed revenue from exporting raw cotton and other staple products.

The naval blockade disrupted established intraregional trade patterns. Thus, the blockade offers an opportunity to examine the costs of trade disruptions and a region's ability to minimize these costs. While we might assert that the blockade forced the Confederacy to less efficient avenues of trade and transportation, this is not a sufficient argument that such dislocation imposed high costs. Shifting from established coastwise trade to an increased emphasis upon Southern railroads and shifting the focus of foreign trade from New Orleans to Charleston and Wilmington probably raised shipping costs, but by how much? Were Charleston and Wilmington reasonable substitutes for New Orleans as entrepots? Were the railroads only a marginally more expensive mode of transportation than coastwise vessels? To answer these questions, we need to establish what the antebellum trade patterns were and why they developed as they did. An important facet of the antebellum trade was the coastwise trade, which, in the absence of customs records, remains ambiguous. However, the coastal trade was important, and although the war itself would disrupt such trade, the use of Southern coasters to transfer produce from region to region might have spared the railroads from excessive use, lowered shipping costs, and hence allowed resources to be used elsewhere. The blockade disrupted this transportation system and imposed a cost upon the Confederacy. Was this increased cost significant?

Raw cotton was an important factor in the Southern hopes for independence. Antebellum Southerners were confident about the outcome of any possible hostilities with the Northern states. In addition to their presumed military prowess, Southerners boasted of a potent economic weapon: their domination of the world market for raw cotton. During the waning days of the antebellum period, the South supplied the western world with 75 to 80 percent of its raw cotton. British observers bemoaned Lancashire's dependence upon Southern-grown raw cotton, and parliamentary investigations highlighted the inability of East India to produce a satisfactory substitute for Southern cotton. Northerners, too, admitted that Southern dominance of the raw cotton market might play a role in the upcoming struggle. Abraham Lincoln's secretary of state, William Seward, took pains to insure that Europeans received a flow of Southern-grown cotton, and Lincoln implemented policies to get cotton out of the South for textile manufacturers. Southerners were aware of European and Northern uneasiness regarding the South's dominance. South Carolina Senator James Hammond boasted, "No, you dare not make war on cotton. No power on earth dares to make war upon it. Cotton is king!"[10] Even the more sober Jefferson Davis couldn't resist claiming that "cotton would pay all debts of war and force New England into penury and starvation."[11]

The South had two obvious strategies for using its price-setting power: either attempt to coerce European intervention by withholding *all* exports of raw cotton or attempt to create a cartel that would reduce the quantity of exports to a level that earned monopoly profits. Throughout the South there was widespread belief that an informal embargo on the export of raw cotton from Southern ports would coerce Europeans into intervening in any potential war, but the belief was mistaken. Southerners only belatedly grasped cotton's true potential as an economic weapon. The latter strategy of exploiting the region's price-setting power could have been implemented by placing an export duty on raw cotton or indirectly by drafting white men into the military or slaves into a military construction corps.

Because of raw cotton's importance, I will focus more upon Southern exports of raw cotton during the Civil War than do most books on the blockade. It differs in two key ways from previous attempts to gauge the blockade's effect on Southern raw cotton exports. It is the first attempt to measure the shortfall in revenue from exports of raw cotton during the war. While previous historians have either noted the significant price differential between raw cotton prices at Southern ports and New York or Liverpool, or the drastic reduction in the volume of raw cotton exports from the Southern states during the war, no one has combined the two effects and attempted to gauge the blockade's effect upon Southern revenues from raw cotton. This omission is surprising, since raw cotton was the most important Southern export staple. A significant reduction in revenue from raw cotton exports would have disrupted the Southern economy, and such a disruption would have weakened the region's ability to wage a war. Second, because the Southern states were the main supplier of raw cotton to Europe and the Northern states, they possessed price-setting power in the market for raw cotton. By acting collectively and reducing the supply of raw cotton, Southerners could have increased their profits, and such an exploitation of their price-setting power would have made the Confederacy economically and militarily more formidable, thereby enhancing its chances for independence. Therefore, I will develop a counterfactual comparing actual revenue from exporting raw cotton during the Civil War with a hypothetical revenue stream earned by a South exploiting its price-setting power. However, some contemporary observers and historians believe that the world demand for raw cotton was on the verge of a sharp temporary or prolonged downturn. Since the state of the world markets for raw cotton and cotton textiles is important both for ascertaining potential revenue from exporting raw cotton and for the diplomatic history of the Civil War, I analyze the available data on the markets. The best guess is that the upheavals in the markets for raw cotton and cotton textiles were caused by the wartime shortage in the available supply of American-grown raw cotton and not by any imminent downturn in demand.

The South's price-setting power did not enable the Confederacy to gain its independence. Europeans did not intervene when confronted with the informal embargo on raw cotton exports, while the South's collective price-setting power netted little in the face of an unexpectedly stringent Union naval blockade. While the latter point might seem to imply that the Confederacy could never have been able to use its price-setting power, it is important to emphasize how surprising the blockade's stringency was. Ex ante, Europeans and Southerners alike did not think that the North was capable of effectively blockading the South. In the unlikely event that the North established such a blockade, many Southerners assumed that the European powers would, in their thirst for raw cotton, sweep away the Union warships. Instead, the blockade reduced exports of raw cotton, but Southerners did not gain from the ensuing price increases. The dramatic increases in the cost of transporting raw cotton from blockaded Southern ports to European and Northern ports accounted for almost all of the increase in prices in Europe and the North.

Part I

THE ANTEBELLUM
SOUTHERN ECONOMY

1

AN OVERVIEW OF THE ANTEBELLUM SOUTHERN ECONOMY

I. Antebellum Imports and Exports

Southern ports were leading exporters of domestic produce. Although New York was the largest, New Orleans, Mobile, Charleston, and Savannah ranked second through fifth. New Orleans had about 90 percent of the value of New York's domestic exports, while the other three Southern ports easily outranked Boston (the sixth largest exporter). Richmond and Texas also were significant export centers, rivaling Philadelphia in terms of value. New Orleans was the great Southern trade center, dwarfing all of the remaining Southern ports. Indeed, the value of its domestic exports was more than the remaining Southern ports combined. The antebellum South exported primarily staple products, ranging from raw cotton to naval stores. Raw cotton, of course, dominated the value of exports, but other staples such as tobacco, rice, naval stores, and lumber were at least locally important (Table 1.1). New Orleans exported almost half of the South's raw cotton, as well as the bulk of foodstuffs and provisions from the Mississippi valley (including goods from the upper Mississippi). Mobile was a large exporter of cotton, as were Charleston and Savannah. Richmond and New Orleans were the two main Southern exporters of tobacco. New Orleans exported $7.4 million worth of tobacco, while Richmond exported $3.0 million. Richmond's other lucrative export was wheat flour ($1.9 million). New Orleans had only $0.5 million worth of flour exports. Charleston had almost $1 million worth of rice exports, and Savannah also exported rice. Wilmington's exports were largely naval stores. Charleston had a smaller share of this trade. The Texas ports exported hides and a growing amount of raw cotton.[1]

Southern imports of foreign goods were relatively small. The region's imports ($30 million) were only one-seventh the value of its exports.

Table 1.1. Value of Domestic Exports from Leading
Southern Ports (in Dollars)

(Year ending June 30, 1860)		
Port	Total Value	Raw Cotton Total Value
New Orleans	$107,812,580	$ 96,166,118
Mobile	38,670,183	38,533,042
Charleston	21,179,350	19,633,295
Savannah	18,351,554	17,809,127
Texas	5,772,158	5,744,981
Richmond	5,098,720	41,483
Wilmington	650,092	0
Key West	580,165	401,919
Norfolk	479,885	14,783

Source: U.S. Department of the Treasury 1860, 317, 350.

However, this ratio understates the Southern imports of foreign goods, much of which were reexported from Northern ports. Still, an examination of Southern imports is illuminating. In terms of value of foreign imports, New Orleans took in over five-sixths of the Southern ports' total value. What wartime officials (and historians) would later characterize as luxuries comprised a significant share of the imports. Coffee accounted for over $6 million worth of imports. Surprisingly, no tea imports were listed (New York dominated this import for the United States). Some $275,000 worth of beer, ale, and porter; $600,000 worth of brandy, distilled spirits, and cordials; and over $1.3 million worth of wine (mostly in casks) came through Southern ports. Nor did Southerners neglect to import fine smokes, as some $1.2 million worth of cigars entered their ports. Over $800,000 worth of china, earthen, porcelain and stone wares also was imported. New Orleans imported $122,000 worth of musical instruments. More practical items included manufactured plain cotton worth $390,000; $2.67 million worth of cotton piece goods and other cotton manufactured goods; $700,000 worth of woolen goods; and $370,000 worth of gunny cloth. Fruits (green, ripe, or dried) accounted for another third of a million dollars. Molasses imports amounted to over $750,000. The Southern ports directly imported relatively trivial amounts (fewer than 7,000 pairs) of foreign boots and shoes. However, New Orleans did import $141,000 worth of tanned and dressed leather skins. Southerners imported large quantities of manufactured iron and steel, with railroad iron being the bulk of these imports (almost $2 million worth). Tin imports were valued at $460,000. The Southern ports imported no saltpeter prior to the war and only a handful of small arms.[2]

Although the United States was amply endowed with salt deposits, Southerners often found it cheaper to buy salt from British suppliers. The salt was shipped as ballast to the Southern ports (for return cargoes of raw cotton). Ella Lonn, the authority on the salt situation in the wartime South, cites a report of the adjutant general of Alabama stating that the Confederacy required, at a minimum, 300 million pounds of salt per year. The Confederate army needed half a million hogs per year for pork rations. Confederate authorities believed that fresh pork was unhealthful, so the pork needed to be salted. To salt pork, two bushels of salt (roughly 100 pounds) were need for each 1,000 pounds of pork and a higher ratio of salt was needed to preserve beef. Virginia was the South's leading producer of salt, and the state ranked second in the United States in terms of production and value. However, Virginia's output of 2 million bushels was not nearly enough to supply the entire Confederacy, so Southerners imported 6.5 million bushels of salt in the year ending June 30, 1860.[3]

Northern products and reexports of foreign products were more important sources of supplies for the South. For instance, Boston shipped 182,634 cases of boots and shoes to Southern ports in 1860. Indeed, some Southerners thought that Northern ports such as New York and Boston would not only lose from the cessation of the raw cotton trade but also from the loss of Southern imports of domestic products and foreign products sent via the North. *DeBow's Review* summarized this belief:

> The fact must continually be borne in mind that the Middle and New England States can, of themselves, have little or no trade with England and Western Europe, because they are producers of the same articles. New England competes with Old England in the purchase of raw materials and food, and the sales of manufactured articles. There are no trading interests between them. Of the importations that are brought into New York, a large portion goes to the South, which raised the produce with which they were purchased through New York commercial houses. . . . What England receives is Southern produce, direct from the South; but what she sends to the North, that is to say, New York, is on its way to the South.[4]

While the *DeBow's Review* author simplified the situation, Southerners consumed far more foreign products than indicated by the import statistics.

II. Grain Supplies

Southern agriculture held considerable promise for supplying Confederate armies with foodstuffs. While the antebellum South was not the granary

Table 1.2. Per Capita Agricultural Holdings and Production

	CSA	Non-CSA
Improved Land (Acres)	6.24	4.80
Unimproved Land (Acres)	15.78	4.46
Cash Value of Farms	$203	$217
Value of Machinery	$9.11	$7.36
Horses	0.192	0.203
Mules and Asses	0.090	0.014
Milch Cows	0.297	0.264
Working Oxen	0.094	0.061
Other Cattle	0.765	0.351
Total Cattle	1.156	0.676
Sheep	0.549	0.753
Swine	1.710	0.812
Wheat (Bushels)	3.454	6.378
Corn (Bushels)	31.05	25.12
Oats (Bushels)	2.187	6.914
Potatoes (Bushels)	0.730	4.717
Hay (Pounds)	238.3	1,627.9
Home Manufactures	$1.58	$0.45

CSA: Confederate States of America (eleven states).

Non-CSA: all states except eleven states of the Confederacy.

Source: U.S. Bureau of the Census 1864.

that the Old Northwest was, the region's per capita output of grain was only moderately lower than that of the rest of the nation (Tables 1.2 and 1.3). Although the region was not a large producer of wheat, oats, and potatoes (producing a little more than a third of the per capita output of the rest of the nation), its output of corn made up much of the deficit. While Southern per capita output of grain largely matched that of Northern states in quantity (if not in mix), there were some troubling differences. Since there were generally fewer people per square mile in the Southern states, the available wheat and corn were spread out. Table 1.4 shows the "density" of corn and wheat production. Tennessee had almost double the bushels of corn per square mile of any state in the Confederacy. However, Indiana and Illinois each had almost twice as many bushels per square mile as Tennessee. Exacerbating the spread-out Southern production of grain, the Southern states possessed fewer miles of railroads per thousand square miles. Ohio, Indiana, and Illinois each had almost twice as many miles of

Table 1.3. Per Capita Grain Production in the Southern States (In Bushels)

	Wheat	Corn	Oats	Potatoes	Hay*
Alabama	1.26	34.46	0.71	0.51	129.0
Arkansas	2.20	40.93	1.09	0.96	43.0
Florida	0.02	20.18	0.33	0.13	163.5
Georgia	2.41	29.11	1.17	0.29	87.9
Louisiana	0.05	23.80	0.13	0.42	148.9
Mississippi	0.74	36.72	0.28	0.52	83.2
North Carolina	4.78	30.30	2.80	0.84	365.4
South Carolina	1.83	21.41	1.33	0.32	248.9
Tennessee	4.92	46.94	2.04	1.07	258.6
Texas	2.45	27.31	1.63	0.29	39.3
Virginia	8.23	24.01	6.38	1.44	557.7
Confederate States	3.45	31.05	2.19	0.73	238.3
Non-Confederate States	6.38	25.12	6.91	4.72	1627.9
Kentucky	6.40	55.42	4.00	1.52	274.3
Missouri	3.58	61.67	3.11	1.68	678.6

* Hay is in pounds

Source: U.S. Bureau of the Census 1864.

railroads per thousand square miles as any Confederate state except for South Carolina. In addition, the three Northern states had many navigable miles of canal, river, and lake transportation.

Historian Louis Schmidt wrote in 1920 that the Southern states bought 10 million bushels of wheat per annum from outside the region. Three states produced significantly less grain than the region as a whole and were importers of grain whether intra- or interregionally: Florida, Louisiana, and South Carolina. South Carolina probably received much of its grain from neighboring states. Louisiana received most of its grain from upriver.

Although New Orleans was losing her preeminence as an exporter of western grain, the city continued to receive much of its grain from the Old Northwest. The exports of grains and flour from New Orleans fell sharply between 1858 and 1859. Concurrently, the amount of flour retained in New Orleans gradually increased over time, but some of the grains "retained" at New Orleans were distributed throughout the region. During the four years 1857–61, an average of over half a million barrels of flour per year were retained in New Orleans (see Table 1.5). Receipts of wheat and the amount of wheat retained in New Orleans had dwindled to insignificance

Table 1.4. Concentration of Grain and Railroads in the South

State	Bushels Per Square Mile Corn	Wheat	Railroads*
Alabama	646	24	15
Arkansas	340	18	1
Florida	48	0	7
Georgia	531	44	24
Louisiana	349	1	7
Mississippi	627	12	18
North Carolina	668	105	20
South Carolina	615	52	40
Tennessee	1,113	119	26
Texas	70	6	1
Virginia	625	214	29
Ohio	1,768	364	75
Indiana	2,060	450	63
Illinois	2,081	436	52
Kentucky	1,700	196	15
Missouri	1,082	63	12

* Per 1,000 square miles.
Source: U.S. Bureau of the Census 1862, 121, 200, 221–28.

Table 1.5. Grain Receipts, Exports, and Retained at New Orleans

Year*	Flour (barrels) Receipts	Exports	Retained	Corn (sacks) Receipts	Exports	Retained
1856	1,120,974	729,442	391,532	1,990,995	1,676,075	314,920
1857	1,290,597	904,910	385,687	1,437,051	711,628	725,423
1858	1,538,742	1,052,756	485,986	1,289,665	858,905	430,760
1859	1,084,978	605,500	479,478	759,438	175,583	583,855
1860	965,860	386,511	579,349	1,722,039	652,370	1,069,669
1861	1,009,201	448,893	560,308	3,833,911	1,545,490	2,288,421
1862	281,645			315,652		
1863	264,601			165,220		
1864	399,897			410,138		
1865	790,824			553,273		

Note: No export figures were listed for 1862 on.
Retained: May include flour and corn that was later shipped upriver.
*ending 8/31, i.e. 1856 = September 1, 1855, to August 31, 1856.
Sources: New Orleans *Price Current,* "Annual Reports."

U.S. Bureau of Statistics (Treasury Department) 1900, "Monthly Summary of Commerce and Finance, No. 7, Series 1899–1900.

Hunts' Merchants' Magazine 53 (1865), 254–55.

prior to the war. Apparently, almost all of the flour consumed in New Orleans came from outside the city, as fewer than 80,000 sacks of wheat were retained in the city during the four years 1857–61. Corn receipts jumped in 1860–61 due to a bumper crop in the northwest states, and the amount retained at New Orleans reached over two million sacks. Thus, the city appeared dependent upon interregional sources for its grain food-stuffs.

The city also distributed Louisiana's sugar crop and Mississippi valley molasses. Most of these commodities were either consumed in the South or shipped to Northern ports, as relatively small amounts of sugar or molasses were exported to foreign ports.

Antebellum New Orleans served as a distribution point for Southern coastal towns and along the Mississippi River system. Unless the local harvests were particularly sparse, the grain went to New Orleans and was backshipped up the Mississippi as far as 300 or 400 miles. In addition to the river trade there was a considerable Gulf trade. Although the weekly totals of exports of foodstuffs from New Orleans to Gulf ports are incomplete, they suggest that significant shipments of flour and corn went to Texas and Mobile. Most of the cotton and foodstuffs received at the port or distributed among the Gulf ports moved on the Mississippi River or via coastwise vessels, since New Orleans was not a major railroad center. Mobile could receive supplies from the interior of Alabama via the Tombigbee and Alabama Rivers. Although some of the foodstuffs originated in Tennessee and Kentucky, much of the grain and packed meat came from Northern states.

The South's hay output was a potential problem. The states in the upper Confederacy had the South's highest per capita output of hay, but even Virginia, the region's largest producer of hay, produced only one-third the per capita output of the non-Confederate states. While Southern livestock probably subsisted to a greater extent upon forage and fodder such as corn-stalks than their Northern counterparts, the region's need for hay imports was ominous.

The region's holdings of livestock appeared adequate. The Confederate and non-Confederate states held similar per capita stocks of horses, but the Confederate states held advantages in working oxen, mules, and asses.

III. Meat Supplies

The South was well endowed with meat products. The wartime shortages of meat supplies did not occur because the region lacked livestock, but because the region possessed inadequate distribution and transportation.

1) Antebellum Beef and Pork Supplies

Pork was the main source of meat for Southerners, while beef was the second most important source. A cursory examination of census data indicates that the Southern states were amply endowed with swine and cattle (Table 1.6). The Confederate per capita holdings of swine were more than double those of the other states; in addition, the eleven states of the Confederacy possessed 1.156 head of cattle per capita, while the Northern states possessed less than 0.7 head per capita.

Tables 1.7 and 1.8 show lower and upper bounds for the "adult male equivalent" per capita supply of pork and beef in the South on the eve of the Civil War (see Appendix 1 for calculations underlying these tables). The assumptions underlying the tables are combinations of those used by Robert Fogel and Stanley Engerman, Robert Gallman, and Marvin Towne and Wayne Rasmussen. Although the antebellum per capita consumption of pork and beef in the South is ambiguous, most estimates place the consumption between 150 and 225 pounds per year. The high estimate of meat supply appears excessive, as the level shown would imply that, unless consumption was at unrealistically high levels, the Southern states were exporting meat, even if we exclude Texas. The low estimate implies that the states comprising the Confederacy, excluding Texas, produced slightly less than a half pound of beef and pork per day (for an adult male). Of course, Texas was the great potential meat export source for the South.

William Hutchison and Samuel Williamson also estimated the potential supply of meat in the Confederacy, aside from Arkansas and Texas. Their estimates for the beef supply are slightly higher than the "upper" bound estimates shown in Table 1.8, while their estimates for the pork supply fall between the low and high estimates shown in Tables 1.7 and 1.8. The attraction of Hutchison and Williamson's estimates is their attempt to link corn and other feeds to estimates of average weights of swine. The estimates show that Kentucky, Tennessee and Virginia possessed the largest swine in the South, while the swine in Louisiana and South Carolina were only half that size.[5]

Tables 1.7 and 1.8, along with Hutchison and Williamson's estimates, present a broad range of potential supply of beef and pork for the Confederate states. We need other evidence to decide which set of estimates is more likely. A piece of evidence tending to support the lower bound over the upper bound estimate is that, while the South was not a large importer of meat products, some meat was imported into the South from the Northern states (particularly the Old Northwest states of Kentucky and, perhaps, Missouri).

Table 1.6. Per Capita Holdings of Swine and Cattle in the Southern States in 1860

State	Population	Swine	Per Capita	Cattle	Per Capita
Alabama	964,201	1,748,321	1.813	773,396	0.802
Arkansas	435,450	1,171,630	2.691	567,799	1.304
Florida	140,425	261,742	1.864	388,060	2.763
Georgia	1,057,286	2,035,826	1.926	1,005,627	0.951
Louisiana	708,002	634,525	0.896	516,807	0.730
Mississippi	791,305	1,532,768	1.937	729,509	0.922
North Carolina	992,622	1,883,214	1.897	693,810	0.699
South Carolina	703,708	965,779	1.372	506,776	0.720
Tennessee	1,109,801	2,347,321	2.115	764,732	0.689
Texas	604,215	1,371,532	2.270	3,535,779	5.852
Virginia	1,596,318	1,599,919	1.002	1,044,467	0.654
Total Confederacy	**9,103,333**	**15,552,577**	**1.708**	**10,526,762**	**1.156**
Kentucky	1,155,684	2,330,595	2.017	835,959	0.723
Missouri	1,182,012	2,354,425	1.992	1,170,082	0.990
Total Southern	**11,441,029**	**20,237,597**	**1.769**	**12,532,803**	**1.095**
Northern States	20,002,293	13,275,270	0.664	13,083,216	0.654
Non-Confederate	22,339,989	17,960,290	0.804	15,089,257	0.675
United States	31,443,322	33,512,867	1.066	25,616,019	0.815

Source: U.S. Bureau of the Census 1864.

Albert Kohlmeier estimated the amount of foodstuffs shipped from the Old Northwest to the South. Since he was studying another question, he did not adjust the figures to reflect actual consumption of northwest-produced foodstuffs in the South. Albert Fishlow used export figures from New Orleans to adjust Kohlmeier's estimates and calculated the consumption of northwest-produced foodstuffs by the South. Table 1.9 shows a similar set of calculations, using the New Orleans *Price Current.* The results are broken down by year, whereas Fishlow used averages for four-year periods. The differences between the estimates in Table 1.9 and Fishlow's Table 1 are minor, and most of the differences may be the result of converting the various units of measurements into a common unit. The important finding is that an average of roughly 550,000 barrels per year of beef, pork, and bacon was consumed in the South during 1859–61. A barrel contained 200 pounds of meat, or roughly enough for an adult male's yearly consumption; in other words, the estimated shipment of packed meat into the South was sufficient for 550,000 adult males. There were 6.56 million adult equivalent males in the Confederacy. Confederate commissary officer Frank Ruffin

Table 1.7. Lower Bound Estimate of Southern Pork and Beef Supply (in Pounds)

State	(1) Beef Per Capita	(2) Pork Per Capita	(3) Meat Per Capita
Alabama	57.7	129.2	186.9
Arkansas	93.8	192.7	286.5
Florida	203.0	132.1	335.1
Georgia	69.1	137.7	206.8
Louisiana	50.8	61.3	112.1
Mississippi	65.5	136.8	202.4
North Carolina	50.4	135.2	185.6
South Carolina	52.0	97.4	149.3
Tennessee	49.2	150.8	200.0
Texas	433.5	161.3	594.7
Virginia	46.7	70.8	117.5
Confederate States	83.8	121.1	204.9
Without Texas	59.0	118.2	177.2
Kentucky	51.5	143.1	194.6
Missouri	70.1	140.4	210.6
Southern States	79.1	125.3	204.4

(1): Slaughter ratio of milk cows and oxen is 0.166666 (Gallman 1970, 12).
  Slaughter ratio of "other" cattle is 0.2 (Gallman 1970, 12).
  Live-weight of cattle is set at 500 pounds (Gallman 1970, 12).
  Dressed-to-live weight ratio is set at 0.53 (Fogel and Engerman 1974b, 95).
  Calves-to-enumerated cattle ratio is .31 (Towne and Rasmussen 1960, 283).
  Slaughter ratio of calves is set at .1 (Towne and Rasmussen 1960, 283).
  Live-weight of calves is set at 135 pounds (Grossman 1992, 225).
  Dressed-to-live weight ratio of calves is set at 0.53 (Fogel and Engerman 1974b, 95).
(2): Slaughter ratio of swine is 0.5 (Gallman 1970, 14).
  Live-weight of swine is set at 140 pounds (Gallman 1970, 14).
  Dressed-to-live weight ratio is set at 0.73 (Gallman 1970, 15).
(3): To calculate per capita rates, the populations of the Southern states were converted into
  Adult Male Equivalents. Children are weighted at 0.5 of an adult male; all females 15 and
  over and males 60 and over are weighted at 0.8 (Gallman 1970, 18 sets this ratio at .75).
Source: U. S. Bureau of the Census 1864.

Table 1.8. Upper Bound Estimate of Southern Pork and Beef Supply (in Pounds)

State	(1) Beef Per Capita	(2) Pork Per Capita	(3) Meat Per Capita
Alabama	89.2	319.6	408.8
Arkansas	145.0	476.4	621.4
Florida	313.8	326.8	640.6
Georgia	106.8	340.4	447.3
Louisiana	78.5	151.7	230.2
Mississippi	101.3	338.4	439.7
North Carolina	77.9	334.4	412.2
South Carolina	80.3	240.8	321.1
Tennessee	76.0	372.9	448.9
Texas	670.2	398.8	1,069.0
Virginia	72.2	175.1	247.3
Confederate States	129.5	299.5	429.0
Without Texas	91.2	292.4	383.6
Kentucky	79.6	354.0	433.5
Missouri	108.4	347.3	455.7
Southern States	122.3	309.9	432.2

(1): Slaughter ratio of milk cows and oxen is 0.166666 (Gallman 1970, 12).

Slaughter ratio of "other" cattle is 0.2 (Gallman 1970, 12).

Live-weight of cattle is set at 750 pounds (Fogel and Engerman 1992b, 302).

Dressed-to-live weight ratio is set at 0.55 (Gallman 1970, 19).

Calves-to-enumerated cattle ratio is .31 (Towne and Rasmussen 1960, 283).

Slaughter ratio of calves is set at .1 (Towne and Rasmussen 1960, 283).

Live-weight of calves is set at 170 pounds (Towne and Rasmussen 1960, 283).

Dressed-to-live weight ratio of calves is set at 0.55 (Gallman 1970, 19).

(2): Slaughter ratio of swine is 0.866 (Towne and Rasmussen 1960, 283).

Live-weight of swine is set at 192 pounds (Gallman 1970, 14).

Dressed-to-live weight ratio is set at 0.76 (Gallman 1970, 15).

(3): To calculate the per capita rates, the populations of the Southern states were converted into Adult Male Equivalents. Children are weighted at 0.5 of an adult male; all females 15 and over and males 60 and over are weighted at 0.8 (Gallman 1970, 18 sets this ratio at .75).

Source: U. S. Bureau of the Census 1864.

Table 1.9. Estimated Consumption of Imported Packed Beef, Pork, and Bacon in the South (in 200-pound Barrels)

Year	(1) Imports	(2) Less Exports	Beef (3) New Orleans Consumption	(4) Plus Coastwise	(5) Southern Consumption
1856	61,059	36,179	24,880	1,346	26,226
1857	30,958	18,726	12,232	366	12,598
1858	32,672	19,511	13,161	536	13,697
1859	54,554	21,813	32,741	1,720	34,461
1860	44,934	21,699	23,235	3,019	26,254
1861	23,389	6,834	16,555	4,378	20,933
1862	13,622				
1863	41,355				
1864	53,082				
1865	26,541				

Year	(1) Imports	(2) Less Exports	Pork/Bacon (3) New Orleans Consumption	(4) Plus Coastwise	(5) Southern Consumption
1856	588,021	326,742	261,279	129,299	390,578
1857	575,132	298,962	276,170	121,398	397,568
1858	592,174	251,486	340,688	119,773	460,461
1859	589,397	210,372	379,025	132,135	511,160
1860	561,163	175,825	385,338	159,832	545,170
1861	479,701	134,727	344,974	123,989	468,963
1862	48,964				
1863	147,010				
1864	184,548				
1865	104,365				

Year: ending 8/31.

(1): Receipts at New Orleans "from the interior."

(2): Less the total exported from New Orleans.

(3): (1) – (2).

(4): Add back the amount of meat exported from New Orleans to "Other Coastwise," assumed to be Southern ports.

(5): (3) + (4).

Note: pork and bacon were reported in varying containers; the containers were converted into 200-pound barrels using weights reported by Leavitt (1934, 21).

Source: New Orleans *Price Current,* "Annual Statements."

testified that the states comprising the Confederacy consumed 40 percent of the three million hogs commercially packed in the United States during 1860–61. Ruffin believed that fewer than 20,000 of those hogs were packed in the Confederate states, although many probably originated in Tennessee and Kentucky.[6]

Given the south Atlantic states' probable need for imported meat products, northeastern ports such as New York, Boston, Philadelphia, and Baltimore loom as possible sources of meat. The antebellum coastwise movement of packed meat between northeastern and south Atlantic ports remains obscure. Some clues may be found in the price current sections of various Southern newspapers. The Savannah *Daily Morning News* intermittently listed prices for "Western" and "Tennessee" mess beef and "Western" and "New York" mess pork during the late antebellum era. During the same period, the Wilmington *Journal* listed prices for "Western" and North Carolina bacon, as well as "Northern" pork. However, the Richmond *Whig* and the Charleston *Daily Courier* did not list prices for western- or Northern-packed meat. Economic historian Eugene Genovese didn't believe that any significant trade in packed meat existed between the northeast and Southern ports. The trade reports for the northeastern ports support Genovese's belief. The Boston Board of Trade's *Review of the Market* shows that fewer than 15,500 barrels of pork and beef were exported coastwise in any given year during 1857–61, and much of this probably was shipped to nearby New England ports. The New York Chamber of Commerce *Annual Reports* did not reveal any information regarding shipments of packed meat coastwise. The Chamber's *Annual Review of the Provisions Trade of New-York for 1861* provided a description of the trade: "The packing of provisions for 1862 commenced under most unfavorable circumstances. The stock of hogs was unprecedentedly large. There was a general feeling of insecurity consequent upon the rebellion. The holders of hog product had met with serious loss upon their balance of stock of the packing for 1860 and 1861. There seemed little hope packing would result more profitable [sic] for 1861 and 1862. The rebels were threatening the principal packing points, and almost universal distrust and apprehension prevailed among the farmers and packers."[7] This description is interesting for two reasons. First, previous Chamber of Commerce *Annual Reports* did not cover the provisions trade, and second, no mention was made of any loss of coastwise shipments to Southern ports. The Philadelphia Board of Trade's *Twenty-Ninth Annual Report* did not list any coastwise movement of packed meat, although the report described the growing consumption of packed meat within a fifty-mile radius of the city. The surrounding region appears to have consumed most of the city's packed meat. Baltimore's meat packing had fallen off in the face of western packers, and the Baltimore *American and Commercial Advertiser* described the beef trade as being for "ship stores." Surprisingly, south Atlantic ports shipped small amounts of packed pork and beef to Philadelphia and New York City in 1860.[8]

In addition to the packed meat imported into the Confederacy, there were shipments of livestock. The best-documented movements of livestock were from Texas and also down the Mississippi to New Orleans and Mobile. Of course, the cattle shipped or driven from Texas are an intraregional movement, and this movement will be discussed later. The number of "Western" cattle shipped into New Orleans averaged 20,000 head per year just prior to the Civil War. The difficulty with the "Western" cattle is that such cattle may have originated in Arkansas, Missouri, or other states. A similar difficulty exists with the live hogs that arrived at New Orleans. Kohlmeier didn't believe that much livestock from the northwest states went to New Orleans, although his northwest states do not include Missouri or Kentucky. An unknown quantity of livestock was driven from Kentucky and Tennessee into South Carolina and other states. One clue is the report of some 15,000 head of cattle per year being shipped by the South Carolina Railroad into Charleston during the final years of the antebellum era.[9]

However, the rosy picture of the potential meat supply of the Southern states should be tempered by the realization that while those states were collectively self-sufficient in meat products, considerable intraregional movement of meat might be required. The ability to use the South's holdings of livestock to supply armies and civilians would depend not only on the number of animals but also the distribution. A situation where the animals were uniformly distributed would create different problems than one where the animals were concentrated.

Using county census data, a per adult male equivalent annual consumption of 180 pounds of beef and/or pork, and the parameters underlying Table 1.7, counties of significant surpluses or deficits can be identified. Table 1.10 shows the surplus or deficit by state. Tennessee was the eastern Confederacy's best source of pork, although the state's combined beef and pork surplus was rivaled by Arkansas, Georgia, and Florida. Most of Tennessee's surplus pork holdings were in the western part of the state, accounting for Nashville's prominence as a packing center. Growers in the Mississippi valley also depended upon outside sources of pork and beef. Louisiana alone required 17,000 tons of meat imports. The trade statistics reveal New Orleans' appetite for packed meat. More than 30,000 tons per

Table 1.10. Estimated Surplus/Deficit of Beef and Pork by State (in Tons)

State	(1) Deficit	(2) Surplus
Alabama		2,403
Georgia		10,120
Louisiana	17,932	
Mississippi		6,410
North Carolina		2,399
South Carolina	7,776	
Tennessee		7,949
Virginia*	28,000	
Total	53,708	29,281
Arkansas		16,542
Florida		7,849
Texas		90,128

(1) and (2): Supply of beef and pork taken from Table 1.6. The demand for beef and pork is estimated by multiplying the number of adult male equivalents in each state by 180 pounds.

* Virginia does not include the counties that eventually comprised West Virginia. These counties had a deficit of almost 8,000 tons.

year of packed beef and pork/bacon were retained in New Orleans during the late antebellum period. In the three large states of Georgia, Alabama, and Mississippi, whatever surpluses existed were confounded by collection and transportation difficulties. There were no obvious pools of surplus livestock in these states from which to draw meat supplies. Many of the counties with surpluses did not have convenient transportation, while the counties with deficits typically relied on shipments from other areas. Virginia and the Carolinas were collectively a region of deficit. Virginia required the largest import of meat products, up to 28,000 tons in the counties outside of those that would comprise West Virginia. However, if Hutchison and Williamson's thesis is correct that Virginia (and Tennessee) possessed the best swine in the South, then the estimate of the state's deficit is exaggerated slightly. Richmond and the other major towns in Virginia were the main areas of deficit, but during peacetime, these towns could easily draw pork and beef via railroads and, more importantly, water transport. However, given the influx of troops, government workers, and other incoming civilians, Virginia was going to require even larger quantities of imported meat.

As Table 1.10 shows, outside of Texas, Arkansas, and Florida, the Confederate states were 24,000 tons short of providing 180 pounds of pork and beef per adult male equivalent. During peacetime, the Southern consumption was augmented by a modest importation of packed meat from the western states and possibly an influx of livestock, suggesting a consumption level closer to 200 pounds.[10]

In general, then, Southern cities were the primary markets for meat products. Indeed, the largest importing areas—New Orleans, Mobile, Savannah, Charleston, Norfolk, and Richmond—required a combined 24,000 tons or more of meat products, but all these cities were easily accessible by water. Given access to the sea, the primary deficit regions could easily be supplied with meat. Other counties near the sea, on navigable rivers, or served by railroads also tended to import meat products. The counties that were relatively isolated generally possessed enough livestock to meet local needs and perhaps a little more. However, outside of Texas, Arkansas, Florida, and Tennessee, there were few convenient pools of livestock to draw upon to ship to troops in Tennessee and Virginia.

If the huge reservoir of meat possessed by Texas could be tapped, then the South need not have any meat shortages. Even under the low estimate of meat supply, the inclusion of Texas cattle raises the Confederacy's per capita supply of beef and pork by twenty-seven pounds, to over 200 pounds per capita. Such a supply, supplemented by poultry, fish, and other meats, would have provided almost two-thirds pounds of meat per day.

2) The Potential Supply of Meat in Texas, Arkansas and Florida

As shown earlier, the Confederate states east of the Mississippi (including Louisiana) were collectively almost self-sufficient in meat. While up to 10 percent of the meat consumed in the South was imported from northern states, Texas certainly possessed enough beef to offset the effects of losing the northern sources of supply.

Texas was the great reservoir of cattle for the Confederacy, and Arkansas and Florida were but poor runners-up. The 1860 Census listed over 3.5 million head (including milch cows and working oxen) in Texas. The difficulty was in getting cattle to the populous regions of the South. Since there were no railroads connecting Texas to New Orleans and the eastern Confederacy, cattle had to be trailed or shipped by water.

New Orleans was the most consistent antebellum market for Texas cattle. The extent of the Texas-New Orleans trade in cattle is reflected in the Jefferson City (an antebellum suburb of New Orleans) cattle market. The New Orleans *Price Current* published an annual review of this cattle market. The number of cattle imported from Texas increased from 31,518 in the year September 1859 through August 1860 to 37,467 in the following year (see Table 1.11). In addition, New Orleans had imported large numbers of "Western Cattle," although some of these cattle may have originated in Arkansas and Oklahoma Territory (Cherokee territory) or from further north. Between September 1859 and August 1861, receipts of "Western" and Texas cattle amounted to roughly 55,000 per annum. Texas cattle outnumbered "Western Cattle" in receipts during this period.

Of the Texas cattle received at New Orleans, Ralph Bieber believes that a greater number were driven overland than by sea, and were driven via two routes. On the first route, from central and eastern Texas, the cattle crossed the Sabine en route to Shreveport, Alexandria, or Natchitoches, Louisiana, where they were shipped down the Red and Mississippi Rivers to New Orleans. The ranchers in western and southern Texas drove their cattle to Liberty on the Trinity River, Beaumont on the Neches, and across the Sabine, Calcasieu and Mississippi Rivers to New Orleans.[11]

Texas cattle also were driven to other regions besides the Gulf. The Brayers reported that several drives were made to Memphis, Tennessee, in 1857. The lower Mississippi valley may have received Texas cattle, too. Attempts to market Texas cattle in Mexico met with failure due to lack of demand.[12]

Driving cattle overland was limited by both the extent of grazing land and the access to open land. Droughts significantly diminished the number of cattle that could be driven, while developed farmland impeded driving. In some cases, railroad construction could have alleviated the need for extensive overland movement of Texas and Florida cattle. One proposed extension was from Orange, Texas, on the Texas/Louisiana border, towards New Iberia, Louisiana, which would have shortened the overland drive between Texas and New Orleans. However, rail shipment was not a panacea. Shipping cattle by railroad elicited much unfavorable comment. A congressional investigation during the 1880s revealed that prior to improvements, "shrinkage" of cattle en route between Chicago and Boston averaged fifty pounds. The *Report of the Commissioner of Agriculture* in 1870 described the deleterious effects of rail shipments, concluding that "a thousand miles' ride takes 100 to 500 pounds of flesh from an animal."[13]

The alternative to overland driving and/or rail shipment of Texas cattle was shipping across the Gulf of Mexico. Shipping cattle from Texas to New Orleans or Mobile via the Gulf avoided the constraints of scarce grazing land and other obstacles to trailing cattle to the eastern Confederacy. Mobile Bay, in particular, was conveniently located, as railroads emanated from the bay to key areas in the upper South. One railroad ran directly north from Mobile into Mississippi up to Corinth, a major railroad junction just south of Tennessee. Another railroad system started from Tensas (across the Bay from Mobile) and passed through Montgomery, Alabama, to Atlanta, Georgia, and points east.

In fact, an important feature of the data shown in Tables 1.11 and 1.12 is the preponderance of Gulf shipping of cattle relative to other avenues of transporting Texas cattle to New Orleans in 1859–60. For the year ending August 31, 1860, the Jefferson City market received 31,518 Texas cattle, of which 24,313 reached New Orleans via the Gulf.

A steady number of Longhorns were shipped from Galveston and Indianola to New Orleans. There are good reasons to believe that Indianola was the more important of the two. First, the cattle could be driven to the dock and onto the ships at Indianola, whereas they had to be ferried to Galveston Island or shipped by rail. More importantly, Indianola was located nearer larger numbers of cattle. Although the bulk of the Texas cattle were not located near Galveston and Indianola (the two main port areas), there were still enough head in these regions to ease the needs of the Confederacy. There were 550,000 total cattle in the nine-county region around Indianola, more than twice as many as were near Galveston. In addition, there were more people living around Galveston than Indianola, curtailing Galveston's export potential. Apparently cattle did not comprise a significant enough portion of the Galveston economy, as two Galveston newspapers, the *Weekly News* and the Galveston *Tri-Weekly News,* did not always mention cattle in their annual summaries of Galveston trade before the Civil War. Nor did these newspapers list freights for cattle. The *Galveston News'* annual report for September 1, 1856, through August 31, 1857, listed shipment of 5,200 head of cattle from Galveston port. Historian Charles Hayes listed the receipts of cattle at Galveston as 4,494 in 1859 and 11,245 in 1860. Many of the cattle reflected in these figures were probably shipped from Indianola to Galveston en route to New Orleans. Sabine Pass, Brazos Santiago, and Matagorda were relatively minor exporters. The *Texas Almanac* reported that Sabine Pass exported 4,531 head of beef cattle for the year ending June 1, 1858, and the data does not indicate any significant increase in that amount. Lavaca drew upon the same sources of supply as Indianola, being west of the latter port on the same bay.[14]

The Mobile cattle trade was of considerably smaller scale than the New Orleans trade (see Table 1.13). Some of the cattle arriving at New Orleans were transshipped to Mobile, as some 2,500 head per year were shipped into Mobile via the Gulf from New Orleans or Texas. Indeed, most of the cattle shipped into Mobile came from New Orleans (although these may have been reshipped Texas cattle).[15]

Table 1.11. Receipts of Livestock at New Orleans

Month/Year	Western Cattle	Texas Cattle	Swine
September 1859	140	4,217	2,229
October	451	3,827	1,671
November	1,507	3,952	5,734
December	2,482	3,967	2,240
January 1860	4,549	2,491	3,389
February	3,525	1,159	2,282
March	5,328	540	4,331
April	2,885	1,062	3,415
May	1,743	2,540	1,949
June	741	2,246	1,045
July	360	3,203	1,317
August	444	2,314	1,320
Total	24,155	31,518	30,922

Month/Year	Western Cattle	Texas Cattle	Swine
September 1860	294	2,537	734
October	1,696	3,327	3,698
November	1,849	5,650	3,190
December	1,600	3,719	3,532
January 1861	2,705	2,257	2,833
February	3,273	1,332	4,306
March	3,300	2,069	3,088
April	2,268	1,734	3,022
May	359	2,393	708
June	2	4,844	462
July	0	4,130	632
August	0	3,475	435
Total	17,346	37,467	26,640

Note: For 1859–60, Western Cattle were off by 60 from the published total of 24,095. Texas Cattle were off by 1,000 from the published total of 32,518. Figures were double-checked against the daily receipts.

Source: New Orleans *Price Current* (September 1, 1860 and September 7, 1861).

Table 1.12. Shipments from Texas to New Orleans via the Gulf of Mexico

Month	Bales Cotton	Beeves	Other Cattle	Hides
September 1858	1543	1,087	767	354
October	3,858	1,292	358	36
November	3,562	1,473	461	2,198
December	4,375	1,088	30	857
January 1859	3,228	539	118	1,569
February	2,807	657	4	2,885
March	4,115	1,689	30	493
April	5,889	2,237	0	2,855
May	3,053	1,765	0	2,883
June	1,547	1,840	101	1,402
July	590	2,678	0	1,900
August	852	3,078	98	2,373
Total	35,419	19,423	1,967	19,805
September 1859	3,033	3,023	108	0
October	4,674	2,440	0	1,400
November	5,300	1,728	0	562
December	3,929	2,330	5	63
January 1860	3,340	1,535	22	782
February	4,070	721	0	5,098
March	8,327	582	0	5,205
April	4,099	2,062	56	448
May	1,593	2,973	68	1,669
June	1,517	2,142	0	2,938
July	189	2,437	0	801
August	613	2,340	522	1,249
Total	40,684	24,313	781	20,215
September 1860	1,073	2,161	349	466
October	2,884	2,287	119	1,715
November	3,289	1,821	11	915
December	2,620	1,397	0	1,275
January 1861	3,589	713	0	630
February	2,610	1,209	0	530
March	1,908	1,030	0	260
April	3,828	1,146	0	709
May	2,311	2,111	0	1,561
Total	24,112	13,875	479	8,061

Note: "Other Cattle" includes cows, yearlings, and calves.

Source: New Orleans *Price Current* and New Orleans *Picayune*.

There were two supposed disadvantages to shipping by sea: weight loss during shipment and high freights. The voyage between Galveston or Indianola and New Orleans took two days under normal conditions. According to a census report, the cattle were not provided with feed during the trip. The weight loss or shrinkage was exacerbated by the refusal of the cattle to lie down while on board, and Galenson estimated an average weight loss of between three and four and one-half percent of total body weight per day. In addition, rough weather that caused heavy rolling was very detrimental to the cattle: "Mr. Ruff claimed that the transportation of live cattle by sailing vessels was more satisfactory than by means of steamships, for the reason that in storms schooners, not being obliged to make the fast time required by the mail contracts held by the steamship company, could lay off and prevent the heavy rolling of the vessel, so disastrous to cargoes of cattle carried by steam vessels. To illustrate this fact he cited the instance of a severe gale to which a Morgan steamer and one of his own schooners were both exposed. The steamer lost 150 cattle, while his sailing vessel lost but one."[16]

The most unfortunate gap in our knowledge of the Texas cattle trade regards the costs of shipping. Observers rarely reported any information on freight rates charged by shippers. The business newspapers of the times listed freight rates for cotton (and occasionally for other goods), but they did not report freights on cattle. What information we possess is anecdotal. A correspondent with the Commissioner of Patents reported that in 1850 cattle from the Red River area of Texas were shipped down the Red River to New Orleans at a cost of $5 to $6 per head. An anonymous author wrote to *DeBow's Review* in 1859 discussing the potential for shipping 30,000 beeves by steamer from Indianola to New Orleans. The author cited a current freight rate of $7 per head, which, if true, certainly was competitive with shipping via the Red River. The postwar shipping rate for beeves from Texas to New Orleans was quoted at $6 per head. Given the preponderance of Texas cattle shipped via the Gulf rather than trailed, Gulf shipping rates must have been competitive.[17]

Aside from Texas, Arkansas and Florida held promise as meat exporting states. Arkansas possessed a greater export potential (about 16,500 tons) than Florida, but much of its export potential lay in the isolated western half of the state. Some export potential existed in the counties bordering Memphis, Tennessee. Aside from a small rail network around Memphis, the state's only other railroad was a short line near Little Rock. The Arkansas River might have been another potential means of transporting meat to the eastern Confederacy, but, in general, the state's potential as exporter was

Table 1.13. Imports of Cattle into Mobile by Railroad/Water

Date	Listed Cattle	Estimated Cattle
January 1858	255	265
February	123	128
March 1859	193	227
April	40	50
May	306	398
June	306	398
July	315	425
August	18	29
September	0	0
October	262	487
November	204	253
December	338	480
Total March–December	1,982	2,747
January 1860	271	488
February	410	446
March	530	530
April	307	349
May	121	156
June	41	53
Total January–June	1,680	2,022

Note: Very few cattle came into Mobile by railroad or by inland rivers.

The estimate is based on multiplying the cattle listed by the ratio possible issues for the month/existing issues). The newspaper did not publish Monday issues, and it is possible that Tuesday issues contained more listings than any other day of the week; however, any resulting distortion is liable to be minor.

Source: Mobile *Daily Register.*

confounded by poor transportation.

Florida boasted a surplus of over 7,500 tons. Perhaps 25 percent of Florida's export potential lay in the areas comprising present-day Tampa and St. Petersburg, but these towns were inconveniently outside Florida's scant railroad network. The only Florida railroad to connect with a railroad in another state lay in the western panhandle. A main line between the Gulf port of Cedar Keys and the Atlantic port of Fernandina (on the Atlantic near the northern border) could have been useful in ferrying Texas cattle across the state and avoiding the long sea voyage around the peninsula. Since Florida's eastern railroads did not connect with any in

Georgia, all Florida cattle required overland driving, unless shipped coastwise. In fact, there was a small coastwise movement of cattle prior to the war. James McKay began shipping cattle from Tampa Bay to Havana, shipping an average of 400 steers per month in 1860.[18]

Prior to the war, then, Texas, Arkansas and Florida cattle possessed a tantalizing promise. Certainly the three states possessed enough beef to supply large Confederate armies. Unfortunately, the states' isolation posed a challenge to the transportation system. Shipping via the Gulf would be crucial to tapping Texas' promising beef supply, while shipping coastwise would be useful to exploiting Florida's supply.

IV. Manufactured Goods

The Eighth Census provides a useful starting point in comparing output between the North and the South. In most manufacturing categories, the Southern states produced less than 10 percent of the value of the total United States production (see Table 1.14). The South's production of woolen goods, men's clothing, and boots and shoes were each less than 5 percent of total national output, while the region's production of cotton goods and leather were only slightly more than 5 percent. The Southern output of agricultural implements was roughly 6 percent of the nation's output. The census did not even list any Southern production of shovels, spades, forks, hoes, and scythes, although some of these tools may have been produced by blacksmiths on plantations or in the towns. Southern output of wagons and carts was about 16 percent of the national output. Southern output of railroad iron (12,180 tons) was about 5 percent of the national output. All of the car wheels were produced by Northern firms, as were all but 19 of 470 locomotive engines. The South produced less than 4 percent of pig iron (36,790 tons). The region also lagged in producing machinery and steam engines and guns. The Southern states produced about 14 percent of the value of flour and meal. Virginia was the nation's fifth largest producer of flour and meal, and that state produced half of the South's value. Virginia was the nation's second largest producer of salt, but its output was only a twelfth of the nation's. Southern states produced a trivial proportion of the nation's output of provisions. The Confederate states did produce more home manufactures than the rest of the country.

The South's deficient manufacturing capability meant that the Confederate government needed to import artillery, shoulder arms, munitions, uniforms, blankets, and medicines. Supplying the needs of its armies would be a daunting task.

Table 1.14. Value of Manufacturing Production (in Dollars)

	Confederate	Total U.S.
Agricultural implements	$ 1,018,913	$ 17,597,960
Scythes	0	552,753
Shovels, spades, forks & hoes	0	1,638,876
Boots and shoes	3,973,313	91,889,298
Cotton goods	8,072,067	107,337,783
Firearms	72,652	2,362,681
Flour and meal	37,996,470	248,580,365
Bar, sheet and railroad iron	2,449,569	31,888,705
(Bar—tons)	14,072	227,682
(Rail—tons)	12,180	235,107
(Boiler plate—tons)	0	30,895
Car wheels	0	2,083,350
Locomotive engines	133,000	4,866,900
(Number of engines)	19	470
Machinery, steam engines	5,750,650	46,757,486
Pig iron	953,903	20,870,120
(tons)	36,790	987,559
Men's Clothing	2,573,045	80,830,555
Provisions	145,000	31,986,433
Salt	451,484	2,289,504
Ship and Boat Building	772,870	11,667,661
Wagons	1,381,887	8,703,937
Woolen goods	1,995,324	61,895,217

Source: U.S. Bureau of the Census 1865, clxxviii–clxxxvi, 715–18, 733–42.

V. The Confederacy's Ability to Build a Navy

The Confederacy also had to supply its infant navy with manufactured products, particularly iron plating. In April 1861, the North had forty-two commissioned warships, while the Confederacy had none. Although the Confederate states began the war without a navy, the initial disparity in naval forces was not necessarily decisive. With only forty-two warships, the Northern navy was not large enough to effectively blockade every significant Confederate port. Nor did the North possess warships to control the western rivers. The Confederacy's initial lack of a navy was further mitigated by three other factors. First, Union naval superiority would take time to manifest itself, since the North would have to recall its existing naval warships from distant stations. To implement its blockade, the North would also need to buy and build blockading vessels. Second, naval technology was changing rapidly during the late antebellum period. The changing technology, particularly that of protecting warships with iron armor, had potentially rendered most of the Union vessels obsolete, while a Confederate navy built from scratch could immediately exploit the latest technology. Confederate Secretary of the Navy Stephen Mallory understood the opportunity presented by the new technology, especially the importance of ironclad vessels. He realized that the South could not compete in building standard wooden vessels, so he opted for a Southern navy based upon ironclad vessels.

> I regard the possession of an iron-armored ship as a matter of the first necessity. Such a vessel at this time could traverse the entire coast of the United States, prevent all blockades, and encounter, with a fair prospect of success, their entire Navy. . . . If to cope with them upon the sea we follow their example and build wooden ships, we shall have to construct several at one time; for one or two ships would fall an easy prey to her comparatively numerous steam frigates. But inequality of numbers may be compensated by invulnerability; and thus not only does economy but naval success dictate the wisdom and expediency of fighting with iron against wood, without regard to first cost.[19]

Finally, Mallory's hopes to gain naval superiority via ironclad vessels received a boost from Union Secretary of the Navy Gideon Welles's initial hesitance in building ironclads. Welles obtained funding to build ironclads for the Union navy only in the summer of 1861. After appointing a board of naval officers to examine the various plans for ironclads, Welles settled on three designs. The actual construction of the famous *Monitor* started only in late October.[20]

With the various delays facing the Union in assembling its naval might, the Confederacy was granted a grace period of several months to build its own navy. If the Confederacy had acted quickly to build several ironclads, its navy might well have temporarily, at least, contested control of much of the American waters.

The South possessed at least a limited shipbuilding capacity. Although the antebellum Southern shipbuilding efforts were dwarfed by Northern shipbuilding, the South was not starting from scratch. The Eighth Census listed 33 Southern "Ship and Boat Building" establishments with 546 workers. The Southern states built 84 of the nation's 1,071 vessels, including 45 of the 264 steamers. Virginia, North Carolina, and Louisiana built the most vessels. The Confederacy was blessed with two major shipbuilding facilities: Norfolk and New Orleans. When the Federals abandoned Norfolk in 1861, they failed to destroy the large Gosport naval yard, making possible the resurrection and transformation of the USS *Merrimack* into the CSS *Virginia*. Norfolk contained a large amount of ordnance and also was relatively close to the Tredegar Iron Works in Richmond (a firm with a history of producing naval ordnance and which could produce iron plating). The naval ordnance at Norfolk was critical. The Confederates distributed the ordnance among the various ports, and the ordnance enabled the Confederates to hold some of the ports against the wooden vessels blockading them. New Orleans had the facilities to build ships, too. Unfortunately for the nascent Confederate navy, the vessels produced in antebellum New Orleans were probably river craft, and it is unlikely that any warships or ocean steamers had been constructed there. Despite the city's inexperience at building warships, the attempt to complete two ironclads there before Farragut's fleet captured the city was testimony to the city's shipbuilding potential. Therefore, while Mallory did not believe that the South could immediately build a warship capable of sailing along the coast and engaging the Federal warships, he thought the South would eventually be able to construct quality steam frigates.[21]

Besides the limited shipbuilding facilities, the Confederate navy faced other difficulties. Domestically-manufactured iron products were destined to be in short supply. While there were considerable pig iron deposits within the South, much was located in remote areas. The Southern iron mills typically received their iron ore from Pennsylvania. The South possessed some iron mills (notably Tredegar in Richmond), but the region had always imported most of its railroad iron. At the outset of the war, Mallory sent a naval officer to Tennessee and Georgia to see whether any rolling mills could roll iron plating. The officer reported that, outside of Kentucky, none of the existing Southern iron mills were capable of rolling the two-inch plates needed to armor warships. During the war, three Southern rolling mills adapted their machinery to roll two-inch iron plate. Mallory pressed the Confederate Congress to create incentives to get iron mills to adapt their machinery to produce such plates. Machinery was also a problem, as the South had only a limited ability to produce the boilers and machinery. The Eighth Census listed 115 Southern establishments that manufactured steam engines and associated goods, and these establishments employed 4,570 workers. Southern steam engine manufacturers comprised about 10 percent of the total United States steam engine capacity, but most of these Southern shops were capable of producing machinery only for small vessels. Even the machine shop at the Norfolk naval yard was inadequate.

Mallory informed Jefferson Davis that this machine shop was incapable of producing heavy steam engines, and that Tennessee possessed the only machine shop capable of doing such work. There were several establishments in New Orleans capable of producing machinery, given time to adapt to the needs of warships.[22]

The Confederacy's lack of manufacturing capability was most glaring in its naval buildup. The Confederacy faced significant disadvantages in building a strong navy using domestic resources, and, indeed, relying upon domestic resources was probably the worst way for the Confederates to obtain a strong navy.

VI. The Antebellum Transportation System in the South

On the eve of the Civil War, the railroads of the Southern states did not form what could truly be described as a system. One could, upon a cursory examination, trace a rail route between Richmond and the Mississippi River and even on to New Orleans. This "system" ran through southwest Virginia into Tennessee. The rails then ran through southern Tennessee before drifting into Mississippi. At Corinth, Mississippi, the rails went west to the Mississippi River or south through Mississippi to Mobile. Further west, at Grand Junction, Tennessee, two railroads formed a route to New Orleans. Although several railroads comprised this east-west route, only at Lynchburg and Petersburg, Virginia, were there changes in gauge (from 4'8.5" to 5'). A more important problem than the gauge changes was the inability to "through ship" goods. Through shipments were impeded either by the railroads' refusal to allow their cars to be run on other rail lines or by the lack of physical connections between the different roads. The lack of connections between rail lines aggravated the problem of differing gauges throughout the South.

Unfortunately for the Confederacy, this combination of railroads formed the sole east-west rail link between the Atlantic states and the Mississippi River, New Orleans, and Mobile. Elsewhere, although railroads pierced many Southern counties, there were many troublesome gaps. A second east-west system was taking form from Savannah and across central Georgia, Alabama, and Mississippi to Vicksburg (and then across the Mississippi by boat to Monroe, Louisiana). This chain also branched off to Mobile and New Orleans. The chain was broken between Meridian, Mississippi, and Uniontown, Alabama (to the west of Selma), and between Selma and Montgomery, Alabama (the sluggish Alabama River provided a link of sorts between these railroads). Because of the Selma to Montgomery gap, west-central Alabama and central Mississippi were isolated from southeastern Alabama. The Montgomery to Girard, Alabama, segment (across from Columbus, Georgia) was of 4'8.5" gauge, while the rest of the route was of 5' gauge. Yet another gap occurred at Columbus because of the unbridged Chattahoochee River. At Savannah and Charleston, gaps occurred because the different roads were not physically connected, proving a boon to drayage, hotel and other local businesses of those cities.[23]

Two states, Arkansas and Texas, did not have rail connections with the other Confederate states. Antebellum Texas had the fewest miles of railroad relative to area of any state in the Confederacy. The railroads were largely concentrated around Houston (where five relatively small railroads converged). Outside of the Houston hub, there were two small lines in northeastern Texas and a small line connecting Victoria, Port Lavaca, and Indianola. In the case of sea investment, Texas was easily detached from the Confederacy, as there were no railroads between the Texas border and New Orleans or Baton Rouge. The closest to an interstate Texas railroad was the line to Orange, just within the Texas border, which was separated from Louisiana by the Sabine River. Arkansas had a railroad terminating just across the Mississippi from Memphis, Tennessee.

Florida's railroads were also inadequate for wartime shipping. Far western Florida was connected by rail to Montgomery, Alabama. None of the railroads in eastern Florida connected with any railroad in Georgia.

Due to a rail gap between Danville, Virginia, and Greensboro, North Carolina, only the Wilmington & Weldon and Petersburg railroads linked Richmond with Wilmington, North Carolina and, from there, Charleston and Savannah. Finally, the Gulf cities of Mobile and New Orleans each possessed only railroads to the north (the other roads around New Orleans were local carriers only), as no railroads connected these two cities. The two cities were linked via a large coastwise trade.

The Southern railroad web was quite vulnerable. The loss of Weldon, North Carolina, or Petersburg, Virginia, would render the defense of Richmond almost hopeless, especially later in the war when supplies of arms, munitions, and food run through the blockade became increasingly crucial. Losing Corinth, Mississippi, would sever (in terms of rail transport) western Alabama, Mississippi, and the three western Confederate states from Richmond. Even worse for the Confederacy, Corinth was near the Tennessee River, a river pointed dagger-like at the Deep South.

Many of the Southern railroads were primarily designed to ship cotton to navigable rivers, seaports, or to protect local commercial interests. The railroad lines were not intended for, and were inadequate for, rapid or massive transit of men and materiel over long distances. As an example of cotton's importance to many Southern railroads, cotton comprised over 75 percent of the freight weight of the leading articles carried into Charleston by the South Carolina Railroad prior to the war. Railroad shipments into Savannah reflected a similar emphasis upon cotton. Compilations from the Savannah *Daily Morning News* show that roughly 350–400,000 bales per annum were imported into the city by rail. Wilmington differed from these other Atlantic ports. In 1860, fewer than 23,000 bales of cotton were exported from that port. Naval stores, particularly rosin, formed the bulk of Wilmington's exports.[24]

Even had the Southern railroads filled in the gaps, established a standard gauge, and made linkages in the cities, their carrying capacity would still have been questionable. Few Southern railroads were double-tracked, since the antebellum volume of traffic did not warrant the expense. Unfortunately, the prevalence of single-trackage impeded an increase in rail traffic. One official reckoned that a double-tracked line could handle *five* times the volume of traffic as a single-track railroad.[25]

Thus the war began with Southern railroads incomplete and inadequate to the needs of east-west shipments. Changes in the operations between rail lines, improved connections between lines, increased trackage to bridge gaps between the lines, and double-tracking were needed not only to meet the demands of new wartime shipping patterns but also to offset the loss of water traffic. It should not be forgotten that the antebellum railroads were complemented by coastwise and river movement of goods. Water transportation was crucial for moving bulk goods. Historian Archer Jones provides a good assessment of the merits of railroads and river steamers: "Although the railroads . . . were primitive by modern standards, they enabled armies far from water transport to supply themselves. Yet the slow, short trains, which carried 10 to 15 tons of cargo per car, were less efficient than large river steamers, which could carry 500 tons of cargo. A river could easily carry more steamers than a rail line could trains, a factor counterbalancing the higher speed of locomotives. Sabotage or destruction by raiders could disable railroad tracks far more easily than it could harm steamers in a river."[26]

Animal-drawn transport was another mode of conveying supplies. Wagon transport required relatively large numbers of animals. A wagon carrying a ton of cargo required six mules. Outside of short hauls, poor roads and mounting forage requirements hampered wagon transport, so for long hauls, wagon transportation was prohibitively expensive. The Confederate states did not possess much wagon-producing capability, and, according to the census, the peacetime output of wagons in Southern states was one-fifth of the Northern states' output. Virginia, Tennessee, and Alabama were the largest producers of wagons in the Confederacy.

Collecting horses and mules was a difficult task. According to the Eighth Census, Virginia's per capita holdings of horses and mules were below the average of the Confederate states. In the case of mules, Virginia possessed fewer than three mules per hundred people compared with a Confederate average of nine per hundred. Tennessee had a relative abundance of horses and mules, but the Confederate troops in that state would need most of the animals. The largest per capita holdings of horses and mules were in Arkansas and Texas. To the South's misfortune, the areas best able to supply horses—Texas, Arkansas, Tennessee, Missouri, and Kentucky—were, for various reasons, unable to significantly meet the Southern military's animal requirements, so the need became more pressing as the war continued. Even if the requisite number of animals had been collected, there was another daunting problem: Feeding the large concentration of horses and mules, which was an even greater challenge than feeding the troops.

In conclusion, the Southern railroads, while boasting more total miles than most European countries possessed at the time, faced severe limitations. Although Union military leaders worried about potential Confederate use of "interior lines" (the ability to transfer troops from one region to another faster than your opponent because you are essentially cutting across the arc of a curved line), Southern "interior lines" rested upon a railroad pipeline of limited capacity. The Confederates might have been able to shift a few troops and supplies from Virginia to Tennessee quicker than the Federals could, but they could not switch large numbers of men or masses of materiel quicker in most cases. As the war continued, deterioration of the roads reduced even this modest capacity. Slower train speeds and inept handling of loading and unloading cars further negated whatever "interior lines" potential the Confederacy might have possessed. Thus, Southern railroads embarked on a mission for which they were ill-suited.

Jefferson Davis should have been aware of the severe deficiencies of the Southern railroads. When summoned to assume the Presidency, he undertook a railroad journey from Vicksburg (near his plantation on the Mississippi River) to Montgomery, Alabama. Instead of heading directly east all the way to Montgomery, the gaps in the rail lines between Jackson, Mississippi, and Montgomery forced him to head north at Jackson to Grand Junction, Tennessee. From Grand Junction, Davis headed east to Chattanooga, Tennessee. From there he journeyed to Atlanta. Finally, at Atlanta he traveled southwest to Montgomery. The trip was tiring, and one can only speculate on Davis's thoughts about his roundabout journey. The trip did not bode well for the Southern railroads' wartime capacity.[27]

VII. Conclusions

While the South possessed sufficient foodstuffs to supply field armies, the lack of fodder, isolation of much of the beef supply, and lack of manufacturing capacity augured ill if the infant country could not maintain its sea-lanes. Southern railroads were a fragile foundation to bear the burden of distributing supplies intraregionally.

2

THE CONFEDERACY'S ABILITY
TO SUPPLY TROOPS AND
CIVILIANS IN VIRGINIA

Although Confederate armies and civilians throughout the South were typically plagued by shortages of arms, munitions, fodder, manufactured goods, and foodstuffs, the most dramatic effects were felt by Lee's Army of Northern Virginia. What was the antebellum South's potential to supply troops in Virginia and civilians in Richmond? If there were sufficient supplies available within the Confederacy, did the distribution system fail the army? Did the influx of civilians into Richmond hinder supplying the troops? How did the Union military forces affect Lee's supply situation?

The late antebellum trade patterns, an important issue in their own right, offer clues on how Confederate troops and civilians in Virginia might have been supplied during the war. Did the South have the ability to redistribute available supplies to Richmond, in order to meet the demands of two concentrations of hungry mouths: Lee's army, including its unprecedented concentration of draft animals, and the burgeoning civilian population in Richmond?

Antebellum Virginia was typically well-supplied with grain and fodder and less well-supplied with pork and beef. However, even if the state supplied most or all of its food and fodder requirements, the initial distribution of these supplies would be important in determining the state's ability to maintain a large army. A situation in which the supplies were evenly distributed throughout the state would create different logistical problems than if the supplies were concentrated. If the state imported food and fodder, the sources of the imports would be an important factor. Food and fodder imported from the North might become unavailable during wartime. Conversely, food and fodder exported from Virginia might be retained to supply an army.

Information on the antebellum coastwise trade is useful in assessing Virginia's food and fodder supplies. The coastwise trade was not subject to customs, so the records are scattered. Previous commentators on the coastwise movement, including economic historians Robert Fogel and Albert Fishlow in 1964–65 and historian Diane Lindstrom in 1970, have been unable to definitively measure the patterns. Data compiled from cargo manifests published in various antebellum newspapers will shed new light upon these movements.

Virginia was the South's largest wheat producer. According to the 1860 Census, the state produced twice as much wheat as any other Southern state. Tennessee and North Carolina were the next largest wheat producers. The wheat supplies for troops in Tennessee and Virginia were conveniently located. However, in eastern Tennessee and the region of Virginia that eventually became West Virginia, Unionist sentiment was high and the grain supplies from these regions were less secure.[1]

Virginia also produced half the value of flour and meal of the Southern states. Indeed, enough flour was produced in Virginia to supply the state's citizens and to allow for some exports. Therefore, the state was likely to be able to supply an influx of soldiers and civilians by retaining flour that might have been exported during peacetime.[2]

Coastwise and foreign exports reveal the extent of Virginia's surplus of flour. The New York *Shipping and Commercial List, and Price Current* provides data on the coastwise trade in grain and flour. This newspaper listed the daily arrivals of ships and their cargoes from Southern ports. Table 2.1 shows the flow of flour into New York. Richmond, Norfolk, and other Virginia cities shipped over 250,000 barrels of flour per annum to New York during 1858 and 1859, while 225,000 barrels were sent in 1860 before the growing hostilities surrounding Lincoln's election reduced the flow of flour. In addition to the flour produced in Virginia, there was reason to hope that the Carolinas and Georgia might be able to produce a surplus of these commodities. Savannah and Charleston combined to ship 84,000 barrels in 1858 and 50,000 barrels in 1859 to New York, but fewer than 2,000 in 1860.

The south Atlantic ports also shipped flour to Boston, Baltimore, and Philadelphia, although these cities imported less Southern flour than did New York. The Virginia ports sent about 100,000 barrels of flour per annum to Boston during 1858–60. Philadelphia received smaller quantities of flour from Virginia. The Richmond *Daily Whig* showed that Richmond's exports of flour (by steamer) to Philadelphia between 1858 and 1860 fell from over 30,000 barrels in 1858 to below 8,000 per year in 1859 and 1860. The Philadelphia Board of Trade's *Twenty-Seventh Annual Report* listed 10,211 barrels of flour imported from Richmond, Charleston, and other south Atlantic ports during 1859. Richmond also exported large quantities of flour to foreign ports. Richmond millers sent almost 600,000 barrels of flour to South America during the two calendar years 1858–1859.[3]

The south Atlantic ports exported more flour than wheat. Table 2.1 shows the relatively small amounts of wheat sent to New York City from south Atlantic ports. The other major northeastern ports also did not import much wheat from the South.

The Southern states produced large quantities of corn. Much of the corn was fed to livestock. Still, corn was an important part of Southerners' diet. Virginia produced less corn per capita than the Confederate states as a whole. Tennessee produced the most corn per capita, but much of its output would be needed to sustain troops and animals stationed within its borders. The south Atlantic ports exported much more corn than they did wheat, but the shipments of corn to northeastern ports were volatile. New York's and Philadelphia's imports of corn from these ports diminished considerably between 1858 and 1860 (see Table 2.1 for New York). According to the Philadelphia Board of Trade's *Twenty-Sixth Annual Report,* the south Atlantic ports shipped more than one million bushels of corn to Philadelphia in both 1857 and 1858. However, the *Twenty-Seventh Annual Report* did not list any corn imports from south Atlantic ports during 1859. In addition, cargo manifests for vessels entering Philadelphia from the Southern coast did not list any corn imports during 1860. South Atlantic ports did not export much wheat or corn to foreign ports. According to the 1859 *Report of the Secretary of the Treasury on the Commerce and Navigation of the United States,* between 130,000 and 170,000 bushels of corn and wheat per annum were exported from south Atlantic ports to foreign ports during the late antebellum era. Sailing vessels conveyed most of the coastwise shipments of flour and grain. Indeed, corn was rarely shipped by steamers, while flour and wheat were increasingly shipped by sailing vessels. About half of the rice shipped coastwise went by steamers.

Where did the grain exported from south Atlantic ports originate? Aside from that produced within its borders, Virginia received much of North Carolina's grain and flour. *DeBow's Review* stated, "Most of the flour and wheat of [North Carolina] finds ports and market in Virginia." The counties in the extreme northeastern portion of North Carolina produced relatively large amounts of corn, and Norfolk received most of the excess corn grown in the northeast part of North Carolina. The eight small counties in this corner of North Carolina produced almost four million bushels

Table 2.1. Grain Imports into New York from South Atlantic Ports

| | Wheat (bushels) | | |
| | | Calendar Year | |
Originating Port	1858	1859	1860
Richmond/Norfolk	92,618	113,301	34,282
Other Virginia	26,643	19,333	930
North Carolina	46,553	83,221	58,037
Charleston	28,346	22,800	0
Savannah	166,240	28,570	408
Other ports	0	1,252	294
Total South Atlantic	360,400	268,477	93,951

| | Flour (196-pound barrels) | | |
| | | Calendar Year | |
Originating Port	1858	1859	1860
Richmond	155,709	149,338	137,655
Other Virginia	109,772	102,751	87,333
North Carolina	4,208	3,202	5,967
Charleston	33,260	15,549	106
Savannah	51,224	34,645	1,739
Other ports	3,433	97	2,118
Total South Atlantic	357,606	305,582	234,918

Note: in 1858, 55,972 sacks of flour from Charleston and Savannah were sent to New York. Sacks are of unknown size (presumably less than a barrel).

| | Corn (bushels) | | |
| | | Calendar Year | |
Originating Port	1858	1859	1860
Richmond	12,635	2,812	10,700
Norfolk	566,676	213,231	188,281
Other Virginia	289,682	44,632	63,511
North Carolina	232,482	62,767	34,873
Other ports	71,627	5,202	0
Total South Atlantic	1,173,102	328,644	297,365

| | Rice (tons) | | |
| | | Calendar Year | |
Originating Port	1858	1859	1860
Charleston	14,507	12,664	12,292
Savannah	2,612	5,381	4,994
Total	17,119	18,045	17,286

Source: daily compilation of New York *Price Current.*

of corn. About 68,000 people lived in these counties, and after allowing thirty bushels per capita, almost two million bushels of corn remained for export. The area did not possess much excess wheat or hay, but its corn surplus held great promise. According to *DeBow's Review:* "Receipts of corn are estimated at 2 million bushels [in 1859], of which there were received by the Dismal Swamp Canal [connecting Norfolk with the northeast portion of North Carolina] 1,443,065; by Seaboard and Roanoke Railroad, 54,363 bushels, and the balance from other sources."[4]

Did the northeast ports ship flour and grain to south Atlantic ports? The fact that southeast ports, especially those in Virginia and North Carolina, shipped flour and grain to Northern and foreign ports does not prove that the southeast did not import these commodities, too. The region might be an importer of a certain grade of flour, even while exporting another grade of flour. For instance, Richmond's flour was renowned for its quality and its ability to resist spoilage in tropical heat. These qualities led to most of Richmond's flour being exported, while the surrounding area provided the city's consumption of flour.[5]

The evidence suggests that south Atlantic ports were not significant customers for flour and grain from northeastern ports, except when Southern crops were poor: "In the South, which had for the past few years grown sufficient wheat for its own consumption, there was an entire failure. Consequently a good demand prevailed from that quarter until early in November [1860], when the political crisis so much destroyed confidence as to embarrass and derange both the financial and commercial interests of the country."[6] A report by the secretary of the treasury described the coastwise trade: "Grain and flour from the James river, the Chesapeake, and the coasts of Maryland and Delaware, have been carried to the eastern States in great quantities." The report made no mention of shipments of foodstuffs from northeast ports to south Atlantic ports. Boston exported coastwise fewer than 11,000 barrels of flour and 25,000 bushels of corn and wheat combined per annum during 1857–60. Baltimore was probably a larger conduit for Northern grains and flour to the South. Baltimore's total coastwise shipments of wheat and corn during 1857–60 averaged over two million bushels per annum, but Boston and Providence, Rhode Island, received significant proportions of these coastwise shipments of grain. Charleston received at least 150,000 bushels of corn from Maryland in 1860 and smaller amounts in previous years. Baltimore was a relatively large coastwise shipper of flour, as there was a residual of perhaps 600,000 barrels per annum during 1858–60. Where the Baltimore flour was shipped is not clear from the records. Some was probably shipped to Charleston, as the Charleston *Daily Courier* listed prices for Baltimore, Philadelphia, and "Western" flour. Even if it were all shipped to Southern ports, the south Atlantic region would still probably be a net exporter of flour. The south Atlantic ports shipped almost 400,000 barrels of flour per annum to New York and Boston between 1858 and 1860, besides the flour shipped to South America. It is unlikely that the entire residual of flour at Baltimore was shipped south. Large shipments of Baltimore flour ended up in Boston and Providence. The region around Baltimore probably consumed some of the residual, too. Did Philadelphia ship much grain to south Atlantic ports? The Philadelphia Board of Trade's *Twenty-Sixth Annual Report* estimated that 200,000 to 250,000 barrels of flour were exported coastwise, but Boston took 15 to 20 percent of this flour. The report also stated, "All of the coasting trade of Philadelphia from the north and east, carries more or less of flour to the British provinces, Maine, and the nearer New England ports." The *Twenty-Seventh Annual Report* described the outward trade southward: "All forms of iron, iron manufactures and machinery, carriages, wagons, marble sculptures, furniture, and manufactures of wood, are very largely sent, making up the bulk of the trade." Some dry goods were also sent, but no mention of foodstuffs was made. The extent of New York's exports of grain and flour to southeast ports is unknown. None of the major southeastern ports' prices current listed "New York" corn, wheat, or flour prices.[7]

Charleston received a large proportion of its corn from North Carolina, and the South Carolina Railroad delivered much of Charleston's flour and grain. Lindstrom believes that rail shipments of grain to Charleston and Savannah originated in Tennessee, Georgia, Alabama, and the Carolinas.[8]

To summarize, Virginia and the south Atlantic region were usually net exporters of flour and sometimes of grain. In years of normal or bountiful crops, the south Atlantic states were able to export modest amounts of flour and grain to northeastern ports. During wartime, such produce that was exported to northeastern ports might have been retained to sustain Confederate troops in Virginia. However, any net exports of grain were not so large as to prevent a poor crop, such as in 1860, from forcing a reversal of the flow of grains. The war would also curb Virginia's ability to maintain or increase its grain and flour output. Since Virginia produced trivial amounts of cotton, the enlisting of white Virginians into the army could not be fully made up by switching slave labor from growing cotton to producing foodstuffs. The concentration of draft animals into military service limited the food production and hindered local transportation of goods to railheads and ports. Finally, the inability to replace deteriorating farm implements due to wartime and blockade-induced obstacles hampered food production.

Since Virginia and the south Atlantic states were not large producers of livestock, supplying troops and civilians in Virginia with meat was problematic. Virginians did not appear to have imported much packed meat from northeastern ports during the antebellum. Richmond may have drawn packed meat via inland waterways and railroads. The Richmond *Daily Whig* listed a total of 375 tons of bacon imported into Richmond by canal and railroad for the three year period 1858–60. For the three-year period, Richmond received 3,600 head of cattle and 25,000 hogs via canal and railroad. The city also received livestock from other unspecified sources, as, according to the January 7, 1861, issue of the Richmond *Daily Whig,* the city received over 8,000 head of cattle and a similar number of hogs from other sources during 1860 alone. Baltimore received some cattle from Virginia, although the livestock may have originated in Tennessee: "Some 13,000 head of the Cattle offered [at Baltimore during 1857] were received from the West, via the Baltimore and Ohio Railroad, and the remaining 31,000 head were driven here from various points, but principally from Virginia." The south Atlantic cities probably drew little packed meat from New Orleans. For the six years ending August 31, 1860, New Orleans shipped a maximum of 50,000 barrels of beef and pork in any given year to "Other Coastal Ports" (American ports other than New York, Boston, Philadelphia, and Baltimore), and much of these shipments of packed meat probably ended up at other Gulf ports, particularly Mobile. The south Atlantic ports were net exporters of meat products to other countries. However, the amounts were negligible, as fewer than 1,100 barrels of beef, hams, bacon, and pork were exported in any of the three years ending June 30, 1861. Exports of live animals were trivial.[9]

The meat supply problem might have been eliminated or mitigated in the absence of an effective blockade. The Confederacy could have imported packed meat from Northern, British, or Canadian producers. Shipping Texas cattle to Florida via the Gulf also might have alleviated any shortages. However, if these sources were unavailable, the meat supply might be inadequate.

Another potential supply problem threatened to overwhelm the distributional system. Civil War era armies required large numbers of horses and mules, as oxen were used infrequently. While horses and mules could transport more than men, they also required far more foodstuffs than men. Forage, hay, oats, and corn were crucial in keeping cavalry, artillery, and transport animals healthy. The official Federal army ration per horse was fourteen pounds of hay and twelve pounds of oats, corn, or barley per day. The daily ration for mules was slightly less, a combined twenty-three pounds. During campaigning, the animals often received much less than the official ration.[10]

According to the census, the eleven Confederate states produced just over one million tons of hay or 5.6 percent of the total United States output. Historian Sam Hilliard believes that the census understates the extent of available fodder in the South, as corn stalks were often used as feed for hogs and cattle. Regardless of the census underestimate, the Southern states typically imported hay from the Northern states. For instance, New Orleans received 150,000 bales (25,000 tons) of hay from upriver during 1859–60. The Confederate troops in Virginia were fortunate that the state was a large producer of hay. Virginia produced 558 pounds of hay per person, more than double the per capita output of any other Confederate state except North Carolina. Given the state's low per capita holdings of livestock, the state was relatively well-supplied with hay to sustain existing animals. There were two potential drawbacks with the state's supply of hay. First, almost one-third of the hay was produced in counties that would eventually comprise West Virginia. Second, the Shenandoah Valley was Confederate Virginia's major hay producing region, and three counties in the valley—Rockingham, Augusta, and Rockbridge—produced one-sixth of Confederate Virginia's hay output. The real problem was shipping enough hay to supply the Confederate army's large concentration of animals. Imports of hay by rail and canal into Richmond rose from 728 bales in 1858 to 12,554 bales in 1860, but railroads were unlikely to become major hay transporters. On a per pound basis, the price of hay was comparable to corn, but hay was much less valuable than wheat or flour. Coastwise shipments into Richmond were more economical and amounted to 75,000 bales over the same three year period, 1858–60.[11]

As shown earlier, Virginia was not a relatively large producer of corn, although the state did produce a large amount of oats. In summary, the state might possess enough hay to feed an influx of animals, but it would require imports of corn and oats. The main problem was collecting and shipping the requisite quantities within Virginia.

The rail, inland water, and coastal transportation system supplying Virginia was adequate for peacetime shipments, but the system's ability to transport larger quantities or to accommodate new trade patterns was suspect. Virginia's railroads had many of the characteristic drawbacks of Southern railroads. They lacked connections in Richmond and Petersburg, consisted of single- instead of double-tracking, had tenuous connections with railroads in other states, used flimsy wooden stringer/strap iron rails on a heavily-used section of the crucial Richmond & Danville railroad, and depended upon imports of British rail iron. The state's ability to manufacture railroad locomotives, cars, and supplies was better than most of the other Confederate states, thanks to the Tredegar Iron Works, but was still severely deficient. Given the military's monopolization of Tredegar's output, whatever ability antebellum Virginia had to supply its railroads probably was reduced.

Virginia's railroads were going to need help from water and wagon-borne transport. Wagons, for reasons discussed earlier, were unlikely to provide an adequate substitute for rail and water transportation. If the Confederacy could maintain control of Virginia's waterways and Chesapeake Bay, the transportation system might prove sufficient; otherwise, the rail system was likely to break down.

In summary, there were adequate supplies of food and feed available to supply Confederate troops in Virginia, provided that the transportation system functioned well. Virginia's antebellum system relied heavily upon water transportation, especially as the railroads' ability to significantly expand their carrying capacity was doubtful. The state's railroads would be hard-pressed to compensate for any loss of water transportation.

Part II

THE BLOCKADE'S EFFECTS ON THE CONFEDERATE WAR EFFORT

The war and the Union navy's blockade deranged the intraregional movement of goods within the South. The Union navy's control of the American waters contributed to the Confederate armies' chronic supply shortages throughout the war. By its blockade, the Union navy suppressed, if not totally prevented, coastwise shipment of goods between Confederate ports. Historian Stephen Wise dismissed the coastwise vessels because they were not bringing in war materiel from foreign ports: "their impact was negligible . . . they did little to support the war effort and nothing to relieve the growing shortages in the Confederacy."[1] However, the coastal vessels still could have made a valuable contribution by conveying Southern foodstuffs and raw materials between Southern ports; the coastwise vessels would have improved the supply situation and lessened the strain upon the railroad system. The blockade affected the movement of food in the Mississippi valley, especially the movement of cattle and pork. The stringency of the blockade often meant that the Confederate armies either went without certain supplies or were forced to rely increasingly upon a rickety railroad system. The blockade also diminished the ability of Southern railroads to distribute the available goods by depriving the railroads needed imports of supplies, equipment, and rails.

$$3$$

THE BLOCKADE'S EFFECTS
UPON THE MISSISSIPPI
VALLEY'S ECONOMY

Wartime shipping patterns were destined to differ from antebellum patterns. The concentration of troops and animals forced rearranging the movement of goods. The loss of Northern-produced foodstuffs shipped down the Mississippi or shipped coastwise needed to be offset. What were the war's effects upon the Mississippi valley?

I. New Orleans's Food Supply

The advent of the Civil War and accompanying trade restrictions quickly led to shortages in New Orleans. The trade restrictions immediately disrupted the meat supply. The outbreak of the Civil War reduced New Orleans's receipts of "Western Cattle," but the Texans were able to make up some of the shortfall. Texas cattle continued to arrive at New Orleans up to the time of the city's capitulation, and there was a resumption of sending Western cattle to the city in early 1862. Despite these shipments, the supply of bacon, hams, and pork rapidly dwindled, and, by as early as September 27, 1861, the *Daily Crescent* reported, "We shall have to fall back on Creole beef and mutton."

Grain supplies also were disrupted. On November 9, 1861, the *Daily Crescent* lamented the "steadily increasing scarcity of breadstuffs." Federal occupation of areas along the Tennessee and Cumberland rivers further constricted supplies. For the year ending August 31, 1862, the receipts of grain and flour were just a fraction of the antebellum levels, with the receipts of flour plummeting to fewer than 300,000 barrels as compared to over a million barrels received during the year ending August 31, 1861 (of which 560,000 were retained in New Orleans). Receipts of corn at New Orleans exhibited an even more marked decrease than that of flour. The receipts for the year ending August 31, 1862, were one-twelfth of the amount in the bumper year of 1860–61, and, more importantly, the amount retained must have been well below the antebellum levels. In the face of the trade upheavals, prices rose quickly (see Table 3.1), and families of soldiers were among the first to suffer from privation. A relief effort, including a free food market, was started in August 1861. By February 1862, the relief funds were severely taxed with 2,000 families receiving assistance. Clearly, the diminution in "receipts from the interior" combined with the Federal navy's blockade to disrupt the entire Gulf of Mexico distribution system. Mobile and Florida ports, as well as upriver towns and plantations were left without their usual convenient sources of food.[1]

To cope with the rising prices and deepening privation, the mayor established a price control on bread, with further action occurring on March 23, 1862, when the provost marshals at New Orleans implemented more comprehensive price controls. Price controls for grains were set as follows: $16 per barrel of flour, $2.50 per bushel of wheat, and $1.25 per bushel for corn. The New Orleans *Daily Crescent* expressed its approval of the price controls: "had the authorities [not] acted . . . flour would at this time been held at $25 to $30 per barrel." The paper believed that growers would still make plenty of profits even with the price controls, as "the last *Shreveport Southwestern* . . . quotes [corn] at 50 to 55 cents per bushel." Therefore, according to the *Daily Crescent,* the growers still had incentives to forward provisions. If the price controls didn't work or if the growers didn't comply by forwarding foodstuffs, the newspaper advocated imposing martial law over the entire Confederacy. Ironically, a week later the paper's market report stated that the small receipts of flour for the week were due partly to the price control.[2]

Before the Federal navy launched its April 1862 attack against the forts guarding the river south of New Orleans, Confederate and city authorities were pleading for provisions, citing the reduction of the city's slender stocks due to demands by the Army of the Mississippi. The New Orleans mayor's request for flour to be sent from Richmond, in exchange for sugar and molasses, was an indication of the paucity of available regional supplies. The New Orleans board of provost marshals informed Jefferson Davis that the city required two freight trains of provisions per week. The *Daily Crescent* did not fear the Federal navy as much as it feared the specter of starvation, stating that "the only way the great city of New Orleans can be captured by the Yankees is by starving it out."[3] As Mansfield Lovell, the commanding general of New Orleans, reported to Secretary of War George Randolph: "The occupation of Tennessee by the enemy, the low

Table 3.1. Prices at New Orleans and Richmond (In Dollars)

| | April 1861 | |
	Richmond	New Orleans
Flour (barrel), Superfine	$7.88	$ 5.05
Extra	8.25	NL
Family	8.77	NL
Corn (bushel)	0.64	0.57
Corn meal (bushel)	0.70	0.60 to 0.75
Wheat (bushel)	1.35	1.25 to 1.50
Bacon, sides (pound)	0.15*	0.10 to 0.115
Bacon, shoulders (pound)	NL	0.07 to 0.075
Hay, Timothy (100 pounds)	1.25	2.00 to 2.30

| | April 1862 | |
	Richmond	New Orleans
Flour (barrel), Superfine	$7.00 to $7.25	$14.00 to $15.00
Extra	7.50 to 7.75	17.00 to 18.00
Family	8.25 to 8.75	17.00 to 18.00
Corn (bushel)	0.80 to 0.90	1.20 to 1.50
Corn meal (bushel)	0.90 to 1.00	1.80
Wheat (bushel)	1.15 to 1.25	2.50
Bacon, sides (pound)	0.26	0.28 to 0.30
Bacon, shoulders (pound)	0.24	0.25 to 0.27
Hay, Timothy (100 pounds)	1.85 to 1.90	3.00 to 3.25

* Only one price listed for Richmond bacon.
Note: Many of the New Orleans prices were set by the provost marshals.
Source: New Orleans *Daily Crescent,* April 15, 1862 for 1862.
　　　Lerner 1954, for 1861 Richmond prices.
　　　New Orleans *Price Current,* April 3, 1861 for 1861 New Orleans prices.

water in Red River, the interruption of the railroads at Decatur, and the want of communication by rail with Texas, all combined, have brought about a scarcity of provisions here." By the time Farragut steamed past the forts guarding the mouth of the Mississippi, Lovell reported that provisions for only eighteen days remained in the city.[4]

II. Collapse of Trade at New Orleans

The Federal naval blockade and interdiction of river trade combined with the Confederate embargo on cotton shipments to sharply curtail activity at

Table 3.2. Volume and Value of Receipts Received at New Orleans from
the Interior

Year	Cotton	Sugar	Molasses	Tobacco	Value ($)
1856–57	1,573,247	43,463	84,169	58,928	$158,061,000
1857–58	1,678,616	202,783	339,343	90,147	167,156,000
1858–59	1,774,298	257,225	353,715	85,133	172,953,000
1859–60	2,255,448	195,185	313,840	95,499	185,211,000
1860–61	1,849,312	174,637	313,260	43,756	155,864,000
1861–62	38,880	225,356	401,404	7,429	51,511,000
1862–63	22,078	85,531	202,616	4,774	29,766,000
1863–64	131,044	75,173	143,460	15,547	79,234,000
1864–65	271,015	9,345	18,725	16,346	111,013,000

Year: September 1 through August 31.
Cotton: in bales.
Sugar: in hogsheads.
Molasses: in barrels.
Tobacco: in hogsheads and bales.
Value: value of all receipts received from interior.
Source: New Orleans *Price Current,* "Annual Reports."

Table 3.3. Arrivals of Steamboats and Salt Water Vessels at New Orleans

Year	Steamers From Interior	Salt-Water Vessels From Gulf
1856–57	2,745	1,934
1857–58	3,264	1,905
1858–59	3,259	1,998
1859–60	3,566	1,918
1860–61	3,171	1,579
1861–62	1,456	241
1862–63	655	2,045
1863–64	1,414	2,981
1864–65	1,481	1,449

Year: September 1 through August 31.
Source: New Orleans *Price Current,* Annual Reports.
For 1861–62, *Hunt's Merchants' Magazine* 49 (1863), 253.

the port of New Orleans prior to April 1862 (see Table 3.2). New Orleans cotton factors urged the planters not to ship their cotton to New Orleans until the blockade was abandoned. Although the planters generally heeded the call not to ship cotton, enough was shipped to prompt the cotton factors to petition the governor in late September 1861 to make the embargo official, and Governor Thomas Moore ordered that no cotton be brought to New Orleans. The blockade did not deter all trade, as some 300 vessels ran through the blockade during the ten months prior to Federal occupation. However, the number of arrivals from the Gulf was less than a sixth of the normal number of arrivals, and many of these blockade runners were probably relatively small coastal vessels (see Table 3.3). Foreign trade probably came to a near standstill after the early months of the war. There were only a few arrivals of ocean-going vessels between late June 1861 and the fall of the city in late April 1862. Arrivals of steamboats from the Mississippi River were also dramatically reduced. In 1860–61, 3,171 steamboats arrived at New Orleans, but the arrivals shrank to 1,456 during 1861–62 (and diminished even more in 1862–63).[5]

Table 3.2 shows the depressed condition of the Southern staples trade in New Orleans. Prior to Fort Sumter, Southern growers had hurried their produce to Southern ports, so the decrease in trading didn't really start until September 1861. For New Orleans, the standstill in the raw cotton trade was especially devastating. The receipts during the fall of 1861 were fewer than 5,000 bales, compared with 187,500 during the fall of 1860. Instead of receiving the usual 1,800,000 bales of raw cotton per commercial year, the city received fewer than 40,000 during 1861–62 and worse was to come in 1862–63. Tobacco receipts fell off precipitously, too. Only sugar and molasses receipts remained strong in 1861–62, and, in fact, these receipts actually increased (because Louisiana growers could not ship their produce up the Mississippi to Northern consumers). The aggregate value of imports received at New Orleans from the interior tell a stark tale: receipts fell more than 15 percent in 1860–61 from 1859–60 and were only one-third as much in 1861–62 as in 1860–61.[6]

Thus the blockade, trade embargo, and depredations against the producing regions combined to cripple New Orleans trade. The *Daily Crescent* began to have doubts as to the desirability of the embargo on Southern staples, and began to call for an easing of the embargo by early 1862. The newspaper cited two reasons for the easing. First, the embargo made it easier for the Union to say that its blockade was effective. By allowing exports, the newspaper thought that the blockade's inefficacy would be revealed to the European powers. Second, the paper claimed, "If the quantity [of raw cotton exported] were ten times these figures, we think our community would have been gainers." The paper cited the need of planters and the Confederacy to raise purchasing power, so they could purchase necessary foreign manufactures, military supplies, and foodstuffs.[7]

III. Conclusions

The Confederacy showed little ability to supply New Orleans as long as trade with the upper Mississippi valley was prohibited and as long as Federal warships contested Confederate access to the Gulf of Mexico. In addition, the blockade diminished New Orleans's value as an export center, embargo or no embargo. The fall of New Orleans removed one supply headache from the Confederacy's long list of supply headaches. Indeed, had Farragut's vessels not made their famous run past the guns at Forts St. Phillip and Jackson, New Orleans would have suffered from food shortages and civilian discontent.

The remainder of the Mississippi River in Confederate hands could have continued to furnish some supplies (such as meat, sugar, grain, and molasses) to Confederate troops in Tennessee and Mississippi, although the lack of railroads would have minimized the amount of supplies that could be shipped beyond Mississippi. The Yazoo, Red, Arkansas, and White rivers could have shifted northern Texas, Louisiana, Arkansas and Mississippi produce to regions needing supplies.[8] However, the siege of Port Hudson sealed off the Red River. Federal gunboats, moving downstream after the capture of Memphis, denied free passage of the Mississippi River along the Arkansas-Mississippi border. The fall of Vicksburg and Port Hudson in 1863 reduced Confederate trade across the river to furtive attempts to evade Union gunboats.

$\overbrace{\quad 4 \quad}$

The Blockade's Effects upon the Beef and Pork Trade of the Confederacy

The blockade affected the Confederacy's ability to exploit its meat supply. What happened to the beef and pork supplies of the eastern Confederacy during the war, and what were the ramifications of the shortage of meat upon the Southern armies? How did the blockade and the Union control of the lower Mississippi prevent the potential Texas beef supply from being used effectively?

I. Wartime Meat Supplies

The commissary-general of subsistence for the Confederate army, Lucius B. Northrop, was unenthusiastic about the Confederacy's meat supply. As early as August 1861 he reported to President Davis: "The real evil is ahead. There are not hogs in the Confederacy sufficient for the Army, and the larger force of plantation negroes. Hence, competition must be anticipated by arranging for the purchase of the animals and getting the salt to cure them. Furthermore beeves must be provided for the coming Spring; cattle must be collected from Texas before the rains set in, and be herded in ranging grounds convenient to the Mississippi. I am arranging for that matter." Northrop initially attempted to procure bacon from Maryland and Kentucky during the summer of 1861, but his efforts had netted little. He was still aggressively pursuing meat from Kentucky even as late as November 1861: "we must look to Kentucky, and as the hopes predicated on a more rapid advance from beyond our lines, where our currency will not answer. Gold is necessary, but its price is from 20 to 25 per cent. premium; but pork and beef are one-third less costly, and meat bought and cured from them will be cheaper than what is obtained within our own land. To get this gold . . . army regulations must be violated." Later, in January

1862, Northrop claimed better success for his between-the-lines endeavors: "On commencing the organization in Montgomery it was known that supplies, especially of salt meats, could not be obtained to an adequate extent except in the enemy's country. Accordingly, appropriate steps were taken to reach them. The stores of bacon and pork thus acquired, at a cost to the Government of much less than one-half the current rates, are still being issued."[1]

Despite Northrop's efforts to get meat from the border states, Tennessee provided the bulk of the meat products consumed by Confederate troops. Fortunately for the Confederacy, the presence of the initially large supply of hogs in Tennessee allowed for the easy feeding of the large Confederate army in Tennessee, thereby avoiding much of the inconvenience resulting from a shortage of barrels for packed meat. As Commissary-Major Frank Ruffin reported: "Tennessee then became the main reliance for a supply for the future use of the Army, which, together with the accessible portions of Kentucky, had been so ravaged by hog cholera and injured by short corn crops for three years preceding the year just closed [1861] that the number slaughtered at the porkeries had dwindled from 200,000 head to less than 20,000. It was into this field, just recovering from these disasters, and almost the sole resource of the Army, the planters, and the inhabitants of cities, that this department had to enter as a purchaser—dubious of a sufficiency, but assured of a heavy and active competition."[2] Ruffin's lament aside, Tennessee provided the Confederate armies with half of their pork supply and a significant portion of their beef supply in the first year of the war. By January 1862, Ruffin reported to Commissary-General Northrop that 250,000 hogs had been secured for the Confederate army, of which half came from Tennessee and 20,000 were from Kentucky. The rapid depletion of Tennessee's meat supply and General Bragg's retreat from Kentucky in 1862 placed a severe strain on the Confederate armies' supplies: "General Bragg's army since leaving Kentucky has drawn its supplies chiefly from the reserves of Atlanta. These drafts have been of such magnitude that there is but about 500,000 pounds here. It is quite certain that want awaits both armies [the armies in Virginia and Tennessee], even on the supposition that our efforts to import from England are far more successful than heretofore. Not one of the contracts to import from the North has been fruitful."[3] Northrop's reaction was to demand a reduction in the field rations, and eventually his wish was granted.

Even with the disastrous retreat from Kentucky, the October 1862 beginning stock of bacon on hand (5.15 million pounds) was greater than that held in October 1861. Despite the larger stock, the commissary-general was gloomy about the prospects of the supply of meat for 1862–63. Although Tennessee supplied 12 million pounds of bacon in 1862, Northrop claimed he could expect none in 1863. He also bemoaned the growing scarcity of fresh meat (primarily beef), claiming that "The future of beef supply for the Army is so nearly exhausted that this Bureau does not know whence more is to be obtained."[4]

Aside from the depletion of Tennessee's livestock holdings, there were other reasons why obtaining meat from Tennessee was becoming less feasible as the war continued. Much of the supply route between Tennessee and Virginia ran through Unionist east Tennessee. The route was susceptible to Union cavalry raids, and one such raid disrupted the supply of Lee's army in early 1863. The situation was serious enough to prompt Lee, normally reluctant to release any of his troops for any reason, to offer to send men and wagons to transship the supplies between the gaps in the lines. The alternate rail routes, through Atlanta, across Georgia and South Carolina, and north through Charlotte or Wilmington, North Carolina (where changes in the rail gauge necessitated transshipment), were inconvenient. In addition, the railroads around Wilmington were burdened by eastbound shipments of raw cotton to that port. Having to ship beef through Wilmington was likely to overtax these railroads. By the end of 1863, Northern troops controlled most of Tennessee, completing the disruption of the supply of meat from that state. Hog cholera struck Georgia and other states during 1863, further depleting supplies and diminishing the possibility of obtaining bacon and pork from states in the Deep South.[5]

By the middle of 1862, the Union navy's control of the Mississippi between Vicksburg and Memphis cut off Arkansas's meat supplies from the eastern Confederacy. With the loss of middle Tennessee and Federal operations around Vicksburg, beef from Florida loomed larger in the Confederate supply equation. Because Florida beef was the closest alternative source to Tennessee, many groups lobbied for the beef. Even troops in Tennessee received meat from Florida during 1861–62, but the competition for the meat was intensifying. At times, the Confederate army in Tennessee hijacked meat bound for troops in Virginia. Confederate General Bragg requested 400,000 pounds of beef to feed his troops in March 1863 in Tennessee, but received less than half this amount. Troops and citizens of Charleston, South Carolina and Virginia also requested beef from Florida, and some Florida beef was used to sustain troops defending Charleston. In excess of 30,000 head were exported from the state in 1863, but fewer were shipped in 1864. These numbers were not enough to sustain soldiers and citizens (especially the population of Charleston).

Cattle in southern Florida could not be driven to the railroad in the northern part of the state, and Florida's potential as cattle supplier would not be significantly improved. To better tap Florida's resources, a railroad between Albany and Thomasville, Georgia, was proposed, but it was not built. Although some officials believed as late as the winter of 1864 that hundreds of thousands of head awaited in Florida, census data and the opinion of Commissary-General Northrop argued to the contrary: "The dream about the oceans of cattle in East Florida has no foundation. If they can meet the demands of the troops in Georgia and South Carolina, so as to save the bacon in these states and furnish from Georgia some surplus hither, all will be realized which should be reasonably expected."[6] The chief commissary officer in Florida, Major P. W. White, bluntly stated that the beef supply in Florida was exhausted under the existing conditions: "As to beef, we are unable at present [April 1864] to supply the army here with it, and you need expect none from this State, until General Beauregard shall realize the necessity of opening the communication with the southern portion of the peninsula, and giving protection to our operations there, and until the War Department shall grant us the means of bringing them out."[7]

Historian Robert Taylor estimates that the government purchased 75,000 head of Florida beef during the war. In addition, some cattle were shipped on private account. Aside from the limited capacity of Florida to export beef, the lack of railroad connections and inability to ship coastwise because of the blockade forced overemphasis on driving cattle to railroads in Georgia. The driving could only be done seasonally (March through September) and was limited by available water and grazing. Finally, collecting and driving cattle required skilled wranglers, but the availability of such wranglers was limited by conscription policies. Thus, Florida proved an inadequate source of beef for the Confederacy.

The lack of railroads or water transportation certainly magnified the shortcomings of Florida's beef supply. Even when cattle reached railheads, shortages of special stockcars and delays along the route often led to the cattle arriving emaciated. In recognition of this, some shipments were designed to move cattle to forage areas, prior to final movement to slaughterhouses. Aside from blockading Florida's ports, the Union navy launched raids against salt works, railroads, and cattle herds, thereby further diminishing the accessibility of Florida's cattle.[8]

An alternative to driving the beef or to shipping live beef by rail was to slaughter and salt it. This avoided the deleterious effects of prolonged rail shipment upon livestock, reduced the amount of rolling stock needed (especially of the scarce stockcars), and could be done efficiently in areas relatively far from the front. For instance, General Joseph Johnston estimated that five carloads of livestock would require just two cars as packed meat. Countering these advantages were the scarcity of salt and the often-terrible taste of the salted meat, leading to a high rate of wastage as troops discarded the meat. One Virginia meatpack complained that "in December 1861 he did not have one day's supply of salt on hand and that he could slaughter 8,000 to 9,000 hogs a day if he were kept supplied with salt." Private packers were not the only ones complaining. Army officers, too, lamented the shortage of salt that prevented them from processing local supplies of meat. Commissary-General Northrop, in a sarcastic vein, reported one good side effect of the salt shortage: "In consequence of the insufficient quantity and inferior quality of salt among the inhabitants, much of their meat is spoiling. The high prices fixed by the county committees, and the fear that the commissioners of appraisement might not reach prices high enough to satisfy avarice, has doubtless stimulated every one who could spare any meat to bring it out, and the fear of its being fly-blown and spoiled in their hands has strengthened the patriotic desire of feeding the soldiers."[9]

The meat shortages manifested themselves quickly. When the supply of hogs dwindled, beef increasingly became a more important component of the Confederate soldier's ration. The inability of Tennessee and Florida to succor all the demand for meat resulted in the gradual reduction of the meat ration to one-quarter pound of beef per day from an initial twelve to twenty ounces per day. While the one-quarter pound ration might have been sufficient for garrison troops, some of the Confederate generals believed the scanty rations affected the health and fighting ability of their combat troops.[10]

The reduced beef rations occurred despite the antebellum Southern states appearing to possess sufficient holdings of swine and cattle, even without Texas. Was there an actual shortage of livestock in the Confederate states? Were the meat shortages due to problems of distribution? The loss of key meat-producing regions?

The real prices of pork, bacon, and beef during the Civil War offer ambiguous evidence of shortages. The rapid changes in the price level, the stock of money, the velocity of money (the rapidity with which money changes hands), and the real output make interpreting commodity prices difficult. Deflating a commodity's price by a general price index to find the "real price" may yield information on the commodity's changing relative price, but may not inform us of the commodity's scarcity. As Milton Friedman discussed in 1952, if the change in the price level is predominantly due to changes in the money supply or of velocity, then a rise in the real price of a commodity signifies either an increase in demand for it or a decrease in supply of it. However, if the change in the general price level is primarily caused by changes in real output, the inference is more complex. A commodity could have become scarcer even though its real price had fallen (other goods may have become even more scarce or faced different elasticities of demand).

Schwab's prices for bacon (the only meat in his data) show that the increase in currency price for bacon tended to be greater than the increase in currency price for gold. Lerner's deflated bacon prices in Richmond, Augusta, and Wilmington showed fluctuation around the antebellum real prices, and, indeed, the deflated bacon prices sometimes fell below the initial 1861 real prices. More suspiciously, the deflated Wilmington bacon prices were generally higher than similarly deflated prices in Richmond (both cities deflated by their respective price index). This occurred even though Wilmington became the entrepot for bacon shipped from Britain, New York, and Canada, while Richmond was besieged by mid-1864. Clearly, the deflated bacon prices are of limited use in inferring the available supply of bacon.[11]

Eugene Lerner collected beef prices for both Augusta and Wilmington. For Augusta, beef prices were available only beginning in 1862, and these deflated prices fell in mid-1862. A similar pattern occurred in Wilmington, but thereafter deflated beef prices fluctuated. In Wilmington the real prices were generally 20 percent higher during the latter half of the war than the real prices in early 1861. Observers in Richmond, such as war clerk John Jones, reported a huge jump in nominal beef and bacon prices during the war. However, given Richmond's spectacular increases in prices, the deflated meat prices may not have risen by much and may have fallen, especially as all supplies in Richmond were severely reduced (particularly during Grant's siege from mid-1864 until April 1865).

The prices are also unlikely to reveal the true extent of any shortages for another reason. Confederate impressment and purchasing policies were very unfavorable to producers. For a farmer taking an extra hog or cow to the Richmond market, there was the risk of the livestock being impressed or forcibly purchased by Confederate authorities at prices often far below the market prices. Such policies discouraged producers from exposing their commodities and contributed to the shortages in the cities and around military encampments. Indeed, the despised Yankees often paid better than the "friendly" Confederate authorities.

The meat prices, then, provide ambiguous evidence. Instead, we must rely on anecdotal evidence of individual diarists, newspaper accounts and military reports, as well as our assessment of the antebellum supply of meat in the South. The military leaders and political leaders believed that the shortages of beef and pork were real. Apparently the impressment officials were so diligent in their endeavors that they were depleting even the breed livestock, so the Confederate Congress decided in March 1865 to revise the impressment laws to exempt breeding stock. One officer in Savannah lamented that "I have exhausted the beef-cattle and am now obliged to kill stock cattle."[12] Since the states of the eastern Confederacy may have imported only 10 percent of their pork and beef supply before the war, losing the Northern sources of supply, while forcing some cutbacks, certainly should not have been an insufferable loss, especially if Texas, Arkansas and Florida could contribute more meat. However, the eventual depletion and loss of Tennessee's supply of meat was a harder burden. Since Tennessee possessed the best hogs in the Confederacy, Tables 1.7 and 1.8 would understate her role as a supplier of pork. In addition, Tennessee's convenient location placed less strain upon the Confederate transportation system. Even if Georgia, Mississippi, and Alabama had possessed large surpluses of meat, such surpluses would have been far less accessible to the frontline troops.

Certainly, distribution difficulties exacerbated any shortage of meat in the Confederacy. Even at the end of the war, significant amounts of supplies existed in the Confederacy (if not enough to fully supply the armies, enough to protract the struggle a little longer), but supplies obtained through blockade running or between-the-lines trade often accumulated at rail depots. Near the end of the war, the faltering railroad system leading into Richmond curbed the movement of whatever supplies were available. According to documents published in the *Southern Historical Society Papers* in 1876, the Commissary Department reported the existence of 11.5 million rations of meat in Virginia and North Carolina and another 5 million in East Tennessee in February 1865, but obtaining these supplies depended upon restoring communication between Tennessee and Virginia, adequate purchasing power, and local transportation. The loss of the Central Railroad and the James River Canal had already cut off two million of the meat rations listed above. Federal cavalry raids and movements also disrupted rail transport of supplies. Moreover, the crumbling railroad system was partially the result of the blockade's stringency: The blockade was primarily responsible for the inability of Southern railroads to import rail iron and also for creating the rail bottleneck south of Richmond (because of the inability to use Chesapeake Bay and the James River).

The Confederacy's financial difficulties also contributed to the inability of commissary officers to obtain sufficient meat supplies. Certainly Northrop blamed the funding as the chief culprit: "as a consequence of the lack of money and credit, not one-fifth of the hogs which could have been secured have been or will be obtained for the army." To buttress his claims, Northrop attached several reports of commissary officers throughout the South citing the need for funds.[13]

Whatever the cause of the meat shortage in the eastern Confederacy, that shortage, combined with shortages of other supplies, constrained the military operations of the remaining Confederate armies. General Lee wrote to General Longstreet that "The great obstacle everywhere is scarcity of supplies. That is the controlling element to which everything has to yield."[14]

II. Where Were the Texas Cattle?

Could Texas cattle have alleviated the meat shortage in the Confederacy? We've seen that the large cities and armies were hardest hit by shortages of meat. Many of the interior counties were relatively self-sufficient in meat, primarily because of the high cost of shipping meat overland. The fragile, incomplete railroad network and loss of navigable inland waterways made moving cattle from Texas, Arkansas, and Florida to the interior of Mississippi, Alabama, and Georgia a tenuous prospect at best.

However, the shortages faced by Mobile, New Orleans, Richmond, Savannah, Charleston, and the troops in Virginia could have been significantly alleviated in the absence of an effective blockade by shipments of livestock and packed meat across the Gulf of Mexico, along the Atlantic Coast, and up the Mississippi and James rivers. By succoring these cities and the troops in Virginia, the competition for meat products in the interior would not have been as severe, allowing the available meat in the interior to be used for local needs or the troops in nearby locales.

Although the Texas cattle were remote from the main population and military centers, coastwise shipping would have greatly increased the Confederacy's access to these cattle. Even the south Atlantic cities might have been supplied with Texas beef shipped across the Gulf of Mexico to Cedar Keys, Florida; shipped by rail across the Florida peninsula; and then shipped by coastal vessels to south Atlantic ports. The postwar shipments of cattle from Texas to Cuba demonstrate the feasibility of the trans-Gulf movement. According to a report in the Tenth Census, the average trip from Texas to Cuba took four days, compared with two to New Orleans.

If the Confederacy could have maintained access to Chesapeake Bay and the Atlantic, even Richmond and the troops in Virginia could have benefited from coastwise cattle shipments.

The ability to transport cattle across the Gulf from Texas to New Orleans, Mobile, and Florida still existed in April 1861. The New Orleans-Mobile Mail Company possessed five coastal steamers at the beginning of the war: *Alabama, California, Cuba, Florida,* and *Oregon.* These vessels, usually of lighter draft than the ocean-going steamers, were well fitted for the Gulf, and, prior to the war, had conveyed cattle across the Gulf. Even with just these five steamers, 1,000 head per week could have been shipped from Galveston and Indianola to New Orleans or Mobile, as the steamers were capable of carrying up to 200 head each. An additional 50,000 head per annum would have been equivalent to 13,250,000 pounds of beef (assuming 265 pounds per head), which would have been more than Tennessee's contribution in 1862. Such a delivery of Texas beef would have significantly alleviated the shortage of meat in the eastern Confederacy, and, of course, the Gulf ports also possessed sailing vessels with which to convey cattle.

Given the shortage of meat in the Confederate states east of the Mississippi, why weren't cattle from Texas used to eliminate the shortage? Why was Texas's contribution to the eastern Confederacy's meat supply destined to be so modest?

The Civil War disrupted the flow of cattle in the Gulf region. The supply of "Western" cattle was cut off in May 1861, so Texas cattle were used to make up the difference. By late June 1861, the New Orleans-Mobile Mail Company suspended operations upon the arrival of Union warships. The blockade and Confederate confiscation of some steam vessels combined to eliminate shipping between New Orleans and Texas. Some of the steamers were converted into Confederate gunboats, only to be burned to avoid capture, while others later became blockade runners. The New Orleans *Price Current* did not list any arrivals from Texas at the New Orleans port after May 25, 1861 (the *Picayune* listed a few schooners).

With the suppression of Gulf shipments, alternative routes were taken to deliver Texas cattle to New Orleans in the spring of 1861. The shipments from Shreveport took up part of the slack, but overland movement across the Sabine to Berwick's Bay, where the Opelousas Railroad could convey the cattle to New Orleans, became the primary conduit. The increasing price of Texas beef in New Orleans was the impetus for using these heretofore minor routes. In early June 1861, the prices ranged from $10–18/head for lower quality and $30/head for higher quality beeves. By the end of the month, with the shortage of western beeves, the prices had advanced to $10–25/head for lower quality and $35/head for higher quality. These alternative routes were initially able to replace "Western" beef in New Orleans's beef trade, so New Orleans received roughly the same number of beeves during September 1860 through August 1861 as in the previous commercial year. However, the equality in numbers of cattle received at Jefferson City overlooks the fact that Texas cattle were not as valuable as Western cattle, the latter often selling for $10–15 more per head. Nor did the increased flow of Texas cattle make up the shortfall in packed meat that normally came down the Mississippi from "the interior." By the summer of 1861, the flow of packed meat down the Mississippi had practically vanished. The number of barrels/tierces of pork dwindled from 213,982 to 11,452 between 1860–61 and 1861–62, while the amount of bacon imported was less than 20 percent of the 1860–61 level.[15]

Certainly the Texans were more than willing to supply beef. In April 1862, a speaker in the Confederate Congress quoted letters from Texas cattlemen stating that they would be willing to supply cattle to the Confederate army, free of charge, if the government would bear the expense of transportation and driving. The speaker boasted, "The state of Texas . . . could feed the whole world." Plans to drive Texas cattle to Tennessee and Virginia met with failure: "Arrangements were made in 1862–63 to bring cattle from those States [Texas and Florida] and put them on the grass lands of Virginia and Tennessee, but the long drive, want of good grass on the way, caused the attempt that was made with a few droves to fail. Some thousands of beeves have been obtained within the past few months by swimming the Mississippi, and when the river is again in a suitable state and the season admits of it the proceeding should be continued."[16] Moreover, Federal river gunboats gradually interdicted river traffic on the Mississippi, although desperation prodded efforts to swim cattle across it. As New Orleans fell and Federal naval operations moved north from New Orleans and south from Memphis, Confederate Commissary-General Northrop sounded the alarm: "If the enemy shall control the entire navigation of the Mississippi River, we shall be excluded from further receipts of beef from Texas."[17]

In the end, the Texas cattle remained a largely untapped resource for the Confederacy. The Union navy, through its blockade of the Gulf ports and its control of the Mississippi River, impeded the Confederacy's access to the vast Texas herds and thereby contributed to the supply distress of the Confederacy. While the loss of New Orleans and the movement of a Union fleet up the Mississippi River certainly deranged the movement of Texas cattle, the blockade of Galveston and the Texas coast was necessary to seal off the trans-Gulf movement of cattle.

III. Epilogue

Prior to the Civil War, shipments of beeves from Texas to Gulf ports were increasing. During the Civil War, the blockade of Galveston, New Orleans, Mobile, and other Gulf ports curtailed shipment of Texas beeves by sea, causing a greater dependence upon overland shipping. The overland route to Confederate troops east of the Mississippi was fraught with difficulty, due to the scarcity of railroads in the trans-Mississippi, diligence of Federal gunboats, and a lack of good forage and open land en route. Although some Texas beeves were driven to and across the Mississippi River, the overland method proved a very narrow funnel through which to pour Texas cattle.

The Confederate Congress finally decided to help the Texas cattlemen bring beef to the eastern Confederacy. In late 1862 the Congress extended exemptions for stockmen, allowing an additional man for every 500 head of cattle. In addition, by early 1863 they authorized commissary agents to purchase cattle at $25 per head (if rounded up) or $22 per head (if the government had to do the rounding up). Purchases were to be paid for in Confederate currency, which was a method certain to discourage transactions! As usual, the Confederate government placed too low an official price on the cattle, and it was outbid by Federal authorities in New Orleans (who were willing to pay for Texas cattle with gold). By June 1864, the Federals were paying $40 to $60 per head.[18]

The Confederate government's efforts were ineffective, and Texas provided little succor for the eastern Confederacy. The Confederacy was forced to import beef from foreign and New York sources. Thus, because of the blockade and Union control of much of the lower Mississippi River, Lee's men went hungry in 1865, while a Texas cattleman's poverty was, in McCoy's ironic phrase, "estimated by the number of cattle he possessed."[19] The blockade was so effective that the hungry troops and superfluous cattle might as well have been on different planets.

5

THE BLOCKADE'S EFFECTS
UPON SOUTHERN RAILROADS

The Confederate army suffered chronic supply shortages. Although the South's manufacturing sector was unable to fully supply Confederate military forces with ordnance, small arms, ammunition, and other materiel, the big surprise was the inability of the South to adequately feed its troops. After all, the antebellum South was nearly self-sufficient in foodstuffs. Certainly the Confederate states possessed adequate herds of livestock to sustain the troops with healthy allowances of meat. However, General Lee's troops in Virginia and the troops in Tennessee received ever-dwindling supplies of meat. In addition, Confederate troops and civilians often faced shortages of other foodstuffs and commodities.

The inability of the South's intraregional transportation system to sustain the armies (as well as the burgeoning population of Richmond) has been cited as a proximate cause of the South's demise. Robert Black states that "Railroad transportation in the Confederacy suffered from a number of defects, all of which played a recognizable part in the Southern defeat." Frank Vandiver summarizes the railroads' role in the Confederate defeat as being endemic of an overall problem: "Rail lines were the arteries of the South; when they atrophied, decay set in, decay that became chronic, pervasive, strangled the efforts of all supply bureaus, stalled commerce, halted the mail, and sapped the nation's will. The conclusion seems obvious: railroad failure wrecked Confederate logistics. Unfortunately the conclusion is not sound. A large factor in failure was the absence of a comprehensive logistical system in the wartime South. Economic planning came piecemeal, almost spasmodically and in response to crises." Charles Ramsdell, too, is cautious in his assessment of the railroads' role: "It would be claiming too much to say that the failure to solve its railroad problem was the cause of the Confederacy's downfall, yet it is impossible not to conclude that the solution of that problem was one of the important conditions of success."[1] The Union navy's contributions to the Southern intraregional transportation deficiencies have been less noted. While the Southern transportation network was inherently suspect, the Union navy's blockade exacerbated the existing deficiencies.

I. Southern Railroads during the War

1) Attempts to Extend Southern Railroads

There were several crucial gaps in the Southern railroad system. Southerners proposed or completed several major extensions of the existing railroad network in the Confederacy. Of the wartime extensions, the connection between Danville, Virginia, and Greensboro, North Carolina, providing another link between Virginia and North Carolina railroads, proved the most crucial in prolonging the war. Indeed, the Piedmont Railroad became an integral component of the system sustaining Lee's army around Richmond. A second connection, between Selma, Alabama, and Meridian, Mississippi, while only partially completed, was useful in supplying the western armies. A third connection, between New Iberia, Louisiana, and Orange, Texas (on the Sabine River), was never attempted because of the fall of New Orleans. This connection was potentially very useful, as it would have given the cis-Mississippi Confederacy greater access to Texas's vast cattle herds (by remedying the lack of forage facing attempts to trail cattle through this region).

In February 1862, the Confederate Congress approved funding to construct a rail connection between Selma, Alabama, and Meridian, Mississippi. Although this link would have created a rail line from Monroe, Louisiana, to Selma, Alabama (broken only by the unbridged Mississippi River at Vicksburg and the Tombigbee River at Demopolis, Alabama), its usefulness was limited by the trackless stretch between Selma and Montgomery. Filling the gap between Selma and Montgomery would have provided the Confederacy with an east-west system (albeit over many different lines and gauge changes) deep in Confederate territory. An episode in 1863 reveals the inconvenience caused by the gaps in the second east-west rail system. The loss of Corinth, Mississippi, severing the sole east-west rail link, created the isolation of rolling stock between the eastern and western sections of the cis-Mississippi. In late 1863, the need arose to transfer rolling stock from Mississippi to the eastern states. Due to the gaps between Selma and Montgomery and between Mobile and Tensas, Alabama, rolling stock was moved south to Mobile, ferried across Mobile Bay and sent northward from Tensas to the eastern railroads. The Confederate Congress provided $150,000 to fill in the Selma/Montgomery gap, but this amount proved insufficient. By April 1862, Alabama and Mississippi Rivers Railroad officials informed then-Secretary of War Randolph that because of escalating costs and financial difficulties (due to the reduced railroad freight receipts caused by the blockade-induced reductions in cotton shipments), they would require an additional $350,000. In addition, a shortage of iron retarded construction. Although the Shelby County Iron Manufacturing Company could produce iron rails and spikes, the Confederate government monopolized its output. The railroad connection was not completed until late 1862.[2]

In March 1862, the city of New Orleans passed a resolution advocating the formation of a New Orleans and Texas Railroad. This line was to connect New Iberia, Louisiana, with Orange, Texas (and the wistfully named Texas & New Orleans Railroad). The resolution cited the importance of the proposed line to cheaply provide meat and breadstuffs to New Orleans and the Confederacy. Indeed, the resolution claimed that "the construction of this railroad will undoubtedly furnish the city of New Orleans and the Confederate Government a supply of beef and other provisions at a saving on present cost of a sum annually in amount to its estimated cost, and its existence as a means of military transportation will be equivalent to an army of 50,000 men." The resolution concluded by calling upon Louisiana delegates in the Confederate Congress to press for Confederate aid. The New Orleans & Texas president estimated that the proposed 117-mile line would require $1.25 million in bonds. In addition, some $250,000 in bonds was needed to complete the Texas and New Orleans line. On April 19, 1862, the Confederate Congress approved $1.5 million in bonds to complete the railroads, but, within days, New Orleans capitulated and the project was abandoned.[3]

Several minor railroad connections were recommended by the secretary of war in early 1865: "the Chief of Engineers and the Quartermaster-General concur in indicating the following as the most important railroads, the repairs or construction of which are necessary for military purposes, viz: First, the connection of Columbia, South Carolina with Augusta, Georgia; second, the connection of Albany, Georgia with Thomasville, Georgia; third, the connection of Union Spring, Alabama with Montgomery, Alabama; fourth, connection of Montgomery, Alabama with Selma, Alabama; to which the Chief of Engineers adds: Fifth, the completion of the railroad bridge over the Tombigbee River at Demopolis, Alabama."[4] These extensions would have eased the difficulties in transporting supplies across the Confederacy.

Breckinridge did not mention one other line that was being completed as he made his recommendations. The Live Oak, Florida, to Lawton,

Georgia, connection faced various difficulties that delayed its completion until March 1865, but this link gave eastern Florida its first rail connection to Georgia. The link could have been important had it been completed sooner, as it promised to be a conduit for Florida beef.

Near the Live Oak/Lawton link, two connections were proposed near the end of the war. These proposals reflected the fluid nature of the Confederacy's railroad needs. The Federal capture of Savannah in late 1864 severed a coastal rail system. The proposed connection between Albany and Thomasville, Georgia, would have partially compensated for the loss of Savannah and, perhaps more importantly, freed stranded rolling stock south and west of Savannah. In addition, a new link between Augusta, Georgia, and Columbia, South Carolina, was proposed. As was often the case, conscription interfered with the labor pool, and iron was scarce. The railroad officials requested details of skilled labor or sufficient exemptions and permission to take rails from the Federal-threatened South Carolina Railroad or from the remote Spartanburg and Union Railroad.[5]

As Virginia, Tennessee, and the Carolinas became stripped of supplies, the troops in Virginia were supplied increasingly from Georgia and Alabama, thus putting a greater burden upon the railroads. The Montgomery and West Point Railroad provided the only link between central Alabama and Georgia. By 1862, a second link between the states was proposed: from Talladega, Alabama, to Rome, Georgia. The line would have eased the supply of the Army of Tennessee. Another line between Montgomery and Union Springs, Alabama, was proposed in 1864. To help supply the troops in Virginia, a rail extension was proposed for southwest Virginia. The extension would have enabled the Confederate armies to enlarge their range of operations, especially into West Virginia.[6]

Breckinridge's recommendations reveal the slow pace of Southern railroad construction during the war. Many of these lines had been recommended much earlier in the war. Although the shortage of skilled labor was an important impediment to building these extensions, the lack of construction equipment and of railroad iron were crucial deficiencies, too.

2) Rolling Stock and Railroad Supplies

Rolling stock deficiencies became more debilitating as the war continued. Although the Southern railroads possessed car manufacturing and repairing facilities, these facilities were inadequate to satisfy wartime needs. A lack of key supplies for maintaining rolling stock exacerbated the inadequacies of the existing facilities.

Tredegar Iron Works had been the principal Southern builder of loco-motives. Unfortunately, the company quit producing locomotives after 1858. Because the Ordnance Department monopolized Tredegar's output during the Civil War, no revival of locomotive production occurred. The few other shops capable of producing locomotives were stymied by the lack of parts, especially steel boilerplates, sheet-iron, and flues for boilers. The iron needed for parts could have been produced within the Confederacy, especially if new rolling mills were constructed. However, the steel would have to be imported. A quartermaster's report questioned the govern-ment's monopoly on Tredegar's output: "It is estimated, and in my opinion rather under than over the mark, that fifty locomotives now in the Con-federacy are useless for the want of tires, and they can be made either at Atlanta or Richmond in less than six months; but the Government absorbs the work of these shops and the material also; consequently the railroads are impotent."[7]

The Southern freight and passenger car productive capability was less bleak. Virginia railroads, for instance, were able to build a few new cars during the war, although their capabilities were hardly enough to prevent the stock of usable cars from dwindling. More new cars could have been built, except for a paucity of key parts. A railroad official, Walter Good-man, informed Jefferson Davis that 300 or 400 cars could be manufactured for the government if springs could be obtained or manufactured. Trede-gar was the only firm capable of producing steel that could be transformed into springs.[8]

The initial supply of rolling stock was diminished by heavy use, of course, but also by abusive handling. Such wretched usage emanated from two principal sources. First, rolling stock that was placed on "foreign" lines suffered neglect, as carriers were more careful handling their own rolling stock than those of other lines. Typical of the complaints reaching the War Department was that of Georgia Governor Joseph E. Brown in October 1861: "We have let the East Tennessee roads have the use of our cars and engines this summer, and they have abused and broken them till we shall be very hard pressed for motive power and rolling-stock to do our winter's business."[9] A Quartermaster's report of October 1863 echoed Brown's com-plaint: "To complete what the government officers first thought to be the best plan for transportation, but which every railroad man knows to be a most destructive one, the former ordered engines and cars from road to road, irrespective of ownership, and making no provisions for their return." The Quartermaster attributed most of the destruction of the cars to this ill-sighted policy and lauded a new policy whereby owners kept their rolling stock under their own control. Confederate troops were the second contributor to the dilapidation of Southern rolling stock. Railroad officials complained that the troops riding in boxcars tore off the wood side-planks to provide ventilation (and to provide a view).[10]

Whatever the cause, the number of locomotives and cars on the Southern roads dwindled. Maldistribution of rolling stock worsened the shortages. Some lines suddenly became very busy, while other lines sank into a period of relative quiescence. Appeals were made to shift available rolling stock to the lines with the most urgent needs. Mere appeals were inadequate, primarily because of the aforementioned abuse, neglect, and non-return of loaned rolling stock. Even where the government impressed rolling stock, controversy could still erupt. In one case the Quartermaster Department impressed Central of Georgia Railroad's rolling stock to transport cotton to Wilmington, North Carolina, but the impressment angered theater commander General Joseph Johnston who wanted the rolling stock to transport supplies for his troops.[11]

In his April 1863 report to Secretary of War Seddon, Assistant Adjutant-General William Wadley estimated that Southern railroads needed 31 locomotives and 930 cars to make up for the deterioration of existing rolling stock. Wadley believed that the initial rolling stock had deteriorated by 25 per cent in the first two years of the war. All of this diminution in the Southern rolling stock and deterioration of the roads constricted the maximum carrying capacity of the railroads. In addition, the inexorable deterioration of rolling stock exacerbated other shortages. Because deteriorating locomotives lost thermal efficiency, they required more scarce wood fuel per mile.[12]

The condition of the rails proved another detriment. According to the *Report of the Secretary of the Treasury for the year ending June 30, 1860,* Southern ports received 65,000 tons of railroad iron. Almost all of the imported rail iron was from Great Britain. The English rails, even with the tariff and transportation costs, were considered a better deal, partly because of their higher quality. The rails normally lasted from ten to fifteen years, but the increased traffic probably meant a ten-year life. Only three Southern manufacturers were capable of rolling railroad iron: Tredegar, Atlanta Rolling Mill and Etowah Iron Works. The South possessed some iron ore deposits, but the area around present-day Birmingham, Alabama, was undeveloped. The north-central portion of the state was bereft of railroads. As historian C. B. Dew points out, the region possessed much pig iron, but very little was used. Pig iron output in Virginia for twenty-one months during the middle of the Civil War was less than 7,000 tons and was insufficient to keep Tredegar operating at more than one-third capacity. Even had the Tredegar and Atlanta mills received enough iron to operate at full capacity, their output would have been less than 20,000 tons, an amount far short of the 50,000 tons per year needed just to maintain existing tracks. Tredegar failed to roll any rails during the Civil War, and not a single new rail was manufactured in the Confederacy during the war. Some worn rails were rerolled, but this was a limited amount. Proposals to construct new iron works did not relieve the shortage, since attempts to construct new iron mills were futile in the face of labor, machinery, and raw materials shortages. Government price controls further curbed the incentive for developing new ironworks. Clearly, the South could not depend on domestic production to meet railroad needs, to say nothing of other Southern iron requirements.[13]

The government monopolized the meager output of the iron manufacturers for use in its naval construction programs. The exclusive use of iron for ordnance and ship armoring worsened the shortage of iron for railroad use. As iron became scarce, rail prices climbed. In December 1861, the Western & Atlantic purchased 1,100 tons for $50 a ton. By November 1862, the rails would have cost almost four times as much, a rate of increase slightly greater than the general price increase. Bulloch cites a rise from $25 to $1,300 a ton between March 1861 and January 1865. The result was to raise the cost of shipping (as well as eventually reducing the volume of shipping). Although railroad officials and some military officials criticized the government's iron monopoly, an equally vociferous coalition, primarily comprised of naval and ordnance officers, backed the policy.[14]

Even by the end of 1861, rail prices were high enough to induce existing railroads to consider tearing up their rails and selling them to more prosperous lines. Such a drastic measure as the *voluntary* cannibalization of some existing railroads did not provide the needed amount of iron and impaired the internal transportation system.

Two other methods of obtaining rails were employed. Some railroad companies sought to remedy the deficiency of rails by importing them through the blockade. The Federal naval blockade imposed severe restrictions on the flow of commodities in and out of the South. With the increased shipping costs imposed by the blockade, blockade runners preferred to bring in small volume/high value commodities instead of bulky iron rails. Still, the escalating prices drove the railroad companies, in January 1862, to formulate a plan to import railroad supplies. Railroad official D. T. Bisbie suggested to then-Secretary of War Judah Benjamin that the Confederate government help the combined railroad companies in their quest for imports: "The Government can of course get its own immediate wants filled, but not so the others without other combinations. . . . I submit, too, whether the Government could not, through the suggested combination, get its own importations more surely, promptly, and cheaply than through any other method."[15] The Government apparently did not act upon this proposal.

With a shortage of specie, Southern railroad companies resorted to using cotton to purchase railroad supplies. The Mississippi Central Railroad Company requested permission to ship cotton through the blockade in order to purchase railroad supplies. The railroad's president enlisted the help of a Mississippi congressman, and the secretary of war had no objections to the plan. To encourage the import of iron, the Confederate Congress repealed the duty on railroad iron to complete the Alabama & Mississippi Railroad.

The Confederate War Department did help some Virginia railroads in their efforts to import railroad supplies. Although the War Department refused to share space on its steamships, it allowed its agent, Captain John M. Robinson, to help purchase supplies in England. The captain's orders included selecting, purchasing, and shipping the desired supplies for a combination of five Virginia railroads. The president of the Richmond, Fredericksburg & Potomac Railroad, Peter V. Daniel, wrote to the secretary of war lauding Robinson's efforts: "[Robinson] succeeded in effecting very advantageous and satisfactory negotiations for purchasing [railroad supplies]." Daniel recommended that Robinson be enlisted to procure railroad supplies for other Southern railroads, but Secretary of War James Seddon responded unenthusiastically: "I prefer the presidents of the railroads should correspond among themselves or assemble by their own arrangements to consider the subject of procuring supplies from abroad. I am unwilling to intervene officially in matters relating exclusively to their own interest."[16] Thus, Captain Robinson's expertise was not applied to the pressing problem of obtaining railroad supplies.

In June 1864, the Mississippi Central again asked permission to trade cotton for railroad supplies and foodstuffs for its workers, but this time the trading partners were to be Yankees. The president, Walter Goodman, believed that 50 or 60 bales would be sufficient to obtain bacon and railroad tools. Altogether, the Southern railroads' efforts to import railroad supplies probably netted relatively small amounts.[17]

The second method to obtain iron rails was for the government to use its impressment power to cannibalize existing railroads for rails, rolling stock, and supplies. An engineer and special agent to the secretary of war recommended in April 1862 that rails and rolling stock be taken from an unprofitable railroad in Alabama to construct a line between Selma and Meridian. The agent requested authority to impress the materials, arguing that the stockholders would acquiesce in such an impressment. By January 1863, a War Department special order charged two military officers to ascertain what railroads in the Confederacy could best be disposed of and their rails taken up and used to maintain more important lines or to construct crucial new ones.[18]

Florida officials decided to tear up railroad tracks between Fernandina (occupied by Federal forces) and Baldwin and to use the rails to construct a link with a Georgia railroad (no eastern Florida railroad connected with any Georgia railroad). The Florida railroad was joined by four other railroads as candidates for cannibalization. The impressment of railroad property was a source of controversy. Not all of the selected railroads agreed to the decision to remove their rails. State governors, such as Florida's John Milton, jealously defended state authority against encroachment by the Confederate authorities. In some cases, Confederate authorities cultivated the cooperation of governors to obtain railroad property.[19]

The drawbacks of cannibalizing railroads included shrinking the area from which foodstuffs and staples could be drawn and the fluid nature of the military situation. Removing rails from areas threatened by Union forces came at the risk that the rail line might be needed later if the threat disappeared. In any event, the deterioration in Southern rails forced trains to reduce their speed.[20]

Shortages of railroad mechanical parts and construction tools also hampered the Southern railroads. Lack of parts led to increasing numbers of idled rolling stock and reduced thermal efficiency (thereby increasing the need for wood fuel). There was a lack of even such basic tools as axes and shovels, and this lack had deleterious effects on maintaining the railroads. Eventually the Confederate Congress passed a law exempting railroad companies from the payment of import duties on railroad supplies.[21]

3) Freight Rates and Fares/Railroad Finances

The tension surrounding the election of Lincoln and the outbreak of hostilities in April reduced freight shipments. The subsequent informal embargo on exports of raw cotton and the Union naval blockade's growing effectiveness accelerated the reduction of raw cotton shipments. Since raw cotton had comprised the bulk of many Southern railroads' freight, government freight and passenger business became essential alternatives.

In their initial patriotic enthusiasm, several railroad presidents offered to transport military supplies and personnel free of charge. As the realization dawned that the war would be prolonged, more realistic fares and charges were implemented. As early as April 1861, a convention of railroad presidents resolved to charge two cents per mile for troops and military freight at *half* the regular local rates, and they also agreed to accept, if necessary, Confederate bonds or Treasury notes as payment. Unfortunately, railroad liberality with government traffic planted the seeds of financial woes later.

Having become used to such generous terms, the Confederate government was loathe to relinquish them. In addition, the various states clamored for reduced rates, especially on the state-owned lines. Within a year, rising costs and lagging receipts of revenue led some railroads to press for increased rates, and a railroad convention held in December 1862 recommended increased fares and freight. However, throughout the war, Confederate traffic paid less than private parties, but compliance to the reduced rates could be insured by adroit use of coercive conscription laws. The Virginia Central eventually charged less than one-half for government passengers and *one-fourth* for government freight.[22]

With rates for government business artificially low, the companies attempted to raise rates to private parties. This triggered a call for regulated rates for private shipments, but the government refused to enact any such regulations. The secretary of war received a report from Lieutenant Colonel F. W. Sims (the military liaison to the railroads) stating that government freight rates in 1864 were only twice "peace prices" and that "These rates are not excessive, but on the contrary extremely liberal. The roads find their profit in caring for individuals, and if the private rates are cut down by act of Government it is inevitable that Government rates must be advanced. Speculators, etc., are thus indirectly aiding in keeping down the price of one of the heaviest items of Government expense." Sims's superior, General Alexander R. Lawton, endorsed the report and added his own comment: "It is believed that the action of the commissioners could fix rates only for Government transportation."[23]

The disparity in rates charged government and private business naturally led the railroads to favor the latter. Generals Joseph Johnston and Braxton Bragg in Tennessee and Georgia complained about the railroads' preference for private shipments.[24]

Price controls on railroad freight rates and fares for government business did not necessarily benefit the Confederate government. Although the government paid less for freight, the railroads responded by providing fewer rail services. The reduced services received by the government would offset partially, at least, the lower freight rates paid. The reduction in service would depend upon the sensitivity of supply to the artificially low prices. The more sensitive the supply, the greater the reduction in services supplied. Although the short-run sensitivity of supply may have been relatively low, the long-run sensitivity was certainly greater, implying greater cutbacks in services in the long run. Thus, the government benefited less and less from its price control as the war continued. Had the war been relatively short, the price control strategy might have been efficient from the view of the Confederate government. However, as a long-term policy, it was of increasingly dubious merit.

Moreover, by paying market prices to the Southern railroads, the Confederate government would have helped the railroads. Increased revenue would have assisted the railroads in buying cotton, shipping it through the blockade, and purchasing and importing railroad supplies. Although iron rails may have been impractical to import through the blockade, iron rails could have been produced within the Confederacy instead of being used to plate armored warships. Since the iron was not sold in a market context, there was no guarantee that the allocation mechanism was efficient or optimal. Second, a more flexible conscription policy might have provided the railroads with a more adequate labor force, while not significantly weakening the military prowess of the army.[25]

Aside from the government paying lower freight rates and passenger fares, such business had other drawbacks. The Confederate government frequently opted to pay its bills in Treasury notes and bonds, but these demonstrated a marked proclivity towards depreciation. In addition, even such unsatisfactory means of payment was often delayed. The liability incurred for damages to freight en route further injured the railroads' financial situation. With the dilatory effort to unload railroad cars, the cars were sometimes vandalized by soldiers (or stragglers as Governor Jospeh Brown characterized them) and pilferage occurred. The railroads had to reimburse such theft and damage of government supplies. Governor Brown recommended that the Georgia state railroad, the Western & Atlantic, no longer be liable for the cargo it was transporting. He also informed the Georgia assembly that the Western & Atlantic was suffering heavy losses in transporting Confederate freight. He called for charging the Confederate government "one hundred per cent [more] upon the rates now paid for the transportation of Confederate freight."[26]

Railroads that earned profits and paid dividends may have been paying out capital. Since Southern railroads did not explicitly calculate depreciation and because of the rapid rise in inflation, revenue and expense figures for the war years are suspect. The drastic run-up in prices, especially for railroad supplies, and the excessive wear and tear on the railroads were probably not completely accounted for. Although some lines paid higher nominal dividends (in percent of capital invested), the rate of inflation reduced the real dividend; indeed, the greater depreciation incurred by lines running large quantities of government freight may have created a situation in which paper profits were made, but real losses were incurred. In such situations, the dividends represented a cannibalization of the lines' capital. Some lines, such as the aforementioned Western & Atlantic, claimed "heavy losses." The president of the Georgia Railroad claimed that "The more business [the Georgia Railroad] does, the more money it loses, and the greatest favor that could be conferred upon it—if public wants permitted— would be the privilege of quitting business until the end of the war!"[27]

II. The Blockade's Effects upon Southern Railroads

Southern railroads were fragile conduits for the mass of war materiel and foodstuffs required to sustain the Confederate armies and the burgeoning population of Richmond (as well as other urban centers). There were ways to improve the rail system, but obtaining the means to effect the improvements were difficult. The Southern railroads were hard-pressed just to maintain themselves. Domestic resources were woefully insufficient to sustain and improve the existing railroads, but, in the absence of an effective blockade, Southern railroads might have easily purchased and shipped the requisite material from Europe (and perhaps even from the North). After all, the Southern railroads had imported most of their rails and other supplies from Europe and the North during the antebellum period.

In addition to the physical shortages of railroad supplies, many Southern railroads were facing financial difficulties. The initial uncertainty triggered by secession, the imposition of an informal embargo on exports of raw cotton and, later, the Federal naval blockade disrupted the normal flow of raw cotton to the ports, so receipts from shipping private freight plummeted. Several railroads found themselves in financial difficulties early in the war, impeding their ability to maintain themselves.

As the war continued, the Southern railroads' carrying capacity diminished rapidly. A Confederate military officer in charge of monitoring Southern railroads issued a gloomy report in April 1863. He detailed the estimated freight capacity for thirty-four of the key Southern railroads. Fourteen of them were only able to run one or fewer trains in each direction per day. None of the lines were able to run more than three trains in each direction per day. The daily tonnage capacity was equally distressing.

Unfortunately for the Confederacy, the dwindling carrying capacity of key Southern railroads coincided with growing demands for rail shipment due to wartime and blockade-induced changes in shipping patterns. Because the blockade severed water transportation between Richmond and the shipbuilders in New Orleans, the shipbuilders depended on the railroads to ship machinery and iron plating rapidly enough to complete the ironclads at New Orleans and Memphis in time to combat the Union fleets. The wartime dependence on Wilmington as an export center for raw cotton also placed greater burdens on the railroads of North Carolina and the Deep South. The loss of Gulf and Atlantic coastal shipping and the interruption of inland traffic on the Mississippi River and Chesapeake Bay compounded the growing demand for rail shipments.

III. Conclusion

The inadequacies of the Southern railroads contributed to the Confederate defeat. Confederate supply officers claimed that millions of rations (one-third to one-half pounds of beef or pork per ration) were en route to troops in February 1865. Millions of rations of breadstuffs were held at Augusta and Columbus, Georgia, awaiting shipment to the armies. The bottleneck was due, of course, to the ever-dwindling ability of the railroads to haul these rations. The Southern railroad system probably was incapable of efficiently supplying the troops and civilians, but the Union naval blockade helped stymie attempts to improve the existing railroads and compounded many of the inherent inadequacies of these railroads.

1. "Preparing Merchant Vessels for the Blockade." From *Harper's Weekly Magazine*, July–December, 1861. Photograph courtesy of the Naval Historical Foundation, Washington Navy Yard, D.C. Because the U.S. Navy had only forty-two commissioned warships, it purchased and converted many merchantmen. These vessels were hurriedly equipped with some ordnance and dispatched to blockading stations.

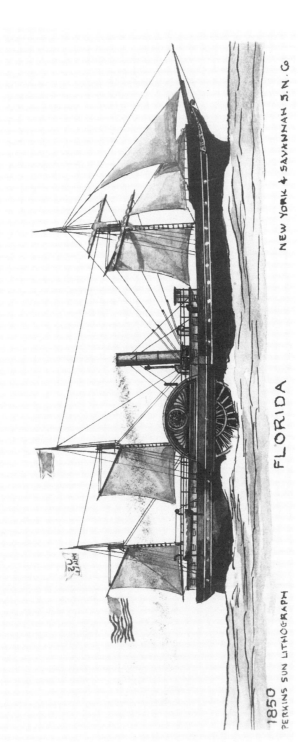

2. The *Florida* provided regular passage between New York and Savannah prior to the war. The U.S. Navy purchased the vessel in 1861 and used it as a blockader. Photograph courtesy of the Naval Historical Foundation, Washington Navy Yard, D.C.

3. The *Connecticut* was built for the New York & Savannah Steam Navigation Co. It is representative of the vessels plying the Atlantic coast. According to Silverstone, the vessel had dimensions of 251'6" x 38'2" x 14'. In comparison, the blockade-runner *Advance* had dimensions of 236 x 26' x 11'8". The *Connecticut* served as a transport, supply, and blockading ship during the war. Photograph courtesy of the Naval Historical Foundation, Washington Navy Yard, D.C.

4. The *Marblehead* is representative of a class of "90-day" gunboats. Most of these vessels were laid down in 1861 and commissioned before the end of the year, although the *Marblehead* was not commissioned until March 1862. The *Marblehead* eventually boasted seven guns. After the war, the vessel served as a merchantman. Photograph courtesy of the Naval Historical Foundation, Washington Navy Yard, D.C.

5. The *Eolus* was built as a merchant vessel in 1864, but it was immediately purchased by the U.S. Navy. The Navy mounted three guns on it and used it for blockade duty. The vessel is a good example of the "unwarlike" nature of many of the purchased vessels. Notice how similar it looks to modern-day sightseeing vessels. Photograph courtesy of the Naval Historical Foundation, Washington Navy Yard, D.C.

6. During the antebellum era, the *Yorktown* conveyed flour and corn between Richmond/City Point and New York. The Confederate government seized the *Yorktown* and renamed it the *CSS Patrick Henry*. The vessel served in the *Virginia/Monitor* battle in April 1862. As with the *Connecticut* and *Florida*, the *Yorktown* was designed to carry large amounts of goods. In the absence of an effective Federal blockade, the *Yorktown* would have been useful in conveying grain from North Carolina to Richmond. Photograph courtesy of the Naval Historical Foundation, Washington Navy Yard, D.C.

7. The *Malvern* was originally the blockade runner *Ella and Annie*, but was captured in 1863. Union naval officers quickly saw that successful blockade runners would be good blockading vessels, so the *Ella and Annie* served as a Union blockader after its capture. Photograph courtesy of the Naval Historical Foundation, Washington Navy Yard, D.C.

8. The *Advance* (also known as the *A. D. Vance*) was a blockade runner that was captured and used as a blockading vessel. The state of North Carolina owned the *Advance* until its capture. Notice the vessel's low silhouette. Photograph courtesy of the Naval Historical Foundation, Washington Navy Yard, D.C.

9. The *Fort Donelson* was another captured blockade runner that was converted into a blockader. As the blockade runner *Robert E. Lee*, the vessel was captured on its fifteenth attempt to breach the blockade. Photograph courtesy of the Naval Historical Foundation, Washington Navy Yard, D.C.

6

THE BLOCKADE'S EFFECTS
UPON MILITARY IMPORTS

I. Arms and Munitions

The blockade also affected the Confederacy's ability to import essential war materiel, especially small arms. The Confederates seized several Federal arsenals prior to Fort Sumter. Major Josiah Gorgas, the Confederate chief of ordnance, reported on May 7, 1861, that the former Federal arsenals located within the Confederacy contained only 159,010 small arms, the majority of which were percussion smoothbore muskets. Ammunition, too, was in short supply, and the report estimated that the captured arsenals contained only twenty to thirty rounds per weapon. The ordnance manual called for 200 rounds per man. The Confederate government would have been unable to fully arm its embryonic army with these captured weapons.

Imports of small arms were necessary throughout the war, as the Confederacy was unable to produce enough for its military. Confederate production of small arms remained minuscule, despite energetic efforts to promote domestic production. Even in November 1863 Gorgas reported that the three Confederate armories at Richmond, Fayetteville and Asheville had produced only 28,000 small arms during 1863. Private producers, "will swell this number to 35,000." At most, Gorgas hoped for 50,000 small arms for the year ending September 30, 1864, from these sources. As a comparison, the Union's Springfield Armory alone produced 350,000 rifles per year, and these rifles were produced at half the price paid to private manufacturers. Revolver pistols produced at Macon, Columbus, and Atlanta, Georgia, amounted to 500 per month, with 1,000 per month as the goal. Clearly this level of production was insufficient for the Confederate army. Confederate small arms production was hampered by various shortages, including a marked lack of skilled workmen, a problem that was exacerbated by Confederate conscription policies and the use of skilled workers as defense units. The futility of this policy is exemplified by the following anecdote: "The battalion made up of workers from the carbine factory and armory had lost one man, John Jones, in action. This seemed relatively small on the face of it, but the loss of this expert barrel-straightener proved far more disastrous than appearances indicated. Without his sure eye and steady hand, the armory production dropped at least 360 rifles per month." The shoulder weapons produced by the domestic producers also were generally of inferior quality.[1]

The Confederacy, thanks to the Tredegar Iron Works, had better success at producing ordnance, but this production was not sufficient to preclude the necessity of imports. Tredegar failed to reach its potential as an armorer. Historian C. B. Dew describes how Tredegar's management refused to adopt the Rodman method of casting cannon prior to the war. This method proved effective in lengthening the life of cannon, perhaps as much as three-fold. In addition, Tredegar was unable to cast the largest ordnance needed at the coastal fortifications. Tredegar also suffered from scarcities in raw materials and skilled labor. Historian Kathleen Bruce indicates that in late 1864, Confederate and Tredegar officials considered importing a new commodity—skilled workmen. These workmen were to have been given immunity from serving in the army. Unfortunately, Bruce was unable to find any evidence whether the men recruited in Europe were ever smuggled through the blockade, but the episode is indicative of a critical handicap facing the Confederacy. In the end, resort was made to hiring prisoners of war. Typically these prisoners would receive better rations in return for working in the Confederate armories; to preclude escape attempts, the names of the cooperating prisoners were forwarded to Federal officials. Another source of weapons was a tenuous and highly uncertain one: battlefield captures. Early Confederate triumphs in 1861–62 netted the South over 80,000 pieces. Of course, the fortunes of war could easily reverse this flow. After Gettysburg and Vicksburg, Gorgas lamented the loss of 70,000 arms.[2]

The Confederate army needed more than these sources to arm itself. Once hostilities commenced at Fort Sumter, both Federal and Confederate agents were dispatched to Europe to purchase war materiel, particularly shoulder arms. Northern arms buyers were often profligate in their purchases (European arms dealers gleefully exhausted their stocks of obsolete shoulder arms), but they drove up the price of all shoulder arms and curtailed the Confederacy's ability to arm its troops. This purchasing of arms also was hampered by the shaky Confederate finances. The blockade, too, raised the final cost of the weapons both from high shipping costs and from actual losses and captures of vessels conveying the Confederate purchases. Gorgas lamented that "a large proportion of his [purchasing agent's] purchases have fallen into the hands of the enemy."[3]

Despite these disadvantages, imports were the main source of small arms for the Confederacy. Historian Stephen Wise estimates that the South imported at least 400,000 rifles, or 60 percent of their total arsenal of shoulder weapons. Indeed, Confederate buyers in Europe gave first priority to procuring small arms. Historian Jac Weller estimates that more than 50 percent of Confederate expenditures were for small arms. Of the 400,000 rifles cited by Wise, relatively few came into the South during the first two years of the war (when the North was still assembling enough ships to create its strongest blockade). Gorgas reported the first arrival of imports on September 28, 1861. From that date until August 16, 1862, just over 63,000 small arms arrived in the Confederacy (only 15,000 through January 1862); 113,504 more arrived between September 30, 1862, and September 30, 1863. The quality of these imports was generally pretty high. Caleb Huse, the purchaser for Gorgas, opted for quality weapons instead of madly buying everything that was available. Weller estimates that of the 375,000 British shoulder arms purchased by the Confederates, some 300,000 were Enfield rifles (in four different models); these weapons, as well as 100,000 Austrian rifles purchased by Huse, were comparable to the rifles possessed by the Union troops. Indeed General Grant found the weapons captured at Vicksburg to be so superior to the ones carried by his troops that he issued the weapons to his men. Despite all of these efforts, a few Confederate soldiers went into combat bearing pikes instead of shoulder arms.[4]

The Confederacy also needed to import niter, saltpeter, and lead. The Confederacy was unable to stockpile enough niter from British India before the blockade became stringent. Since insufficient quantities came through the blockade, the Confederacy established a Niter Corps. This Corps succeeded in providing the South with minimal levels of niter, but the real cost was several times as high as the market price in Britain. Frank Vandiver's list of blockade runners passing through Bermuda reveals the continued need for imported saltpeter and lead. Of the 179 vessels headed into the Confederacy, 52 listed saltpeter on their manifests (roughly 10,000 sacks, bags, and barrels) and 59 listed lead (over 10,000 pigs). Iron was also imported (in bundles, plates, and sheets), especially after 1863. Cartridges and ammunition were imported until 1863, but then fell off in 1864.[5]

II. Confederate Shipbuilding Efforts

While the Confederacy had some shipbuilding capability, the resources were insufficient to meet the navy's needs. The production of iron plating was hampered by a shortage of iron ore (primarily due to the inability of Southern railroads to convey pig iron to the foundries and rolling mills and the loss of some of the iron-producing regions), the need to adapt rolling mills for rolling two-inch plate, and competition for the iron from railroads and other military needs. So strapped were the rolling mills for raw iron, that, even with virtual military monopolization of the available output, the available ore was insufficient to meet the navy's needs for iron plating. The shortage of raw iron offset the efforts to convert rolling mills in Atlanta and Richmond so that they could produce iron plating. During 1864, Mallory reported that the loss of Atlanta compounded the shortage of iron plating, and that although the remaining mills in Richmond are "capable of rolling any quantity, but the material [iron ore] is not on hand, and the amount now necessary to complete the vessels already built would be equal to 4,230 tons." Because of the paucity of iron to make two-inch plates, T-rails from railroad iron were used. The T-rails were not as protective as the two-inch plate. Even such humble items as nails and bolts were in short supply.[6]

As mentioned earlier, there were machine shops in the South, but most had never produced ship machinery. Even those foundries in New Orleans that had built ships before the war were not immediately capable of producing the machinery for the ironclad vessels desired by Mallory. Although some iron, steel, boilerplates, and machinery were smuggled through the blockade, the flow was meager and uncertain. The Navy Department purchased existing steamers and stripped them of their machinery for use in warships. In addition, Mallory hoped that the commerce raiders would capture steamers and that the machinery, especially propellers, could be stripped. The shortages and the inability to rapidly transport iron and machinery within the Confederacy led to delays in completing construction of warships, and such delays were often decisive.

The Union navy helped stunt the embryonic Confederate navy. By blockading the mouth of the Mississippi River, the Federals forced the New Orleans shipbuilders to transport iron and machinery from Virginia and the eastern Confederacy by rail. The rickety Southern railroads proved inadequate in transporting the vital materials. Completion of the *Mississippi* was delayed while a Richmond firm shipped the main shaft (recovered from a vessel that had been burned) across the Confederacy to New Orleans and while railroad iron was collected for the armor. The vessel was not completed in time to contest Farragut's attack on New Orleans, so the unfinished vessel was destroyed to prevent its capture. The blockade depressed Southern purchasing power from raw cotton exports and raised import costs, thereby stymieing imports of iron plating and machinery. Thus, the Federal navy's blockade became a form of self-preservation for that navy: A weak blockade would have eased the South's difficulties in constructing or obtaining a strong navy and possibly sweeping away the blockaders. The stronger the Federal blockade, the more difficult for the Confederacy to contest Union seapower and the blockade. In addition, the Federal navy's capture of New Orleans and Memphis eliminated two of the key Confederate shipbuilding centers.

Given the difficulties faced by Confederate builders in the South and Confederate naval officers in Europe in securing sufficient warships for the Confederacy, was there another way to build Confederate naval strength? James Bulloch advised that the shipbuilding efforts in Europe should be suspended in favor of boosting domestic shipbuilding. He suggested that the South, with its ample timber resources, should import iron plates from Europe: "I would therefore respectfully suggest that vessels be laid down at once, at the various ports in the Confederacy where timber is abundant, then by sending over scale drawings or working plans of their decks and sides, the iron plates, rivets, bolts, etc., could be made here, marked, and shipped to arrive as soon as the vessels would be ready to receive them."[7] In addition, Mallory knew as early as May 1861 that the Confederacy would have difficulty producing iron plating, while Europe, of course, possessed greater capabilities for manufacturing iron plates than did the South. The imported iron plates would have enabled the Confederacy to quicken the pace of shipbuilding, while conserving the scarce iron held in the Confederacy. The Confederates could have more easily imported ship machinery early in the war. The plan also would have avoided violating British and French neutrality and precluded the disappointments suffered by the Confederacy when their ships were seized by British and French authorities, as the importation of iron and machinery was less controversial than the purchase of European-built warships. The shipping of iron plates and machinery also would have avoided the difficulty of making European-built iron armored vessels seaworthy enough to navigate the Atlantic, while still having shallow enough draft to be operable in the coastal waters.[8]

Thus, even as late as Fall 1861, given sufficient purchasing power and the ability to import rolled iron and machinery through the still-developing blockade, the Confederacy might have obtained enough materials to alleviate the shortages and build enough ships domestically to contest the Union navy's control of the American waters. Or, at least, better Southern ironclads might have prevented the Union navy from capturing Southern ports. Historian Raimondo Luraghi believes that this was Confederate Secretary of the Navy Stephen Mallory's intent. In any event, the key would have been to obtain the iron plating and machinery to both speed construction of the *Virginia* and her sister ironclads and to improve these vessels' quality.[9]

While, even with foreign help, the Confederacy was unlikely to win a prolonged ironclad arms race with the North, it could have hoped to gain an initial superiority by early 1862. In retrospect, Bulloch's plan to ship iron plates and machinery looks astute and probably would have improved the Confederate navy, especially had the attempt been made early in the war before the Union navy's blockade became stringent.

III. Conclusions

The Confederate government had difficulty purchasing war materiel throughout the war. While a lack of credit loomed large in hindering the purchases, the blockade-induced increase in transportation costs combined with the depressed prices of Southern staples to further rob Confederate purchasing agents of the ability to get supplies. Attempts to increase credit on the basis of cotton held at Southern ports were only partially useful, as the cotton was typically valued at one-third the price in Liverpool or London. The other half of the purchasing equation, the cost of shipping goods into the Confederacy, became very expensive. Some blockade runners chose to minimize the risk by sailing into Southern ports without cargo. The Confederate government eventually legislated that blockade runners could not carry out Southern staples unless they brought in supplies. In either case, the blockade runners were typically small (compared to the vessels carrying cotton during the late antebellum era), and often were not loaded to capacity, either to improve speed or because cargoes could not be acquired rapidly. While some Southern leaders claimed that the blockade was not effective because insurance premiums were only 15 per cent on blockade runners, the Collie Company's experiences provides an example of the high costs of transporting goods. The Collie Company helped the

Confederate government in its purchasing endeavors and forwarded the following statement in June 1864:

Cost of goods:	$203,451
Expenses of shipping:	$442,568
Purchase of interest in two blockade runners:	$73,000[10]

Few governments are wealthy enough to pay two dollars shipping costs for every dollar of goods imported. The Confederate government was not an exception.

7

The Blockade's Effects
upon Civilian Imports

The blockade suppressed imports of consumer goods in three important ways. First, it surely affected the volume of imports from Northern and European producers. The reexports of European goods via New York, Boston, and Philadelphia, as well as direct shipments of Northern goods, dwindled in volume. The number of arrivals into the Atlantic ports of Norfolk, Richmond, and Savannah were sharply reduced from antebellum levels. However, Secretary of State Judah Benjamin boasted to Confederate agent John Slidell that Charleston imported $5.5 million worth of foreign goods in the first five months of 1863 based upon customs receipts. While Charleston's imports of early 1863 amounted to three or four times more business than in the previous year, such amounts at the Confederacy's busiest blockade-running port did not augur well. Since Southerners imported nearly $30 million worth of goods annually before the war, as well as the imports from Northern producers, $12 million per annum was a mere fraction of the antebellum import level. With New Orleans, Savannah, and Mobile cut off from foreign imports and Wilmington just beginning its rise as the main blockade-running center, Charleston's imports reflected just how constricted the flow was. Benjamin estimated that Wilmington would have $12 million worth of foreign imports annually. Unfortunately for Benjamin's optimistic forecast, Wilmington's imports would not be an addition to but rather a replacement for Charleston's imports, since Charleston's role as entrepot was destined for a year-long slump beginning in July 1863.[1]

The presence of empty store shelves testifies to the inability of Southern merchants to get goods from Northern and European producers. On his journey through the Confederacy, Englishman, W. C. Corsan, described the situation in Charleston in late 1862 (at the peak of Charleston's activity as a blockade-running port): "The regular resident merchants had . . . sold out their stocks long ago, closed their stores. . . . [Formerly busy mercantile streets] were now little more than rows of closed stores, and looked very much as if a perpetual Sunday or holiday prevailed."[2] Corsan also described similar scenes of empty stores in Richmond. Charleston's business activity revolved around the auctions of goods brought in by blockade runners. The regular merchants typically did not participate in this trade. Still, considering the limited number of vessels running the blockade, these blockade runners simply could not meet the demands of Southern consumers and the Confederate government.

Second, the blockade sharply reduced Southerners' ability to purchase imports, as the value of their staple export products fell relative to imported goods. The Richmond market reveals this plainly. In January 1861 cotton received eleven cents per pound at Richmond, while coffee cost sixteen cents per pound. A year later, with the Federal blockade of the Chesapeake, the prices of cotton and coffee were ten cents and seventy-three cents respectively. Imported foreign and Northern goods were not the only ones whose prices rose relative to staple products. Virginia and North Carolina may have been dependent upon imports of bacon even before the war, and sugar and molasses required a lengthy shipment from Louisiana to Richmond and North Carolina. With the Union navy's interdiction of the Mississippi River, sugar and molasses were trapped within the Mississippi valley. Thus, most of the sugar, molasses, and bacon that residents in the eastern states received was either smuggled through the blockade or traded between the lines. The prices of these goods escalated far more rapidly than did cotton.[3]

Although North Carolina benefited by having one of the major blockade-running ports in Wilmington, price data at that city provides clues to the impoverishment of Southerners. The port was not a major cotton-exporting center prior to the war, but Lerner was able to compile a time series of wholesale cotton prices. January prices are shown:

	1861	1862	1863	1864	1865
Cotton, per lb.	.12	.20	.34	1.89	2.21
Bacon, per lb.	.13	.20	.61	2.44	6.87
Flour, per bbl.	7.90	9.80	33.25	120.00	412.50
Sugar, per lb.	.10	.15	.69	3.11	7.25
Sheeting, per yd.	.08	.20	.61	3.63	5.00

A North Carolina cotton planter in 1861 could purchase with one 400–pound bale of cotton: two 200–pound barrels of flour, 100 pounds each of bacon and sugar, and 100 yards of cloth. By January 1865, his bale of cotton would buy less than half. The end result was that cotton lost much of its purchasing power. Since Wilmington was an entrepot for imported goods, one would expect cotton's purchasing power to be strongest there. A comparison with Fayetteville, an inland town, is illustrative (January prices):

	1861	1862	1863	1864	1865
Cotton, per lb.	.10	.09	.19	1.28	1.75
Bacon, per lb.	.12	.17	.52	2.56	6.33
Flour, per bb.	7.75	9.04	30.00	99.38	445.83
Sugar, per lb.	.11	.14	.88	4.00	12.27
Sheeting, per yd.	.09	.18	.37	2.23	3.75

Cotton's purchasing power eroded more rapidly at Fayetteville. Surprisingly, sheeting did not escalate as rapidly in price in Fayetteville as at Wilmington. Bacon was occasionally higher in price in Fayetteville, too. Apple and peach brandy prices at Fayetteville demonstrated the rapidly increasing cost of luxuries. Apple brandy prices rose almost 120-fold between early 1861 and January 1865, while peach brandy prices rose over 60-fold. Various state legislation against distilling grains and fruits contributed to the dearth of alcoholic beverages and may have therefore boosted prices of such beverages. The humble nail, another imported good (although hardly thought of as a "luxury"), increased in price 100-fold by the end of the war. Lerner's price data (corroborated by Schwab's) reveals that commodities primarily imported into the South prior to the war immediately increased in price with the implementation of the blockade. The prices of commodities that the South had exported during the war initially fell in real and nominal terms. Although the absolute prices of raw cotton, tobacco, peanuts, peas and rice thereafter showed dramatic increases, their real prices remained depressed during the war despite a marked reduction in the supply of such commodities. Products that were partly imported or produced domestically tended to fall between the imported and exported commodities. For example, meat was largely domestically produced, although we have seen that the antebellum South may have imported 5 to 10 percent of its supply. The increase in meat prices was far greater than that of cotton but less than that of such imported goods as nails, brandy, silk, and medicines.[4]

Third, the blockade created significant changes in the "relative" prices of imported goods, i.e. the ratio of prices of two commodities. Bulky goods, such as iron, might initially have low per-pound prices compared to, say, medicine or silk cloth. If the per-pound shipping rate increased by two cents, the *relative* increase in the price of a pound of iron would be greater than that of medicine or silk cloth. Shippers naturally brought in commodities that were relatively small in comparison with their value, so such military supplies as fodder, meat, iron, and munitions were less attractive to shippers than high-quality alcoholic beverages, silks, and manufactured clothing. Drugs were popular smuggled items, and Corsan described the gains to be made from a half ton of sulphates, chloroforms, calomel, and gum opium. Given that 1,000 pounds of "medicine" fetched $18,000 from Southern buyers, one can appreciate the attraction of foregoing bulky goods such as meat and railroad iron in favor of smaller, more lucrative goods. Even at the peak of wartime inflation, a ton of railroad iron fetched only $1,300/ton (instead of the peacetime rate of $50 or less), so imports of large bulky items such as rail iron ceased. Economists Robert Ekelund and Mark Thornton have thoroughly demonstrated the effects of changing relative prices on the mix of imported goods.[5]

Some observers have attributed the scramble for imported consumer goods of any kind to civilian "moral degeneracy." However, the descriptions of behavior when the blockade runners docked are reminiscent of descriptions of behavior during hyper-inflations, such as in Weimar Germany. Commodities held their value better than Confederate currency. Civilians bought whatever was available, before their currency almost literally shrank in their hands.

The Confederate government, desirous of getting more of its imports shipped, faced a conundrum. Heavy-handed edicts would drive out blockade runners, who frequently did not care to repeatedly run the blockade even in the absence of governmental regulations. Although Lebergott points out that only about 10 percent of all vessels engaged in running the blockade opted for a second attempt, as specialized steamers became available, owners were more willing to run the blockade repeatedly. The blockade runners also were sometimes hesitant to bring in goods (the insurance rates on blockade runners were around 15 percent), until the Confederate government mandated that no vessel could export Southern staples unless it brought in goods. If the blockade runners ceased to do business, the supply of imported goods would have fallen, exacerbating the redundant currency-driven inflation. Although the blockade runners reputedly made "fabulous" profits, when adjusted for risk the "fabulous" profits are whittled down to less legendary status. In addition, Lebergott estimates that investors in blockade runners might have been as well off had they invested in British war-related speculation. Politically, the government found it useful to accuse the traders of causing the dramatic increases in prices that triggered civilian discontent. Clearly, this accusation (as well as those against speculators hoarding foodstuffs and other Southern products) does not survive scrutiny. The real problems were the excessive currency in conjunction with a likely reduction of output. Unless the Confederate government could solve this conundrum (and it did solve the redundant currency problem, temporarily, by pursuing a new monetary policy in early 1864), debilitating price increases would plague the Southern economy.[6]

North Carolina Governor Zebulon Vance, recognizing the civilian hardships, instituted state action to bring needed supplies through the blockade. Vance decided to purchase vessels to run supplies for the state and to export state-owned cotton. The purchasing agent for the state issued warrants for North Carolina cotton as security for his purchases. The warrants allowed the holder cotton in North Carolina at five pence a pound (compared to twenty or more pence per pound in Liverpool), but the holder was then responsible for getting the cotton out of the South. In late 1863 Vance gave importing cotton cards and machinery for manufacturing highest priority. More than 100,000 cotton cards, which enabled North Carolina residents to produce cloth, were imported. Vance's scheme was so successful that Richmond officials occasionally sought to request supplies from North Carolina's stocks. Indicative of Richmond's heavy-handedness was its demand that the state share its blockade-running vessels with the Confederate government. Georgia Governor Joseph Brown also attempted to alleviate shortages. State-sponsored blockade runners appear to have modestly relieved civilian shortages. However, Confederate policies mandating reserved space for Confederate war materiel and foodstuffs discouraged private and state-sponsored blockade running. Such policies were essentially heavy taxes upon the blockade runners. At a time when the South needed imports, these policies were clumsy at best and more likely detrimental.

Southerners, civilians and soldiers alike, were deprived of their simple luxuries: coffee, tea, alcoholic beverages, sugar, manufactured clothing, paper, medicine, and many other goods. The Confederate government was plagued by a shortage of paper and engraving equipment, hindering its attempts to inflate the money supply. Such Southern produce as fruits and vegetables quickly became scarce throughout the South, primarily because of the region's inability to transport the highly perishable commodities. Norfolk had shipped vegetables and fruits coastwise prior to the war, but most of these products were stranded by Union troops and blockading vessels. Even such basic commodities as seeds were hard to find as the war continued.

Since the blockade runners brought in only modest amounts of goods, Southerners sought other sources. Historian Mary Massey describes the ingenious but ultimately unsatisfactory substitutes that Southerners discovered throughout the war. These substitutes could only alleviate the worst deprivations. Civilians living near the front lines sometimes fared better in obtaining goods, especially if the Yankees were willing to trade. Tales of women smuggling goods through the lines comprise one of the war's romantic genres. Given the paucity of manufactured goods, Southerners attempted to remedy the shortages. Luraghi amply documents the impressive attempts to "industrialize." Southern production of weapons and munitions increased dramatically during the war, but the strenuous efforts were insufficient to supply the troops. Most of the Confederate shoulder arms were imported through the blockade. The Confederate government subsidized niter production, as well as the production of other war materiel. Again, while the Southern efforts were laudable, such efforts inevitably failed to replace Northern and European goods. Confederate leaders, such as Jefferson Davis, described the blockade as a "blessing" for its impetus to Southern manufacturing: "As long as hostilities continue the Confederate States will exhibit a steadily increasing capacity to furnish their troops with food, clothing, and arms. . . . thus daily becoming more and more independent of the rest of the world."[7] Davis made these remarks ostensibly to help bolster Southern morale, but such posturing eventually proved embarrassing. Instead, the relevant question became, "Did the material deprivations damage morale within the Confederacy?" While some historians believe that the deprivations eroded morale and contributed to the demise of the Confederacy, there is difficulty in separating the effects of military reverses from the effects of deprivation. While desertion rates indicate some form of dissatisfaction, ascertaining whether the men deserted because of hungry stomachs, war weariness, or concerns about families is a frustrating problem. As one veteran wrote, "We would not Complain of Rations or hardships if there was a brighter prospect ahead."[8] The blockade-induced shortages of civilian goods surely contributed to the general demoralization of the Confederacy. Unfortunately, we cannot precisely measure its contribution.

8

THE CIVIL WAR SUPPLY
SITUATION IN VIRGINIA

I. Effects of the Civil War upon Trade Patterns

Even if the South had produced sufficient amounts of food and fodder and even if the antebellum distribution system had been adequate, there was a more severe problem: the necessary regional redistribution of food in response to wartime changes in consumption patterns. The concentrations of troops presented a challenge. Essentially Lee's Army of Northern Virginia and the Army of Tennessee became two "mobile population centers," and the extraordinary concentrations of horses and mules exacerbated the situation. Both armies maintained troop strengths of roughly 40,000 to 90,000 men, more than equivalent to the largest cities of the South except New Orleans. Such concentrations of hungry mouths would have created severe dislocations even under ideal conditions, but the Civil War was not an ideal time for such dislocations. The Army of Northern Virginia faced keen competition from civilians in Richmond for scarce rail, canal, and wagon transport. The city became a magnet for government personnel and sundry auxiliaries and its population increased from 40,000 to between 80,000 and 130,000. In addition, Confederate successes on the battlefield created a significant prisoner-of-war population in Richmond. The city's residents demanded ever-greater imports of bulky foodstuffs. If the meat requirement was 180 pounds per adult male equivalent, an increased population of 80,000 soldiers and civilians would have needed another 7,200 tons of meat. Even had there not been an influx of non-Virginians into the state, the collection of Virginians into an army would require collecting and forwarding large quantities of meat, grain, and fodder. With the expanded output of Tredegar Iron Works, there was an accompanying need for greater shipments of raw iron and other metals, thereby heightening the competition for scarce rail cargo space.

The fragile transportation network faced daunting challenges in reallo-
cating food and fodder to the new and fluid population centers in Virginia.
The existing rail network was not designed to supply these new "population centers." Wagon transport was unlikely to significantly assist the railroads. Historian Charles Ramsdell described wagon transportation during
the Civil War:

> By far the greater part of local transportation had to be carried on by wag-
> ons, carts, and teams. There were a few wagon shops in the South in 1860,
> but most of these vehicles, so essential to local needs, were imported from
> Northern shops. As the average period of usefulness of a farm wagon was
> only a few years, those already in use could not be expected to last through
> the four years of war. Under the hard service they broke down rapidly, for
> farmers were often forced to take them long distances over execrable
> roads—nearly all wagon roads were bad in those days. . . . The army needed
> large numbers of wagons and bought so many early in the war that the sup-
> ply left for civilian use was depleted. As the supply declined, many small pri-
> vate wagon shops sprang up, but difficulties beset the operators in the
> scarcity of seasoned woods for wheel spokes and felloes, or iron for axles,
> tires, and bolts, and in the loss of workers by conscription. . . . In conse-
> quence of all these things, wagons and teams had practically disappeared
> from many communities as early as the spring of 1864.[1]

A shortage of wagons manifested itself early in the war, and a Confederate
quartermaster's agent reported: "The committee are satisfied that the
wagon transportation is inadequate, and if the Army was furnished with
the full amount allowed by the present regulations, it would still be insufficient." The shortages of wagons for civilian use also hindered collection
of food taxes from farmers.[2]

The blockade-induced loss of water-borne transportation compounded
the difficulties facing the railroads. The Confederacy needed to use its
complementary water transportation system to augment and to conserve
its railroad resources. Indeed, a wartime railroad conference recommended: "That on all canals, rivers, and other lines of water transportation
as large a number as practicable of boats and vessels of any kind be speed-
ily constructed and used for transporting military supplies, so as to relieve
the railroads of the overwhelming amount of freights now thrown upon
them, and leave them available for transportation of what cannot be carried by water because of its locality or the urgency with which it is
needed."[3] Coastwise shipping would have alleviated much of the logistical
difficulties in supplying troops and civilians in Virginia. River and inland

water transportation, too, would have been very useful in moving the bulky flour, fodder, and grain to Lee's troops and to civilians in Richmond. Richmond could have been more easily supplied by coastal waters in the absence of an effective blockade. Because of the blockade, Wilmington, North Carolina, and Charleston became the main trading ports on the Atlantic. Norfolk became a center for between-the-lines trading. Cattle from Texas and Florida, grains from North Carolina and the Deep South, and other materials could have been collected at coastal ports, shipped coastwise, and then sent upriver to Richmond and other inland towns. Packed meat from northeastern ports sent through the blockade or traded between the lines kept the troops in Virginia from completely collapsing, but Confederate supply would have been much easier if such meat could have been freely imported in the absence of a blockade.

Water transport therefore loomed large in the Confederacy's ability to supply its troops in Virginia. Unfortunately for the Confederacy, Union control of the coast and many of the rivers precluded effective use of water transportation, so the railroads received little relief from this transportation mode. Indeed, instead of relief, the inability to use most of the waterways placed even more of a burden upon the railroads.

II. The Wartime Supply Situation in Virginia

The Confederacy was able to adequately supply its troops in Virginia throughout the first year of the war. To the northwest of Richmond, Thoroughfare Gap became a meatpacking center, while Manassas Junction became the main supply depot. The Confederate commissary had accumulated almost 1,000 tons of meat at these locations. In addition, there were 1,500 tons of other supplies. However, the supply situation began deteriorating in early 1862. General Joseph Johnston's precipitous retreat from northeast Virginia became a logistical disaster. In the Confederate army's hasty departure, most of the stockpiles of meat at Thoroughfare Gap and Manassas Junction were destroyed. Thereafter, the Confederacy never accumulated so much meat in Virginia, and one Confederate general, Jubal Early, lamented that the loss of foodstuffs "embarrassed us for the remainder of the war, as it put us at once on a running stock."[4]

As the war dragged on, Virginia, Tennessee, and the Carolinas became stripped of supplies or were overrun by Federal troops, forcing the troops in Virginia to rely on supplies from Georgia and Alabama. While the Deep South may have possessed sufficient food supplies, getting the available foodstuffs to Virginia was difficult. There was only one railroad linking central Alabama and Georgia, while supplies from northern Alabama and Georgia required a lengthy shipment by railroad.

The rail connections between Virginia and North Carolina centered upon Weldon and Gaston, North Carolina. One line led towards Norfolk and the others moved north to Petersburg. A line from Raleigh ended in Clarksville, Virginia, just inside that state's border, while a Virginia line ended at Danville, just inside the Virginia border. The need for another line binding North Carolina and Virginia quickly became evident. By February 1862, the Confederate Congress approved $1 million in bonds to fund a rail link between the Richmond & Danville and North Carolina railroads.[5]

The forty-mile gap between Danville and Greensboro took more than two years to complete. Labor and tool shortages impeded construction. Secretary of War Seddon appealed to North Carolina Governor Zebulon Vance to encourage his constituents to provide slaves, while the Confederate government would provide carts and tools to the construction efforts. During the interim, wagons bridged the narrowing gap between the rails. Finally, in May 1864, the connection was completed, albeit in a flimsy fashion. However, the timing was providential, as, during the summer, General George Meade and Grant had cut the Petersburg Railroad, leaving the newly built Piedmont Railroad as the only rail line from the south supplying Lee's army.[6]

Another crucial need was to improve the connections in Richmond and Petersburg, Virginia. Several rail lines entered Petersburg, but no through traffic was possible. Cargoes had to be transshipped through the town onto other rail lines. As early as June 1861, Robert E. Lee was advocating linking the railroads in these towns, citing delays in shipping ordnance from Norfolk through Petersburg. The connections were estimated to cost $75,000. Although the railroads involved were not opposed to the connections, the city governments were opposed. Both Richmond and Petersburg had been able to thwart railroad attempts to construct the connections. The railroads thus appealed to Jefferson Davis to override the cities and to allow construction to begin.[7]

These attempts to improve the rail system could not reverse the system's gradual deterioration. The reduced ability to convey supplies came at a bad time, since the railroads not only had to supply Lee's troops but also the burgeoning population of Richmond. According to Assistant Adjutant-General William Wadley's report, many of the railroads were only able to run one or fewer trains in each direction per day. The operating trains were unable to convey adequate amounts of supplies. There were four major lines supplying Richmond, and, according to Wadley, these lines had a combined capacity of 655 tons per day. The South Side railroad brought another 125 tons of supplies per day to Petersburg. Because of the loss of Tennessee and depredations in the Shenandoah Valley and Georgia, the supply situation continued to worsen throughout the remainder of the war.[8]

The relative performances of Southern railroads and U.S. Military Railroads are stunning. The Orange & Alexandria was a railroad linking Alexandria to Gordonsville in northeast Virginia. Union forces controlled the northern part of the railroad in 1863, while the southern part remained under Confederate control. Both Union and Confederate armies were supplied by the contested railroad. Lee's army sometimes received 30 tons of grain per day, while the Federal troops received over 650 tons of hay and grain per day. The U.S. Military Railroads units had refurbished the northern sector of the Orange & Alexandria by building sidings. The improved sector boasted a daily capacity of sixty trains of ten cars each. According to Wadley's April 1863 report, only one-and-a-half trains with a freight capacity of 160 tons could be run in each direction per day on the southern part of the Orange & Alexandria. Another Virginia railroad, the Richmond & Petersburg, shipped fewer than 2,500 bushels of corn into Richmond during July 1863, but the railroad did not even sustain this low level of shipments. In September, the railroad shipped less than half the amount it shipped in July; by January 1864, the corn receipts had dwindled to fewer than 500 bushels.[9]

The railroads were not entirely to blame for the diminishing shipments of grain. Confederate and various state controls and impressment policies discouraged farmers from sending their grain to the larger towns. Historian John Schwab believes that the fears of impressment and very low official prices helped reduce Richmond's receipts of grain from the usual volume of 700,000 bushels to 75,000 bushels in August 1863.[10]

Confederate logistics also were hindered by the fluid nature of the available supplies. Poor crops could cause a rearrangement of supplies, forcing Confederate officials to improvise. Hog cholera wreaked havoc on Kentucky and Tennessee's swine prior to and during the early part of the war. When the Confederacy lost Tennessee and started relying on Georgia's hog supply, the cholera moved into that state in 1863. Grain supplies, too, fluctuated. According to Ramsdell, the Virginia wheat crop of 1862 was less than one-third the usual size, while the rest of the South's wheat crops were damaged by rust and drought. The situation in Virginia and Georgia did not improve much in 1863, as too much rain in Virginia and too little rain in Georgia damaged crops. However, Georgia's grain output improved in 1864. These crop failures increased Virginia's wartime dependence upon the vulnerable North Carolina crops, with one Confederate supply officer stating, "Our great reliance must be on the large producing counties of North Carolina, and unfortunately the richest are in the hands of or under the control of the enemy."[11]

Whatever the cause, the shipments of grain into Richmond were insufficient. Shipments of meat were just as scanty. As Florida was unable to adequately fill the needs of the eastern Confederacy, recourse to alternate sources of supplies was necessary. In 1863, Wilmington became a conduit for meat to Lee's army. Blockade runners brought in meat from Bermuda (meat that often originated in New York or other Northern ports). More than six million pounds of meat was imported through the blockade at Wilmington between November 1, 1863, and October 25, 1864, and the imports of meat continued until the fall of that port. However, blockade running was an unreliable source of supply. Blockade runners were often delayed and, not infrequently, captured, while privately owned blockade runners were reluctant to carry military supplies, preferring other, more lucrative, cargoes. As a consequence, large stocks of meat accumulated in the Caribbean ports. In November 1863 and December 1864, commissary officials reported that three million pounds of meat awaited shipment, much of which rotted away.[12]

Even with the imports into Wilmington, the meat situation was getting desperate by the end of 1863. A report by the Bureau of Subsistence listed the meat supply in the eastern Confederacy. Aside from slaughtered meat, there were fewer than 19,000 head of cattle and 5,300 swine available for the military in Virginia, North and South Carolina, Georgia, Alabama, and Mississippi. The officer compiling the report concluded: "the meat ration on hand, November 15, 1863, in the States east of the Mississippi, being twenty-five days' supply for 400,000 men. It is again presented with the remark that the meat ration is nearly exhausted in Virginia, the last pound here having been forwarded to General Lee's army, and there is no 'reserve depot' to draw upon."[13]

Lee's army eventually required the services of a surprising supplier— the North. Norfolk and eastern North Carolina were the sites of a not-too-discreet "between-the-lines" trade: beef, salt, and other supplies for raw cotton. Meat was traded for cotton at rates of one to three pounds of meat for a pound of cotton. "Large quantities" of cotton were required each week at Weldon, North Carolina, to obtain the meat. An assistant commissary officer, Major Frank Ruffin, believed that Lee's Army of Northern Virginia received the bulk of its meat supply from this source during the last months of the war. In another instance, Lee obtained beef from the

North by theft. In late September 1864, Lee approved a proposed large-scale cattle-rustling operation by one of his cavalry commanders. The raid was successful and netted almost 2,500 head. Even with these sources, Lee's army received only 200 tons of meat during a three-month period in early 1863. Lee was forced to reduce the meat ration to four ounces of beef per day, but, at four ounces per day, the 200 tons would feed 60,000 men for fewer than thirty days. The lack of food and forage began to adversely affect his troops and animals, preventing him from launching a spoiling attack in 1864. Despite all of these efforts, Lee's supplies ran out in December 1864, prompting Jefferson Davis to react by ordering that meat held in reserve for the Confederate navy be "loaned" to Lee. When General U. S. Grant ended the between-the-lines trade in Norfolk, Lee's meat supply quickly ran out again, forcing him to abandon the trenches around Petersburg and move towards Appomattox and surrender.[14]

Since the railroads were unable to adequately supply Lee's troops or the civilian population of Richmond, shortages developed. The growing shortages of supplies led to price increases. Eugene Lerner's data reveal the growing inability of the Southern transportation system to distribute goods. During the early part of the war, flour prices rose more rapidly at Augusta, Wilmington, and Fayetteville than at Richmond. By October 1862, flour prices had quadrupled at Augusta and tripled at Fayetteville, while flour prices at Richmond had slightly more than doubled. As the war continued, Richmond's flour prices shot past the other three cities. By late 1864, Lerner no longer had flour prices for Richmond. Initially, hay prices were lower in Richmond than at Augusta, but the ratio flip-flopped by mid-1862, and subsequent hay prices were typically higher at Richmond. By July 1862, Richmond's corn and bacon prices were the highest of the four cities. After September 1864, corn, bacon, and hay prices were no longer recorded at Richmond. The more rapidly increasing prices at Richmond are suggestive of a general inability to ship adequate amounts of foodstuffs into the city, as even flour became scarce in the city renown for its flour. The scarcity of food was real enough to civilians in Richmond. High prices and shortages of food eventually led to civilian unrest in the form of "bread riots."[15]

How did the supply difficulties affect Lee's army? By the middle of the war, Lee wrote to President Jefferson Davis that a combination of scarce forage and inadequate grain supplies limited the effectiveness of his vaunted cavalry: "Some days we get a pound of corn per horse and some days more; some none. Our limit is five per day per horse." Even near the end of the war, Lee's transportation service alone included almost 14,000 horses and mules; to supply twenty pounds of fodder and grains per animal per day, the transportation service required 140 tons of feed per day. This was the equivalent of 140 wagonloads or ten to fifteen freight cars per day. Certainly, given the Confederacy's inadequate railroad and wagon transport, Lee's cavalry and transport animals could not be kept in one area for extended periods. The lack of fodder forced Lee to occasionally disperse his cavalry and, at other times, to dispatch one of his corps to other areas to save forage and to collect supplies. The fodder problem was never satisfactorily resolved. Lee's biographer, Douglas Freeman, attributed some of Lee's strategic decisions to logistical difficulties. After his victorious campaign against John Pope in August 1862, Lee decided to invade Maryland, hoping for supplies and recruits. Lack of footwear resulted in serious straggling during the Maryland invasion, with Lee ruefully, if exaggeratedly, remarking, "My army is ruined by straggling." Similarly, in May 1863, Lee decided to invade Pennsylvania, in part to procure supplies. Lee did not believe that his troops could subsist in Virginia: "The question of *food for this army* [italics his] gives me more trouble and uneasiness *than every thing else combined;* the absence of the army from Virginia gives our people an opportunity to collect supplies ahead."[16] Lee believed that short rations contributed to the growing desertions early in 1864. To alleviate the suffering, he increased the number of furloughs. Once Grant pinned Lee's army in the trenches around Petersburg, Lee's supply situation deteriorated as Grant gradually cut the remaining supply lines; desertions also began to increase again. The supply situation was so dire that Lee recommended moving prisoners of war and non-essential civilians from Richmond to reduce the diversion of supplies from the army.[17]

III. Conclusions

The stocks of supplies available within the Confederacy in February 1865 argue against a lack of existing supplies being the primary cause of Lee's supply difficulties. After the war, former Confederate supply officers listed millions of rations that were en route to Richmond in February 1865. As one Confederate supply officer lamented, sufficient supplies were available in Virginia and North Carolina pending: "the lines of communication being at once restored and protected . . . the ability of the Treasury to meet the requisitions of this Department, and the Quartermaster-General to provide the necessary transportation for the stores when purchased and collected."[18]

What caused the distributional difficulties? Were the railroads responsible for Lee's supply collapse? Indeed, the railroads' performance, while inadequate to the task, must be seen in a wider context. Rail lines were not the only arteries in the South's transportation system. The war altered trade patterns, and the existing transportation system was not designed to handle the new patterns. The concentration of perhaps 100,000 extra people around Richmond, as well as thousands of animals, amplified the derangement of antebellum trade patterns and created severe challenges to the transportation network. The Union navy prevented the Confederacy from using the one transportation mode that was flexible and expandable enough to meet the new trade patterns: water transport. For instance, Norfolk's corn receipts from North Carolina were sufficient to provide 14,000 animals fifteen pounds of corn per day for an entire year. In the absence of an effective Federal blockade, this corn could have been conveyed to Norfolk by the Dismal Swamp Canal (as during the antebellum era) and then shipped from Norfolk to Richmond by riverboats. Besides supplying Lee's transport animals, such a movement would have alleviated the pressure on the railroads heading into Richmond from the south. The Chesapeake and Atlantic coastline could have accommodated a much greater volume of wartime traffic than it did during peacetime, and a well-managed fleet of ships could have alleviated the dire condition of Southern railroad transportation. The steamers *Jamestown, Nashville,* and *Yorktown* had operated on the Richmond/Charleston to New York routes prior to the war. Each vessel was over 1,200 tons. The *Jamestown* and *Yorktown* often carried over 1,200 barrels of flour and other cargo per trip. Several river and sailing vessels also remained. The Confederate authorities confiscated the steamers and converted them into warships. As warships the vessels were of limited value, but the tightening blockade may have made using these steamers for coastwise trading moot. The blockade also hindered the Confederacy from obtaining meat from Northern (often via illegal trade) and European ports.[19]

The loss of river and coastal shipments has received inadequate attention from commentators on Lee's supply problems. The loss of waterborne transportation was not trivial, and the Federal navy's blockade deserves more credit for helping to subdue Lee and his troops.

Part III

THE WAR AGAINST RAW COTTON

One of the blockade's major contributions to the Union victory was denying the Confederacy badly needed revenue from the export of raw cotton. Southern growers of raw cotton produced the bulk of the western world's supply of the staple. Attempts to create sufficient and reliable alternative sources had failed throughout the late antebellum era. Given that they produced three-quarters of the supply, the Southern growers collectively possessed price-setting power. Such power might be exercised in two ways: reduce the crop to a profit-maximizing output or completely withhold raw cotton in order to induce European intervention. I shall develop a counterfactual that recognizes and incorporates the South's price-setting power in the world market for raw cotton. Rather than contrast actual revenues earned from exports of raw cotton between late 1861 and mid-1865 against 1860–61 revenue levels, the comparison is made against a hypothetical best guess of the South's potential revenues from either directly or indirectly exercising its price-setting power. Although Southerners initially opted for the complete embargo, they eventually saw that they needed to export raw cotton to procure war materiel and to keep their domestic economy from upheaval. In the absence of an effective blockade, the Southern growers would still have had an opportunity to exercise their collective price-setting power.

Since there is some question as to the strength of the world demand for American-grown raw cotton, which would affect the Southern growers' collective price-setting power, I describe the state of the world markets for cotton textiles and raw cotton during 1860–62. Were these markets destined to stagnate in the absence of an effective blockade? Then I examine the quantity of raw cotton exports and the revenue earned from these exports during the Civil War before comparing these actual flows with the hypothetical best guess of the South's potential revenues from exercising its price-setting power. The blockade further reduced the gains from exporting raw cotton by rearranging the intraregional movement of raw cotton. Finally, the blockade's effectiveness, coupled with the capture of New Orleans and Memphis, allowed the Federal government to devise policies to reap benefits from Southern-grown cotton.

9

KING COTTON'S
POTENTIAL

I. The South's Price-Setting Power

King Cotton's reign began in optimism. The Southern states dominated the antebellum cotton market, usually supplying 75 percent or more of the total supply used in Europe and the United States. Southern raw cotton producers collectively possessed price-setting power in the market for raw cotton. The antebellum world demand for American-grown raw cotton was inelastic (perhaps 0.8 in absolute value, i.e. a 1 percent increase in price would decrease quantity demanded by 0.8 percent) and growing at an annual rate of 5 percent. Because demand appeared to have been inelastic, a moderate price increase based on an output decrease would increase total revenue.[1]

Presumably, the South, acting as monopolist, would like to maximize profits, not revenue. Since one of the main gains from restricting output would be the switching of manpower from producing and processing raw cotton to other productive uses (serving in the military or producing food and war materiel), I will use the savings in manpower as a proxy for the reduced costs. Moreover, in 1861 the Confederate government needed to win a war, and the Confederacy's chances were predicated upon revenue (primarily from the exports of staples) and military manpower.

In Figure 9.1, a production possibilities curve depicts the trade-off of labor between producing raw cotton and supplying military needs. Because the South possessed price-setting power and demand was inelastic at the 1860–61 level of output, the production possibilities function would have an upward-sloping section instead of being continuously downward-sloping. Clearly, the South's price-setting power creates a greater production possibilities curve than if the region was a price-taker in the world market for raw cotton.

Figure 9.1 also shows downward-sloping isoquants that depict various probabilities of military/political victory. Each isoquant represents all the combinations of revenue from raw cotton and labor devoted to military needs (instead of producing raw cotton) that afford a specific level of probability of military/political success. The Confederate government presumably wished to maximize the probability of military/political success; to do so, that government wished to attain the highest isoquant possible. Such an optimization occurs, of course, at the tangency between an isoquant and the production possibilities curve.[2]

King Cotton's power is manifest in Figure 9.1. In 1860–61, the South was to the left of the maximum revenue, so cutting the production of raw cotton could generate additional revenue while freeing up labor for other pursuits. Perhaps as important, reducing the crop beyond the revenue-maximizing output level did not entail a precipitous drop in revenue. As will be shown, the revenue falls slowly with respect to decreasing output past the revenue-maximizing level, i.e. the production possibilities curve was relatively flat for a large range around the maximum revenue. Thus, a relatively large reduction in the output of raw cotton (creating a relatively large influx of labor for military needs) might have entailed only a modest reduction in revenue. The relatively flat production possibilities curve implies the possibility of reaching even higher isoquants and likelihood of victory than if the South was a price-taker or was unable to exploit its price-setting power.

One possible exception to the above analysis of King Cotton's power is that, by completely withholding raw cotton, the Confederacy might have been able to coerce British and French intervention. The cotton embargo did not induce intervention. The usual explanation is that a huge overhang of raw cotton held in England doomed the coercive effort. Such an overhang would have also temporarily reduced the South's gains from its price-setting power. The Southern cotton growers had diluted the effectiveness of the embargo by hurriedly forwarding their cotton to market prior to the attack on Fort Sumter, so any "Cotton Famine" would take time to develop. However, the increases in the stocks of raw cotton were not as dramatic as portrayed and would stave off a shortage by only a few extra weeks; in addition, the increased stocks probably signified a desire by producers and speculators to hold more inventory in the face of an uncertain supply rather than a glut. A more serious problem with the coercive strategy was that Southerners underestimated the Europeans' anger at the coercion: "It seems to be quite true that all Cotton exportation has been forbidden by the Confederate Government in order that foreign nations

Figure 9.1. Optimal Allocation of Manpower between Producing
Raw Cotton and Meeting Military Needs

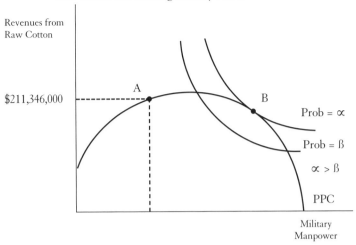

The South has production possibilities curve, PPC. Because the region possessed price-setting power and faced inelastic demand at the original level of production of raw cotton (Point A, netting $211,346,000 in revenues), the curve has an upward-sloping segment (cutting raw cotton output raises revenue). Different combinations of revenue from raw cotton and manpower available to the military (instead of being devoted to producing raw cotton) form isoquants. Each isoquant represents a probability of achieving military/political goals.

The optimal allocation of manpower between producing raw cotton and fulfilling military means is, of course, the point of tangency between the PPC and an isoquant (Point B).

may be forced to take a side in the quarrel. It would ill become England to make herself the tool of such machinations [and intervene against the blockade]."[3]

The Union navy's blockade might seem to have assisted a Confederate embargo on cotton exports or an attempt to exercise its price-setting power. Southern leaders and British observers recognized the combined effects of the embargo and blockade in squelching exports of cotton, but the dearth of cotton exports did not induce intervention. While an effective blockade might have constricted exports to a level commensurate with a price-setting optimum, the increased price and reduced exports would have been due to higher transportation costs, and such higher costs would not have benefited Southerners.

In 1860–61, the receipts for cotton were $211 million (based on a crop of 4,590,000 bales). Given the assumptions discussed in Appendix 2, $247 million would have been the maximum total revenue accruing to the South (based on a slightly larger crop of 4,651,000, because of the 5 percent per annum growth in demand). A reduction to 3,756,000 bales (P = $70) would still raise $240 million, some $29 million more than received in 1860–61.

Even a reduction in the crop to 3,050,000 bales (P = $80) would create $226 million in revenue, or some $15 million more than the revenue earned in 1860–61. The crop reduction of 1,540,000 bales would free up at least 170,000 man-years of labor. As a comparison, the United States navy had spent less than $15 million annually during the three fiscal years ending June 30, 1860. In addition, fewer than a tenth of the workers displaced by reducing the crop by one-third would have been needed to create a regular army larger than that possessed by the United States on the eve of the Civil War, as the army consisted of 16,000 officers and enlisted men on June 30, 1860.[4]

If demand continued to increase in subsequent years, the gains from a restricted crop output would also increase, unless rival raw cotton producers expanded significantly. The evidence on this point suggests that only a modest inroad into the South's market share would have occurred.

II. How to Collectively Reduce Output

The Confederate government would also have needed an idea of the shape of the probability of victory isoquants to choose the optimal level of raw cotton output. Assuming that the Confederacy ascertained the price and quantity of raw cotton that would maximize the chance of military/political victory, the next question is how the Confederate government would have restricted output. The Confederate government could have achieved the optimal price by assessing the correct export duty. The tax revenues could have been used to finance the war. In order to gain political support for the restriction on output, the government could have then offered rebates to growers. The rebates would have been paid conditional on the individual grower adhering to a restricted output (perhaps a fixed percentage of his 1860–61 output). The rebates would be calculated to allow the growers to maintain the same level of income as they earned in 1860–61 and any tax revenue remaining could be used to finance the war. Thus, the Confederate government could plausibly institute a program where Southern growers received the same level of revenue, while allowing for reduced labor inputs and *some* financing of the war. Such a scheme can be envisioned to be politically feasible—i.e. the planters would be at least as well off from a revenue standpoint, while being able to contribute manpower to the military or to other productive endeavors. Therefore, the Confederacy could have waged a modest war at relatively little or no deleterious effect to its economy (in comparison to prewar levels of income), while shifting some of the cost of the war to consumers of cotton goods.

Southerners were not unaware of their potential price-setting power. Antebellum journals carried editorials urging reductions in output, thereby raising prices and profits. To reduce output, some writers urged acreage limits, while other writers believed that a better flow of information regarding the size of the crop would enable planters to get better prices. The planters also seemed to grasp that demand was inelastic, although this view was not unanimous.[5]

As secession loomed, Georgia Governor Joseph Brown pressed for the imposition of export duties on cotton as a diplomatic lever for the South. The duties would have enabled the Confederacy to raise revenue while allowing a reduction in import duties (thereby diminishing the Northern states' share of the Atlantic trade and enhancing the prospects of "direct trade" with Europe). In addition, an export duty would encourage the border states by allaying fears of direct taxation. An export duty's big advantage over an acreage limitation was its ease of administration. The shippers at Southern ports were all familiar with port collectors, as the antebellum United States levied import duties on an array of commodities. It should have been a simple task for the Confederate government to build upon the duty-collecting apparatus at the ports. While some growers might have been tempted to smuggle raw cotton without paying the duties, it is not clear that there would have been much gain from doing so (especially if the export duty was only two or three cents per pound). The idea of an export duty upon cotton had been broached for at least a decade prior to secession. Even in 1849, contributors to *DeBow's Review* were advocating an export duty on raw cotton. In July, H. Smith proposed, "an export duty on raw cotton as will ensure the fabrication of all *coarse* [italics his] cotton goods at home." In December, S. Cockrill suggested that Congress, "shall pass a law, that five dollars per bale be paid into the treasury of the United States upon all raw cotton shipped after the year 1860." Both of these writers advocated export duties in conjunction with the planters shifting some of their capital into erecting cotton mills. J. W. Wilkinson of Charleston was another advocate of an export duty, as he believed that an export duty was the best revenue-raising policy for the Confederate government. He proposed a duty of one cent per pound, roughly a 10 percent duty. Wilkinson's argument is noteworthy in that he explicitly claims that the burden of the tax would fall largely upon foreign nations (he estimated nine-tenths) and that the burden borne by Southerners would amount to two dollars per capita. He also touted the policy's ability to reduce or eliminate the need for import duties and for its ability to eventually lead to direct trade. Neither Brown or Wilkinson explicitly argued for using the export duty to reap a monopoly profit, nor did they discuss what level of duty might maximize government tax revenue. Their proposals were moot as long as the South remained in the Union. During the antebellum era the market for raw cotton remained competitive, since the United States Constitution prohibited export duties that could have created a national monopoly in cotton. The Confederacy revised its Constitution to allow for export duties. Coincident with the greater revenue associated with a smaller output, editorial writers speculated on what to do with the saved labor. Some believed that the "extra" workers could be switched to manufacturing (perhaps in Southern textile mills) or in building Southern railroads.[6]

The strategy of enacting an export duty was not strongly pursued, as Southern legislators were hesitant to enact a significant export duty. Thomas R. R. Cobb wanted to propose such an export duty, but was dissuaded by other legislators. The other legislators were afraid of antagonizing the great powers with either a formal embargo or an export duty. On February 28, 1861, the Confederacy enacted an export duty of one-eighth of one cent per pound on all cotton shipped after August 1, 1861. Unfortunately for the Confederacy, the combination of the cotton embargo and the blockade limited tax revenues from this initial export duty to only $30,000 in specie. In May 1861, Treasury Secretary Christopher Memminger advocated increasing the export duty to at least 10 percent on cotton and other staples, but this was not enacted. In 1863, he again recommended an increase in the export duty, this time to two cents per pound. Finally, his successor, George Trenholm, proposed an export duty of five cents per pound in late 1864. Again, this final attempt to raise the export duties failed.[7]

The general belief that the war would be short and relatively painless is one possible explanation for the Confederacy's timidity in using raw cotton as a revenue-creating vehicle. Historian Douglas Ball and other commentators suggest another reason. Ball believes that the Confederate government was unsure of the strength of public support for the war and was therefore hesitant to levy direct taxes upon a possibly lukewarm population. In a sense, the Confederate government was not too different than most wartime governments; since there is difficulty in assessing just how much citizens are willing to pay directly for a war, many governments desire to camouflage the true costs of war.[8]

With the failure to enact a suitable export duty, the Confederate government might have been unable to directly constrain production or, even if production was constrained, to tap much of the prospective increase in revenue from constraining cotton production. Other ways for the government to have gained from the South's price-setting power would have been to levy an income tax on growers and shippers, legislate acreage restrictions, or purchase the cotton from growers (becoming a de facto monopolist). However, some of the benefits of the South's power could still be realized by passive means, as the war would also assist in limiting the output of cotton. For instance, military manpower needs would certainly reduce the labor force. While slaves would have have served as soldiers, they might have been shifted from the plantations and been used as teamsters, stevedores, or as laborers on fortifications. The reduction of imported foodstuffs from the Northern states caused by the non-intercourse acts and the reduction in food production by white yeoman farmers could have been offset by switching slaves into food production. In any event, a South maintaining its prewar levels of revenue from exporting raw cotton was in a stronger position to finance a war than a South whose revenue from cotton was shackled by a Union blockade that reduced exports and revenue.

Regardless of the Confederate government's failure to directly tap the potential revenue-generating power of raw cotton, some of the financial cost of the war could have been shifted to the Northern and English cotton manufacturers and ultimately to consumers. Southern confidence in King Cotton was not misplaced. An adroit use of her cotton power could have strengthened the Southern economy and war-making capacity; this was the power of King Cotton. However, there is a related question: Would the state of world demand have supported such a price-setting strategy?

10

An Examination of the Antebellum and Wartime Markets for Raw Cotton and Cotton Textiles

In the absence of an effective blockade, Southerners could have used their collective price-setting power in the world market for raw cotton and shifted some of the cost of a war to consumers of cotton goods, while also releasing manpower for her armies. There is a question, however, whether the strength of world demand for American-grown raw cotton would have supported such a strategy. Indeed, the question of the direction of the world demand for American-grown raw cotton during 1860–61 is an important one that has been debated for over a century. If the demand was destined to fall either temporarily or for a prolonged period, then the Southerners were guilty of two miscalculations. First, if the demand for raw cotton was destined to plunge, then the future profitability of raw cotton would become questionable. For instance, a 5 percent annual decline in world demand for American-grown raw cotton would decrease total revenue by $10-15 million per annum in the first two or three years of such a decline. While those amounts seem small, they would have been enough to finance a navy comparable to the antebellum United States navy. A long-term decline in the demand for cotton might have confirmed the truth of historian Ulrich Phillips's argument that slavery was destined to decline (unless slaves could profitably be switched to other endeavors). Therefore, if the demand for raw cotton was destined to fall, then the Southerners might have engaged in a desperate war for a potentially moribund economic institution. If, instead, the war drove any long-term decline in demand, then the South not only lost the war, it also lost the economic peace. Southerners who argued for peace would, in retrospect, look even more statesmanlike, as remaining in the Union and trying to dictate future events within the political arena would have been more astute. Second,

King Cotton's power was a key factor in the Southerners' reckoning of their chances of gaining independence. Jefferson Davis had urged Tennesseans to secede, claiming that "cotton would pay all debts of war and force New England into penury and starvation."[1] Davis did not have to exert much effort to persuade Southerners to agree with him, and Confederate foreign policy was initially animated by the belief that depriving Europeans of cotton would induce intervention on behalf of the Confederacy. However, some historians believe that a "huge reserve" of cotton in stock on the eve of the war dampened the urgency for Europeans to intervene on economic grounds in the war. Howard Jones writes that "fortune had looked kindly on the Union: British manufacturers had a year's surplus." This reserve purportedly reduced Great Britain's need to intervene in the war in order to obtain cotton. Jones is only the latest in a long line of historians to imply that the Confederacy chose a poor time to coerce the European powers.[2]

Arthur Arnold was the first observer to claim that the Civil War-wrought upheavals masked an underlying trend towards decline. Arnold, a British official involved with managing relief for the unemployed Lancashire cotton operatives, believed that the markets for manufactured cotton goods were glutted during 1860–61: "The India and China markets had been over-fed with manufactures until they threatened to burst with bankruptcy.... with reckless cupidity, manufacturers had rushed to divide the profits of the increased trade.... merchants still piled the goods in the warehouses of Bombay, until ruin stared them in the face, and . . . these commodities had become an unmarketable burden." He cited the large stocks of raw cotton and finished cotton goods as evidence of overproduction; in addition, he showed that prices for manufactured goods had not risen commensurately with raw cotton prices early in the Civil War. He concluded that the Civil War masked these underlying trends: "Had there been no war in America, 'hard times' must have come upon all in the winter of 1861. As it was, this event brought relief to the holders of goods, wealth to the speculators in cotton, and a comfortless autumn, with a hopeless winter prospect, to the operatives."[3] Strangely, he did not explain why manufacturers would continue to pump out more 'unwanted' goods.

However, Arnold's contemporaries did not unanimously hold the overproduction thesis. The *Economist's* version of the era differs. Although admitting that some markets were overstocked, on September 6, 1862, the *Economist* cited exogenous factors that disrupted the market: the diminution of the American market because of the Civil War and Morrill Tariff, recurring famines in India, and continuing trade barriers on the European continent. In addition, the *Economist* cited the natural entry of new textile firms and expansion of existing firms spurred by the high prices of 1858–60. By January 31, 1863, the *Economist* still saw nothing untoward in the behavior of the British capitalists and believed that any glut was largely eradicated by the end of 1862.

Still, Arnold's thesis has resonated in the work of subsequent scholars, and there is an extensive literature concerning the direction of the markets for cotton textiles and raw cotton on the eve of the Civil War. Several writers have advanced Arnold's idea that the long antebellum boom in cotton textiles had reached a climax with the expansion of 1858–60 and was destined to be reversed in 1861–62. Each writer presented varying explanations for this reversal. Arthur Dunham expanded the thesis of overproduction and impending crisis to include France, but he also cited large stocks of raw cotton and manufactured cotton goods as evidence of "overproduction." Frank Owsley combined strands of both the *Economist's* and Arnold's depiction of the market for cotton textiles, believing that a combination of factors foretold "destitution in the cotton districts." He cited such factors as the overproduction of cotton textiles, the disruption of the American market, cheapness of rival textiles, fear of large raw cotton stocks in the Confederacy, and the scarcity of American cotton due to the embargo and blockade. Eugene Brady not only rekindled the thesis emphasizing that overproduction caused distress in the market for cotton textiles, but he also concluded that the Civil War-induced shortage of raw cotton simply complemented the necessary check on the production of cotton textiles: "Rather than causing a significant physical shortage of raw cotton, the American Civil War induced expectations [which were never realized] of a future shortage, which greatly increased the price of existing stocks of raw cotton in the United Kingdom. British cotton manufacturers could not have continued to produce beyond world requirements, as they had done just previous to the depression, without adding to an already enormous unmarketable stock of textiles. It appears that the Civil War induced price increases of raw cotton, which reinforced a check upon production that would have been necessary anyway."[4] Farnie cited a different piece of evidence to show the saturation of cotton goods markets: "Mill margins [the difference between the price of a pound of raw cotton and the price of a pound of yarn] . . . averaged 68 per cent upon the price of raw cotton during the decade 1850–59 and had reached 81 per cent in 1860 but were halved in 1861 to a meager 40 per cent."[5]

While these observers are basically describing a sharp but temporary downturn, a second thesis arose that suggests that the timing issue was even worse than previous historians implied (since the overproduction and excessive stocks questions would only temporarily decrease the South's price-setting power). Economist Gavin Wright presented the argument in its strongest form: "The rapid economic growth of the antebellum cotton economy was no more sustainable than the growth of British textiles production, and the hey-day of that industry's expansion was over by 1860. . . . Indeed, in 1860 the textiles industry stood on the crest of a major crisis of overproduction, which would have ushered in this era of stagnation had it not been overshadowed by the Cotton Famine of the 1860's."[6] While Wright's initial calculations showed a per annum decrease of almost 6 percent in world demand for American-grown raw cotton during the 1860s, John Hanson's recalculations lowered the estimate to less than 2 percent per annum. In addition, Hanson demonstrated the importance of the distinction between world demand for *all* raw cotton and world demand for *American-grown* raw cotton. He discovered that world demand for all raw cotton increased during the 1860s (even during the first half of the decade, although he found declining demand for American-grown raw cotton for the same period), while world demand for American-grown raw cotton fell.[7]

The previous debates underscore the importance of identifying whether a sharp temporary downturn or a long-term decline were inevitable or whether the market would likely have remained strong in the absence of the Civil War-induced volatility in the cotton markets.

Antebellum American producers of raw cotton were collectively a Colossus surrounded by smaller rivals (East India, Brazil, and Egypt), or, in economic parlance, a dominant firm with a competitive fringe. The world demand for American-grown raw cotton was the residual of total world demand for raw cotton less the supply of raw cotton by rival producers (for a technical depiction of the subsequent discussion, see Appendix 3). The demand for American-grown cotton could have fallen for three reasons: a decrease in demand for all cotton caused by either a decrease in demand for cotton textiles or by a glut of either cotton textiles or raw cotton, an increase in the supply by rival producers, or a decrease in the supply by American producers that eventually affected the demand.

I. World Market for Cotton Textiles

Since the demand for raw cotton depends on the demand for cotton textiles, it is necessary to examine whether events in the market for cotton textiles had an adverse effect on the demand for cotton, especially American-grown cotton. A decrease in the demand for cotton textiles would adversely affect the world demand for all raw cotton. Given Hanson's findings, the older historical explanation of a glut of cotton textiles suppressing demand cannot be complete, as such an explanation does not indicate why demand for all cotton increased during the same period. However, it is worthwhile to examine the market for cotton textiles, if only to dispel the notion of the market's effect on the diplomatic situation.

Cotton manufacturers were earning high profits during 1858–60, and these profits spurred expansion in the cotton textile industry. Since a permanent expansion of textile production would have entailed long-term investments, it is reasonable to expect a reticence by manufacturers to have made such investments until it could be ascertained whether the increased demand for textiles was ephemeral or would have lasted long enough to have justified the investments. If the demand for textiles persisted, there would have been a natural entry of new manufacturing firms in response to economic profits that would have increased sales volume, decreased prices, and eventually driven economic profits back to zero. Such an expansion also would have supported a strong demand for raw cotton.

Long-term overproduction of cotton textiles could arise if producers expanded too rapidly or if demand decreased permanently. As producers were expanding in response to the increased demand of the late 1850s, was the expansion suddenly confronted by a prolonged decrease in demand, as suggested by Wright? A worldwide permanent decline in demand could have been caused by a decline in the real income of the major consumers of cotton textiles, satiation of existing markets, an invention of a new textile, innovations that led to lower prices for rival textiles, trade barriers to cotton textiles, and changes in taste. Otherwise, it is unlikely that the demand for cotton textiles would evince any permanent decline. Regardless of whether producers expanded too rapidly or demand suffered a permanent decline, prices would fall. However, to distinguish long-term overproduction from a natural and prudent expansion as described above, one needs to establish that in addition to lower prices:

1. These lower prices earned an economic loss.
2. These economic losses were persistent (until, presumably, exit from the industry cut the losses and restored economic profits). At a level of production resulting in persistent losses and the exit of some cotton manufacturers from the industry, the demand for raw cotton would diminish.

Because long-term overproduction implies chronic economic losses, *temporary* decreases in demand for cotton textiles (perhaps caused by a famine or other unanticipated dislocations) would not indict manufacturers of long-term overexpansion. The Arnold version of overproduction implies that the cotton textile manufacturers overexpanded relative to the demand of 1861 or 1862. The demand itself may have fallen, too. In either case, the result would be losses and lower prices (if the overproduction were severe enough). Demand increased in 1859 and 1860, but supply increases lagged or were insufficient to drive prices down to where zero economic profits were earned. The duration of economic losses would distinguish Arnold's thesis of a sharp cyclical downturn in the market for cotton textiles from Wright's suggestion of a prolonged depression.

What about the evidence cited by Arnold and the historians? Do increasing stocks of manufactured goods and declining mill margins unambiguously signal a severe short-run downturn? The implications of rising stocks of manufactured cotton goods are ambiguous since stocks could increase not only because of oversupply but also because of producers deciding to hold more stocks. They might have increased their demand for inventories for two reasons: to speculate on the possibility of higher prices in the future, or, more likely, to maintain or replenish depleted stocks in order to service regular customers. If greater inventories occur because of "excess" supply (either because demand falls or supply increases against a stationary demand), such an excess would result in lower prices and an increase in inventories. If the demand by owners of inventories increases (holding the total supply fixed), price and inventory increase. Of course, it is possible for both the supply to increase and the demand for inventories to increase; in this case the movement of price is ambiguous, depending on which influence is predominant, but inventories increase in any case. Consequently, on a theoretical level, increased inventories are *not* sufficient evidence to establish overproduction. In order to ascertain which of these possibilities caused the inventory increase, we need to examine the path of prices as well. Thus, in one case, prices would unambiguously decline, but in the other cases, prices could increase.

Falling mill margins are another ambiguous piece of evidence. If there was overproduction, then prices should have fallen below their long-term equilibrium level and mill margins, too, would have plummeted. However, normal expansion in response to the years of high profits (and high mill margins) also would reduce mill margins. The new entrants and expansion would have initially created an increased demand for and raised the cost of raw cotton (until the cotton supply expanded in response to the increased demand) and a reduction in the price of textiles, causing mill margins to decline. Falling mill margins would support the overproduction thesis only if the decline pushed these margins below long-run trends, as the long-run trend of mill margins could serve as a proxy for the mill margin that earned zero economic profits.

Therefore, one cannot use price, inventory, or mill margin data separately in order to deduce the state of the market. One must examine these factors collectively to determine what was happening in the market for cotton textiles.

Finally, in addition to fitting these pieces of evidence into a theoretical framework, we need to consider how the Civil War would affect the analysis. The passage of the Morrill Tariff in March 1861 was the first effect of secession upon the market for cotton textiles. Without the secession of the Southern states, the Morrill Tariff could not have been passed. The tariff immediately diverted much of the Northern states' demand for cotton textiles from British suppliers to Northern suppliers, creating a significant dislocation in the market for Lancashire goods.

The second main effect of the Civil War was to restrict the movement of American-grown raw cotton, thereby raising raw cotton prices to cotton manufacturers. Through July 1861, however, the disruption was probably minimal. First, most of the crop harvested in late 1860 had been shipped prior to the outbreak of hostilities, and the summer was typically a period of minimal shipments of raw cotton. Second, the general expectation was that the war would be brief and that the blockade would be porous. Expectations of prolonged and severely constricted raw cotton exports probably weren't inspired until after the Battle of Bull Run (price increases of raw cotton accelerated in August 1861). The subsequent war-induced shortage of American-grown raw cotton was severe enough to dominate any symptoms of the cyclical downturn posited by the adherents of the overproduction thesis. With increased raw cotton prices in Europe and the Northern states due to the shortage, we would expect the supply of cotton manufactures to diminish.

Would we, however, expect the price of cotton manufactures to increase by either the same rate or magnitude as the change in raw cotton prices? Suppose that all cost increases could be passed on to the consumer. Even in this case, the percentage change in the price of cotton manufactures would be less than the percentage change in raw cotton prices, since raw cotton was not the sole expense in producing cotton manufactures. If raw cotton was half the cost of production and if the price of raw cotton doubled, then under certain conditions the price of cloth would increase by less than 59 percent.[8]

Moreover, the Civil War shortage of raw cotton also created a massive dislocation in the cotton textiles market on the demand side. First, the higher prices for cotton textiles (caused by the supply decrease) reduced the quantity of cloth demanded via the substitution effect. If the prices of rival textile products and the implicit price of continuing to wear old cotton clothing initially did not change much in response to the higher prices for cotton textiles, consumers might either buy woolen or linen products or postpone purchases of cotton goods. Second, the price change also created an income effect. According to economists George Shirras and A. R. Prest, cotton clothing comprised perhaps 10 percent of the budget of East Indian and somewhat smaller portions of British budgets. If cotton textiles comprised 10 percent of the budget of a typical consumer, a doubling of the price of cotton textiles would reduce both real income and demand for cotton textiles. Thus, demand could decrease (shift to the left), moderating the price increase due to the supply decrease. In addition, there would be an even larger drop in quantity transacted. As the war dragged on, the implicit price of wearing deteriorating old clothing would rise and, unless new textiles could replace cotton, this "pent-up" demand must eventually manifest itself.

Finally, the Civil War diverted the flow of the Confederate states' demand for cotton goods. First, the prohibition of commercial intercourse between the warring regions prevented Southerners from purchasing cotton goods from New England and probably would have increased their demand for Lancashire goods. However, the blockade restricted Southerners from importing goods from Lancashire, forcing the South to rely upon a meager flow of cotton goods run through the blockade, home production, and wearing existing clothes longer.

The overproduction theories assert that the Civil War and the attendant shortage of raw cotton masked either the onset of a severe cyclical or a permanent downturn in the market for cotton goods. A competing explanation of the events of 1861–62 is that cotton textile producers were expanding in a prudent manner as a result of a prior increase in demand that had raised profits. This competing explanation would attribute the severe dislocation of the market in late 1861 through 1862 to the disruptions induced by the Civil War. The short-term decrease in demand in 1861–62 was the result of the negative income effect from and by consumers postponing purchases because of the war-induced price rise and of the loss of the Southern states' demand for cotton textiles.

The evidence does not strongly support an imminent downturn in the absence of Civil War-wrought disruptions. First, were there excessive stocks of cotton manufactures in Great Britain or India on the eve of the Civil War? In terms of volume, the stocks were large in Great Britain, but stocks relative to supply were not excessively large. Arnold and Forwood commented that ending 1860 and 1861 stocks of manufactured goods of 242 and 293.8 million pounds respectively were inordinately large. The *Economist* attributed the increased stocks of late 1861 to speculative buying. Moreover, the *Economist's* weekly assessment of the cotton goods markets revealed little concern about the stocks, characterizing such stocks as, "moderate for the time of the year," "not very heavy," and "by no means as extensive as might have been anticipated." Only one mention of "heavy" stocks was made on January 18, 1862. Table 10.1 shows estimated closing stocks for several years. Closing stocks for 1856 and 1857 averaged roughly 242.2 million pounds, while the average for the quinquennial 1855–59 was 219.4 million pounds. Consequently, in absolute terms, only the ending 1861 stock is much above the estimated 1855–59 average annual stock. Moreover, this increase in stock of 50 million pounds pales in comparison to the average annual supply of over a billion pounds, and as Table 10.1 shows, the relative stock was only marginally higher at the end of 1861 than in previous years. Thereafter, stocks fell rapidly in absolute and relative terms. The stocks in India are difficult to ascertain, although anecdotal evidence suggests heavier than usual stocks.

If the markets for cotton manufactures were glutted because of over-production, one would expect prices of manufactured goods to fall significantly and for mill margins to decrease below long-term trend levels (indicating economic losses). The real prices of yarn (the market prices deflated by a price index) in the United Kingdom yield little evidence that the market was headed for a downturn. Prices had been strong during 1859–60, fluctuating between 11.0d. and 13.0d. (prior to the war, one British pound equaled $4.86, so a pence was equal to two cents), well above the 1857–58 trough prices (see Table 10.2). While real yarn prices drooped in February 1861, they rebounded modestly through 1861. After August, the upward-movement in prices accelerated and the year-end price of #30 Water yarns (a common type) was roughly 12.5 percent above the ending 1860 price. While raw cotton prices rose more rapidly than the yarn prices, the yarn prices reveal no inherent weakness in the market.

The mill margins (the difference between the price of a pound of yarn and a pound of raw cotton) narrowed throughout 1861, although it exceeded 3.78d. until August 1861, when the margin began to narrow more rapidly. However, the importance of this episode is that the margins never fell to the trough levels attained between July 1853 and March 1858 until after the Battle of Bull Run altered perceptions as to the war's likely duration. After August 1861, expectations about the supply of raw cotton

Table 10.1. Estimated Ending (December 31) Stocks of Cotton Goods in Great Britain (in Millions of Pounds)

Year	(1) Beg. Stock	(2) Yarn/Mfg Produced	(3) Total Supply	(4) Yarn/Mfg Exported	(5) Est.Home Consump.	(6) Total Delivery	(7) Ending Stock	(8) % Stocks Supply
1854							205*	
1855	205*	755	960	558	180	738	222*	23.1
1856	222*	802	1,024	593	180	773	251*	24.5
1857	251*	743	994	579	180	759	235*	23.6
1858	235*	815	1,050	670	180	850	200*	19.0
1859	200*	879	1,079	710	180	890	189	17.5
1860	189	966	1,155	740	173	913	242	21.0
1861	242	900	1,142	674	174	848	294	25.7
1862	294	373	667	413	102	515	152	22.8
1863	152	405	557	392	93	485	72	12.9
1864	72	483	555	404	110	514	41	7.4
1865	41	618	659	476	150	626	33	5.0
1866	33	775	808	626	145	771	37	4.6
1867	37	840	877	688	145	833	45	5.1
1868	45	877	921	720	160	880	42	4.6

* Estimated

(1): Beginning Stock (January 1) = Ending Stock (December 31) of Previous Year, i.e. Beginning 1855 Stock = Ending 1854 Stock.

(2): Weight of yarn and manufactured goods produced during the calendar year.

(3): Column 1 + Column 2.

(4): Weight of yarn and manufactured goods exported during the calendar year.

(5): For 1855–59, Estimated Home Consumption was set at 180 million pounds as per Brady (1963, 158) and Arnold (1864, 46 and 333). The *Economist* (February 20, 1864) implied that average home consumption was closer to 210 million pounds (if true, the ending stocks for 1855–59 would be larger). If 170 million pounds is used for 1855–59 estimated home consumption, then the series is: 189 in 1859; 190 in 1858; 215 in 1857; 221 in 1856; 182 in 1855; and 155 in 1854.

(6): Column 4 + Column 5.

(7): Forwood lists beginning and ending stocks for 1860–68. The beginning stock for 1860 = Ending Stock of 1859. The Beginning/Ending Stocks for 1855–59 are calculated going backward. For instance: Beginning Stock (1859) = Ending Stock (1859) + Yarn and Goods Exported (1859) + Estimated Home Consumption (1859) – Yarn & Goods Produced(1859).

(8): Column 7/Column 3 (in percentage).

Note: Helm's data for 1860–68 showed more yarn and manufactured goods produced than Forwood (or the *Economist,* February 20, 1864), because he (Helm) continued to assume a 10 percent rate of waste in spinning. The other sources increased the estimated waste percentage to 17 percent in 1862 (and kept it above 10 percent for the balance of 1863–68).

Sources: Forwood (1870, Table C) for 1860–68 data and ending 1859 stock.

Helm (1869, Table G) for 1855–59 "Yarn & Manufactured Goods Produced" and "Yarns & Goods Exported." Brady (1963) used Helm's table for some of his computations.

Table 10.2. Real Raw Cotton and Cotton Manufactures Prices in Great Britain

Date	Per lb. Upland Cotton	Yarn #30 Water	Cotton Yarn Margin	Per lb. 60-Reed Gshirt.	Yarn GShirt. Margin
January 1855	5.16	8.40	3.24	9.77	1.37
April	5.40	8.64	3.24	9.95	1.31
July	6.72	9.36	2.64	10.47	1.11
October	6.01	8.90	2.89	10.15	1.25
January 1856	5.66	8.80	3.13	10.34	1.54
April	6.28	9.66	3.38	11.42	1.76
July	6.41	9.68	3.27	11.44	1.76
October	6.61	9.85	3.24	11.01	1.16
January 1857	7.28	10.51	3.22	11.81	1.30
April	7.59	10.79	3.20	12.08	1.28
July	7.91	10.87	2.95	12.54	1.68
October	9.05	12.60	3.55	14.41	1.81
January 1858	6.85	9.77	2.92	11.99	2.23
April	7.51	11.19	3.69	12.83	1.64
July	7.84	11.76	3.92	13.17	1.41
October	8.03	12.58	4.55	14.60	2.02
January 1859	7.29	12.59	5.30	15.04	2.45
April	7.88	12.73	4.86	14.51	1.78
July	7.83	12.52	4.70	14.99	2.47
October	7.48	12.63	5.16	13.69	1.05
January 1860	7.14	13.00	5.86	14.46	1.46
April	7.05	12.60	5.54	14.66	2.06
July	6.75	11.63	4.88	13.27	1.65
October	7.21	11.89	4.68	13.98	2.09
January 1861	7.67	12.79	5.12	14.33	1.53
April	8.02	12.16	4.14	13.18	1.01
July	8.87	12.78	3.91	13.66	0.88
October	12.38	13.66	1.29	15.00	1.34

Table 10.2 continued

Date	Per lb. Upland Cotton	Yarn #30 Water	Cotton Yarn Margin	Per lb. 60-Reed Gshirt.	Yarn GShirt. Margin
January 1862	13.51	15.29	1.78	15.38	0.09
April	13.35	15.62	2.27	16.12	0.50
July	18.00	20.00	2.00	18.55	–1.45
October	26.94	30.93	3.99	25.40	–5.53
January 1863	24.89	30.86	5.97	25.16	–5.70
April	24.33	27.81	3.48	24.92	–2.89
July	22.81	26.78	3.97	24.88	–1.89
October	ua	34.37	—	31.16	–3.22
January 1864	ua	34.53	—	32.02	–2.50
April	ua	32.17	—	30.17	–1.46
July	31.76	37.56	5.80	33.00	–4.56
October	31.91	26.34	–5.57	25.42	–0.92
January 1865	26.46	29.51	3.05	28.50	–1.02
April	15.85	19.94	4.09	18.96	–0.98
July	ua	22.56	—	22.38	–0.19
October	25.46	29.54	4.07	27.41	–2.13
January 1866	22.25	29.33	7.08	27.22	–2.11
April	19.59	26.62	7.03	24.84	–1.78
July	15.00	21.00	6.00	21.45	0.45

Note: ua—unavailable.

Britain yarn prices were for second quality.

Britain Grey Shirtings were 60 reed, 39 inches x 37.5 yards, 8 pounds, 4 ounces (pence per pound).

Sources: *Economist* for Great Britain price data.

Rousseaux Price Index, revised with 1860=100; (eleven-month moving average used to adjust prices).

triggered the beginning of a rapid rise in raw cotton prices and a lagging increase in yarn prices, so the mill margins fell to 1.29d in October 1861 and remained low for a year. However, the mill margins of the 1861–62 period are difficult to interpret, as manufacturers began to blend the cheaper and poorer quality Surat cotton. Adjusting the mill margins for a mixture of American and Surat cotton restores the mill margins to much closer to the normal levels of 3.5–4.0d. per pound. Even without adjusting the mill margins for the mixture of American and Surat cotton, the margins improved markedly during the second half of 1862.

Cotton piece goods prices fluctuated within a relatively narrow band during 1859–60. These prices generally fell over the summer of 1860, but rebounded slightly in January 1861 (to within 1 to 4 percent of their January 1860 levels). Then there was a general fall in prices through June 1861, where the price of shirtings fell to just below the lowest levels of the 1859–60 boom. The events of late 1861 drove the prices down to an overall decline of 1 to 16 percent over the year by the end of December. The margins between a pound of yarn and a pound of a standard grey cloth were declining during 1861, even before the war. The margins became negative in 1862 but, again, the margins are problematic. With rapidly increasing cotton and yarn prices, manufacturers began to adulterate their product with flax and "sizing" (using flour and other ingredients to give cloth adhesiveness and color). Several commentators noted the unusual amount of "sizing" used on the cloth and attributed the use to the rapidly increasing gap between the price of a pound of cotton and a pound of flour. Again, adjusting for "sizing" and quality differences, the margins between the price of a pound of yarn and a pound of cloth are significantly increased, although not by enough to restore margins to "normal" levels.

The prices of yarn and cotton textiles in India revealed a somewhat weaker market. British India had recovered from the economic effects of the Mutiny but was undergoing some localized famines. Still, the Calcutta real prices for shirtings, grey yarn, and colored yarn rose between 1861 and 1862. The Bombay price quotations (Table 10.3) show moderate price decreases during 1860–61, but grey shirtings hardly appear "unmarketable." While the prices in India, combined with the reduced quantity imported, *may* support the thesis of a sag in the Bombay and Calcutta markets during 1860–61, they hardly support the dire prognosis of severe overproduction and/or declining demand. Instead, the modest decrease in prices despite continued large imports and stockpiling of goods in 1860–61 stands as a testament to the strength of demand for cotton manufactured goods in India.

Table 10.3. Nominal Bombay Cotton Goods Prices

Date	#30 Water Yarn	#40 Mule Yarn	54-Reed GShirt.
January 1860	12.8	13.1	ua
April	13.1	13.3	ua
July	13.5	13.5	ua
October	13.5	13.5	108.0
January 1861	12.0	12.0	105.0
April	13.1	12.3	99.0
July	13.9	13.9	102.0
October	15.6	14.1	108.0
January 1862	16.1	15.0	115.5
April	16.5	15.4	114.0
July	20.6	21.0	144.0
October	23.3	22.9	174.0
January 1863	23.6	22.9	168.0
April	29.3	31.1	198.0
July	33.8	33.0	210.0
October	35.3	35.3	234.0
January 1864	39.0	38.3	228.0
April	36.0	30.0	216.0
July	37.5	33.8	246.0
October	35.3	30.0	237.0
January 1865	35.3	30.0	225.0
April	24.0	16.5	147.0
July	29.3	23.3	177.0
October	31.5	27.0	192.0
January 1866	36.0	28.5	198.0
April	33.0	29.3	189.0
July	24.0	26.3	171.0
October	24.8	25.5	168.0

Note: ua—unavailable.

Yarn prices are pence per pound.

Grey Shirtings are 54-reed, 39 inches x 38 yards, 7 pound pieces (pence per piece).

Prices converted to British pence at rate: 1 anna = 1.5 pence

(1 Rs. = 2s.); 12 pence = 1 shilling; and 16 annas = 1 Rupee Shilling.

Sources: *The Times of India (Bombay Times)* and *Imperial Gazetteer of India,* Vol. 1 for currency information.

Table 10.4. An Approximation of Percentage Growth in Demand for Great Britain Cloth Exports (by Regions)

Year	East India/China e =0.5	e =1.0	e =1.5
1857	2.38%	4.66%	6.98%
1858	65.72	74.69	84.14
1859	26.78	28.61	30.46
1860	−10.69	−11.53	−12.37
1861	0.01	0.65	1.29
1862	−37.71	−32.16	−26.12
1863	17.95	36.69	58.42
1864	− 2.13	5.51	13.76
1865	15.04	5.75	− 2.79
1866	19.22	19.46	19.70

Year	United States e =0.5	e =1.0	e =1.5
1857	−17.41%	−20.51%	−23.48%
1858	− 7.97	− 2.71	2.86
1859	46.59	47.76	48.94
1860	− 3.62	− 7.72	−11.65
1861	−66.57	−66.08	−65.58
1862	35.91	41.16	46.61
1863	−20.29	−13.27	− 5.65
1864	− 2.79	5.49	14.47
1865	86.98	83.23	79.56
1866	− 0.02	6.62	13.70

Year	Other Countries e =0.5	e =1.0	e =1.5
1857	− 0.92%	0.39%	1.72%
1858	7.77	13.39	19.29
1859	− 4.44	− 3.70	− 2.95
1860	23.78	19.90	16.14
1861	− 2.30	− 0.97	0.38
1862	−27.58	−23.18	−18.51
1863	17.52	32.07	48.43
1864	18.27	27.05	36.47
1865	2.01	− 1.62	− 5.12
1866	33.78	31.18	28.64

Year: Calendar year.

Source: Ellison ([1886] 1968, Table 2); Helm (1869, 435). Prices deflated by Rousseaux "Overall Index."

The data on stocks, prices, and mill margins provide less support for either an inevitable short- or long-term decline. Prices in Great Britain and India were robust in the face of continued strong production and stockpiling of cotton manufacturers, and the prices do not strongly support the overproduction theory or the idea of a significant long-run downturn in demand. Instead, the modest decline in textile prices suggests that demand remained strong and possibly increased, and that textile producers were acting prudently in expanding output. However, by using an estimation technique described in Appendix 4, we can trace out yearly changes in demand. Since there is a lack of data on world production of cotton textiles, our knowledge of demand centers upon Great Britain's export trade. Moreover, given the disruptions of Britain's markets, such as recurring famines in British India and the loss of the Southern states' demand for British textiles due to the blockade, Britain's export demand may have been the most adversely affected. The demand for British cotton textile exports declined in 1861. A large reduction in exports to the United States was the key to the decline in 1861 (Table 10.4). Total yards exported decreased by 213 million between 1860 and 1861 (a 7.7 percent drop) and, of this decrease, the United States accounted for 152 million yards. Because the United States was not a major importer of yarns or plain cotton cloth, the trade disruption did not significantly affect the growth in demand for these products. Demand for yarn and plain cotton cloth suffered relatively moderate declines in 1861. However, the United States was a large buyer of British printed cotton goods, so the Civil War-induced disruption of trade manifested itself in a large negative growth in demand for British printed cotton cloth exports in 1861 (Table 10.5). This decrease in United States demand for British cotton goods arose from both the Morrill Tariff and from the Civil War itself. Still, the underlying demand for cotton and cotton goods remained unabated in the United States. If anything, American demand probably increased due to military needs—uniforms, tents, and bandages. Indeed, the *Economist* commented on an increase in American demand, "owing to the enormous purchase of military stores and clothing for the army." The North's demand for British cotton textiles rebounded strongly in 1862.[9]

Between 1860 and 1861, British cotton cloth exports to "Other Countries" (all countries except East India/China and the United States) remained stagnant, but prospects for continental demand for cotton goods appeared promising on the eve of the Civil War. British manufacturers could hope for some relief from the 1860 Anglo-French Treaty of Commerce. Indeed, some exports to France immediately increased. Moderate quality goods

Table 10.5. An Approximation of Annual Growth in Demand for Great Britain's Cotton Textiles Exports (in Percent)

Year	Yarn Exports e = 0.5	Yarn Exports e = 1.5	White/Plain Cloth e = 0.5	White/Plain Cloth e = 1.5	Printed Cloth e = 0.5	Printed Cloth e = 1.5
1860	1.31%	− 1.35%	4.17%	0.15%	9.84%	4.76%
1861	− 5.89	2.62	− 2.80	− 0.54	−13.85	−12.24
1862	−42.09	−29.33	−35.04	−22.75	−19.29	−14.00
1863	1.41	63.74	23.93	64.75	3.12	27.78
1864	7.97	21.64	7.56	26.50	14.94	29.35
1865	25.85	6.50	11.95	−0.59	4.92	−1.90
1866	31.52	26.58	26.98	24.53	26.70	25.66
1867	16.04	5.30	5.66	−12.69	−6.39	−14.95
1868	2.27	0.71	−0.35	−9.30	3.18	−3.35
1869	0.30	6.62	−0.58	10.61	5.29	15.27
1870	5.19	−3.39	13.41	2.23	−1.15	−6.98
1860–70	23.63	112.54	42.02	77.41	10.09	35.46
Per Annum	2.15	7.84	3.57	5.90	0.97	3.09

Year: Calendar year.
Source: Ellison ([1886] 1968, Table 2).
Prices deflated by Rousseaux price index with 1860=100.

comprised the bulk of these exports, as the French cotton industry was skilled in producing fine cotton. There were transportation difficulties in France and the continent that retarded demand for the cheaper cotton goods, but the burgeoning railroad network was gradually releasing this demand. Europe was not bereft of trade barriers, and the *Economist* bemoaned the remaining barriers to trade on the continent that enabled foreign producers to cater to captive markets and outbid Lancashire producers. Despite these obstacles, the remainder of the continent appeared to be developing a greater appetite for cotton goods.[10]

We now examine the East Indies and China. The demand in India was crucial for British cotton manufacturers. Unfortunately, this market was highly volatile, with political upheaval, such as the Indian Mutiny, and famines interrupting the expansion of the market. In addition, poor transportation and communication prevented the market from achieving its potential. The East Indian and Chinese demand for cotton cloth was stationary in 1861, while 1860 was the year of decreased demand after two years of massive increases in demand. The 1861 downturn in demand for

Lancashire yarn was mostly attributable to decreased exports to the East Indies and China. Yarn exports to Turkey also decreased.

There is reason to believe that except for the loss of much of the American market, the 1861 downturn in world demand for British products was quite mild, perhaps a 1 to 2 percent drop. In the context of world demand for all cotton goods in 1861, the situation was brighter. The "lost" American demand did not disappear, as Northern demand for cotton textiles probably continued as strongly as ever and was largely filled by Northern textile manufacturers. Southern demand was probably as strong (if not stronger because of wartime needs), but it went largely unfilled because of the blockade and other war-related disruptions. There is little to suggest that world demand for cotton textiles diminished significantly in 1861.[11]

The situation in 1862 is less clear. Again, as seen from Tables 10.4 and 10.5, the demand for British cotton textiles apparently suffered sharp decreases. The East Indies/China market led the decline, but "Other Countries" also suffered large decreases in demand. Surprisingly, the United States' demand for cotton goods surged in 1862 (only to fall off in 1863). Yarn and white/plain cloth suffered larger decreases in demand than printed cloth. In Great Britain, home consumption plummeted to 50 to 60 percent of normal levels. Part of this decrease was due to price increases, but apparently some of it was due to the inferior quality of much of the available cotton cloth. Another cause of the decline in British demand was the inability of Lancashire cotton operatives to purchase as much cotton textiles as they previously had. Moreover, Dunham and Tyson believe a drop in the per capita demand for cotton goods occurred during the 1860s, precipitated by the disruptions of the Civil War that caused higher prices and that lowered the quality of cotton textile goods.[12]

The figures shown in Tables 10.4 and 10.5 probably exaggerate the change in demand between 1861 and 1862. Most of the cotton goods were of lower quality in 1862, so the price increases would have been muted. An adjustment for quality would moderate the changes between 1861–62 and 1862–63. However, the basic results still hold: Demand was largely stable in 1861, fell off sharply in 1862, and rebounded strongly in 1863 and 1864.

The 1862–65 changes in the demand for cotton textiles appear to have been predominantly the effects of the Civil War-induced shortage of raw cotton. The increasing price of raw cotton reduced the supply of cotton goods and sharply raised prices. But what about the long-term state of world demand for cotton textiles?

Long-term world demand for all cotton textiles appears to have been healthy. Most importantly, the existing rival textiles showed only a limited ability to take up the shortfall in cotton textile output. Rival textiles might have posed a threat to the South's cotton power. If the supplies of woolens and linens were elastic (i.e. a 1 percent change in the price of woolens or linens would trigger a greater than 1 percent increase in the quantity supplied of woolens or linens) and if such textiles were close substitutes for cotton manufactures, then we would expect the demand for cotton manufactures to be more elastic. Any attempt to raise raw cotton prices by restricting output would then be less advantageous. However, as world demand for raw cotton displayed inelastic demand, the threat of rival textiles may have been modest. These rival textiles did expand in Great Britain and the United States during the Civil War, but only moderately. During the ante-bellum era, Great Britain's exports of linen and woolen manufactures were dwarfed in volume and in value by cotton. While combined exports of wool and linen textile products rose by 250 million yards between 1861 and 1865, these increases still fell far short of offsetting the reduction in manu-factured cotton exports (roughly 800 million yards a year for 1862–64). Linen exports rose from 133 million yards per annum (1859–61 average) to 237 million (1864–66 average). Woolen exports rose from 182 million yards per annum (1859–61 average) to 267 million (1864–6 average).[13]

The United States increased its imports of linen and expanded its woolen industry. According to Victor Clark, the Northern woolen manu-facturers increased their consumption of wool from 85 million pounds per annum to slightly over 200 million pounds. However, consumption of raw cotton fell from over 338 million pounds per annum to 150 million, so the wartime increase in consumption of wool made up only 60 to 70 percent of the shortfall in raw cotton consumption.[14]

Even in this brief survey, it is clear that rival textiles, even after four years, were able to only offset part of the shortfall in the consumption of raw cotton, much less supplant cotton.

Aside from the inability of rival textile manufacturers to fully replace cotton textiles, there were other reasons to think that the demand for cot-ton textiles would remain strong. First, no new types of textiles were intro-duced during the 1860s. Second, real income across the major consuming countries experienced growth during the 1860s, except for the southern United States. Third, ocean transportation rates were generally decreasing during the 1800s and, combined with the increasing railroad mileage in the world (especially in British East India), promised to open new markets for cotton textiles. Fourth, although Dunham and Tyson theorize that British demand for cotton textiles dwindled during the 1860s, the home consumption figures provided by Forwood for 1866–68 show British consumption gradually returning to antebellum levels, despite the continued higher prices. Despite the dislocations in the market for British cotton textiles, the growth-in-demand figures shown in Table 10.5 reveal growth during the 1860s. Thus, any change in "taste" for British cotton textiles appears to have been modest; indeed, Michael Mulhall estimated that world production of cotton cloth remained constant between the 1850s and 1860s. Given the higher prices of the 1860s, the world demand for cotton textiles must have remained robust and growing during the decade.[15]

Prior to August 1861, the world markets for cotton textiles appeared to have been healthy. Although the Morrill Tariff and Indian famine disrupted the market for Lancashire goods, prices of cotton textiles displayed only a moderate reduction. Moreover, the influx of new manufacturers and expansion of existing producers also exerted a downward pressure on prices. However, the mill margins, while decreasing, were still above the long-term trend up to August 1861. The disruption of the American market represented a diversion of demand by the Northern states towards Northern textile products and a diminution of Southern demand because of the non-intercourse barriers between the belligerents and the early effects of the Union navy's blockade. In summary, the events of the first half of 1861 indicate that manufacturers had expanded in a prudent fashion and that no long-term decline in demand had occurred. Without the Civil War-induced shortage of raw cotton, the world market for cotton textiles probably would have been strong in 1862, with a sharp short-term downturn unlikely.

However, the expectations of a short war and minimal interruption to the channels of trade changed in August 1861 as news of the Battle of Bull Run reached Europe. Combined with the increasing stringency of the blockade and the Confederate embargo on exports of raw cotton, the expectations of a disruption in shipments of raw cotton triggered a rise in the price of raw cotton throughout the world. The prices of cotton textiles responded sluggishly and mill margins fell over the second half of 1861. Cotton textile manufacturers and distributors, fearing eventual shortages, increased their demands for inventory in the second half of 1861.

Prices for cotton textiles began to rise significantly in 1862, a rise tempered by the deteriorating quality of the goods produced. The price increases triggered a substitution effect of consumers either buying woolen and linen goods or postponing purchases of cotton goods. In addition, the sharp increases in prices created a reduction in the real income of consumers, resulting in reduced demand (a shift of the demand curve to the left). Demand rebounded in 1863 and 1864 as linen and wool textile producers were unable to make up the shortfall in cotton goods and as the shadow price of wearing existing clothing increased. In addition, the long-term trends of rising real incomes, population growth, and improved transportation spurred demand for cotton textile products.

These findings cast doubt upon Arnold, Brady, and Wright's beliefs that the market for cotton textiles was either on the verge of a severe short-term or prolonged downturn. The effects of the drastic reduction in the supply of American-grown raw cotton dominated any possible dislocation in the market for Lancashire goods. The supply shock of late 1861 reversed the growth of world demand for cotton textiles, because of the adverse effect upon real incomes and because it led consumers of cotton products to postpone consumption or to buy substitute textiles. However, the underlying long-term world demand for cotton textiles remained healthy and growing; despite all of the dislocations, even the world demand for Lancashire goods grew during the 1860s.[16]

II. World Market for Raw Cotton

Since the world demand for cotton textiles did not appear to have significantly worsened during the early 1860s, the derived demand for raw cotton should have remained robust. There remain three other possibilities. Was there a glut of cotton that threatened the demand for cotton? Did the Southern states suddenly face increased competition from its rival producers, i.e. did British India, Brazil, and Egypt suddenly become more efficient producers and erode the world demand for the American's cotton? Or did the war-induced upheavals in the supply of American-grown raw cotton affect the world demand for such cotton?

What evidence is there that the world demand for American-grown raw cotton was destined to fall in 1861–62 due to overproduction of cotton? The large stocks of raw cotton existing at the end of 1861 have been cited as evidence that the world demand for raw cotton was destined to fall in 1861–62. However, increasing stocks of raw cotton alone are *not* necessarily indicative of falling demand, for if the demand for inventories of raw cotton increased, the stock of raw cotton would rise and so would the price of raw cotton. Thus, the significance of rising stocks of raw cotton can be interpreted only in conjunction with an examination of the price of raw cotton. Second, the stocks are usually quoted in terms of absolute physical volume, but stocks relative to consumption of raw cotton in production is the more relevant measure. Relative stocks affords a better idea of how long the stock would last at current rates of consumption.

However, even an examination of the stocks of raw cotton in absolute terms raises doubts about the thesis of declining demand. Given the inordinate size of the 1859–60 American cotton crop, it is hardly surprising that the volume of stocks of raw cotton were high in Europe during 1860 and 1861 (see Table 10.6). Stocks of cotton reached a peak in June 1860 (1.3 million bales). They remained high even in December 1861, but a transformation had occurred. Where the bulk of the stock during 1860 had been American cotton, by the end of 1861 much was East Indian cotton. E. J. Donnell's data provides evidence that this "large" stock of raw cotton could not prevent the rapid exhaustion of raw cotton supplies. Stocks at Liverpool (comprising the bulk of the total United Kingdom stock) continued to fall during July and August 1862, reaching a low of 57,342 bales on September 5 (from 212,000 at the end of June). This included only 16,082 bales of American-grown cotton. Although heavy imports of Indian cotton during October helped push the stock levels back over 200,000 bales, cotton stocks were largely depleted a little more than a year after the war began. This depletion certainly casts doubts on Brady's assertion that a cotton shortage was never realized. Indeed, the *Economist* was concerned about the dwindling stocks of raw cotton in early 1862: "Theoretically . . . by the middle of the summer nearly every mill in England, Scotland, and Ireland will be stopped for actual want of the raw material. . . . There is no exaggeration in this picture; indeed, some of our correspondents would have us make it much darker. The condition we have thus depicted may last for a long period—*will* [italics theirs] last till the American blockade is ended, or till it has lasted so long and seems so interminable, that we have provided ourselves against its consequences by tardy and uncertain operations elsewhere.[17]

Relative stocks of American cotton in Europe (including Great Britain) were *not* large on the eve of the Civil War. At the end of 1860 and 1861, despite large importations of American-grown cotton, the relative stock rose only to just over eight weeks' supply (at current rates of consumption), a level similar to that of 1858. The relative stock of all cotton in Europe at the end of 1860 was enough for 9.3 weeks' consumption at current rates. While this level was higher than for the preceding two years, it was not inordinate. Nor was the 1861 carryover stock inordinate, even though it rose to 11.3 weeks' supply. Given the uncertain availability of the cotton supply prevailing during the latter half of 1861, prudent textile producers might well have increased their demand for stocks of raw cotton. Thus, increasing absolute and relative stocks during this period should not be surprising. In fact, the uncertainty over the supply of raw cotton was man-

Table 10.6. December 31 Carryover Stocks Held in Europe and Great Britain in Weeks of Consumption at Current Rates

(Consumption and Stocks in 400-pound Bales)

Year	American-grown Cotton			East Indian Cotton			All Cotton		
	Consumption	Stocks	Weeks	Consumption	Stocks	Weeks	Consumption	Stocks	Weeks
1851	2,096,130	304,950	7.6	280,683	167,850	31.1	2,571,508	539,183	10.9
1852	2,558,370	438,700	8.9	260,440	128,305	25.6	3,070,450	674,728	11.4
1853	2,429,500	400,975	8.6	321,640	258,060	41.7	2,988,283	764,793	13.3
1854	2,583,385	457,870	9.2	360,798	207,143	29.9	3,170,018	745,063	12.2
1855	2,584,050	328,650	6.6	431,225	124,780	15.0	3,245,073	533,035	8.5
1856	3,191,250	288,600	4.7	486,525	106,275	11.4	3,943,205	436,735	5.8
1857	2,457,520	343,655	7.3	559,360	21,9980	20.4	3,226,460	607,778	9.8
1858	2991,548	460,410	8.0	576,840	66,240	6.0	3,778,263	577,753	8.0
1859	3,535,870	431,035	6.3	416,585	135,720	16.9	4,187,355	598,705	7.4
1860	3,759,480	584,280	8.1	474,220	174,665	19.2	4,454,613	796,435	9.3
1861	3,039,350	477,263	8.2	742,390	372,130	26.1	4,027,420	878,403	11.3
1862	337,700	67,540	10.4	1,034,865	316,590	15.9	1,691,590	437,148	13.4
1863	204,750	44,100	11.2	1,184,040	216,840	9.5	1,931,010	301,180	8.1
1864	246,330	24,840	5.2	1,141,395	391,980	17.9	2,161,703	477,880	11.5
1865	372,860	159,650	22.3	1,455,823	166,425	5.9	2,863,463	406,953	7.4

Year: Calendar Year; stock as of December 31.

Weeks: (Stocks/Consumption) x 52.

Sources: Donnell (1872) and Great Britain, *Statistical Abstract for the United Kingdom* ([1867] 1965) for weight data.

ifested by a strong upswing in the amount of raw cotton sold to speculators. Between August 8 and November 22, 1861 (after the news of the battle of Bull Run), some 700,000 bales were sold for speculation. The corresponding figure for 1860 was 380,000. Unfortunately, a breakdown by source (American or East Indian) is not possible.[18]

Many of the previous commentators on the Civil War market for raw cotton concentrated only on the stocks of raw cotton in Great Britain and not on the entire market. However, the 1860 and 1861 relative carryover stocks held in Great Britain were actually just below the long-term trend in this variable. From 1855 to 1859, raw cotton stocks were significantly below trend, so the 1860 and 1861 increases in relative stocks merely replenished the stocks to their trend level. Brady used Thomas Ellison's data to demonstrate that the relative stock held in Great Britain *rose* during the Civil War and that this fact casts, "serious doubts against the hypothesis that depletion of the cotton stock was responsible for the depression."[19] Ellison's table and Brady's remarks are based on comparing existing stocks with the current year's consumption of raw cotton. During the Civil War, many of the cotton spindles were idle in the Northern states and Europe, and Brady and Ellison's comparisons essentially ignore the amount of raw cotton that the cotton textiles industry could have consumed at late antebellum production levels. Therefore, using current consumption of raw cotton as the denominator in determining relative stocks becomes less illuminating during the Civil War, and a more relevant denominator is the level of consumption of raw cotton in the production of cotton textiles that would have prevailed with the industry operating at normal production levels. The average consumption of the last three years of the antebellum period can be used as a proxy for the normal consumption capacity. Thus, using Ellison's unrevised weekly consumption of all cotton against the stocks of all cotton, we get twenty-one weeks' supply of cotton in stock at the close of 1862 (an increase from seventeen weeks' worth at the close of 1861). At the average rate of consumption for 1859–61, the stock at the end of 1862 was good for only eleven weeks' of consumption.[20]

In summary, the stocks of cotton on the eve of the Civil War were not inordinately large. The slight increase in relative stocks in late 1861 probably reflected an increase in the demand for inventories of raw cotton. Nor did these stocks stave off a physical shortage of cotton during the summer of 1862.

Did raw cotton prices weaken significantly in 1861, signifying a possible diminution in demand for cotton? The nominal Liverpool Uplands raw cotton prices opened at 6.5d. per pound in early 1860. The price gradually drifted down to 5.44d. by mid-summer. Thereafter the price began to rise, ending the year at 7.13d. The price slumped to 6.5d. in late February 1861 but rose to over 7.5d. by May. After a brief drop in mid-May (coinciding with two weeks of large shipments of American-grown cotton), the price resumed its upward climb. By late July, the price per pound was 8.25d. The accounts of the Battle of Bull Run accelerated the price increase, until the price peaked at 11.63d. in mid-November. The "Trent" affair, with its attendant hopes of British intervention in the war, dropped prices down to 10.13d., but the Uplands price closed out 1861 at 11.5d., a 63 percent increase from the opening 1861 price.[21]

The next factor to consider is the reactions of rival raw cotton producers. The South's price-setting power would be undermined if rival producers of cotton became more efficient or rushed in to fill a supply shortfall of American-grown raw cotton.

The total consumption of cotton (from all sources) in Europe and the United States rose at an annual rate of 5.3 percent during 1830–60 (see Table 10.7, upper panel). From 1831–60, consumption of American-grown cotton grew at a per annum rate of about 5.5 percent. However, the rate of increase in consumption differed between the major consumers. Although Great Britain was the largest consumer of American-grown cotton throughout the period, the British per annum increase in consumption of 4.6 percent paled besides the United States' increasing consumption of 7.1 percent per annum (Table 10.7, lower panel) and the rest of Europe's increase (aside from Great Britain and France). Only France showed a slower rate of growth in consumption for American-grown cotton than Great Britain.

These varying rates of increased consumption are reflected in the relative shares of consumption of American-grown cotton. The United Kingdom's share dropped from almost 60 percent to less than 50 percent between 1831 and 1860. France's share of consumption, a steady 18 to 19 percent for the first half of the thirty-year period, dropped to 12 percent prior to the Civil War. The combined United Kingdom and French drop in relative consumption was offset by the United States and the rest of Europe, with the latter region experiencing the largest relative change.

East Indian-grown cotton was the largest rival to American-grown cotton. Consumption of Indian (largely Surat) cotton increased during the antebellum period, reaching 500,000 bales per year just prior to the Civil War. By 1856–60, Great Britain and continental Europe (aside from France) roughly split the East Indian cotton. French cotton textile producers did not import much East Indian cotton until the Civil War. Throughout the antebellum period, Indian cotton served largely as a backup for the

Table 10.7. 1830–1860 Average Annual Increase in United States and European Raw Cotton Consumption

(By Origin of Fiber, By Percent)		(By Region of Consumption)	
East Indian	6.6%	United States	7.1%
United States	5.6	Great Britain	4.6
Egyptian	3.3	France	3.7
Brazilian	–0.5	Rest of Europe	10.5
West Indian	–1.8	Total	5.5%*
Total	5.3%		

*Because Hammond and Watkins data for United States consumption of raw cotton includes consumption by the Southern states, their data differs from Donnell's. Donnell's gives a 6.2 percent per annum increase by the United States for American-produced cotton and a world per annum increase of 5.4 percent.

Dividing the weight data by Ellison's number of bales gave the average weight per bale by origin. Although this was for bales imported into the United Kingdom, there is no reason to believe that bales imported into Europe were appreciably different in average weight. The average weight per bale by origin was then applied to the number of bales by origin consumed by the United States, United Kingdom, and Europe to get the weight of consumption by origin. A trend line was then computed against the natural log of weight.

Sources: Donnell (1872) for number of bales consumed in Europe by origin.

Hammond (1897) for United States consumption of US cotton.

Mann (1860) and Great Britain, *Statistical Abstract for the United Kingdom* ([1867] 1965) for United Kingdom raw cotton imports weight data.

Ellison ([1886] 1968) for number of bales imported into United Kingdom.

years when the American crop was sparse. Although consumption of Indian cotton grew at a higher per annum rate than that of American, the rate of change in consumption of Indian cotton was much more variable. Indian cotton was used only grudgingly and appeared likely to continue in a supporting role for the foreseeable future. East Indian-grown raw cotton tended to have a shorter, more fragile staple. Its inherent inferiority was exacerbated by the indifferent handling it received on the long overland haul to Indian ports and by intentional adulteration. Finally, the East Indian cotton required more care in spinning. These factors accounted for the persistently lower prices paid for East Indian-grown raw cotton relative to American-grown raw cotton.[22]

Before the Civil War, American-grown cotton accounted for 85 percent of total United States, Great Britain and continental European consumption of cotton. As a result of the war, world consumption of raw cotton from all sources shrank from 2.119 billion pounds (1859–61 average) to 974 million pounds (1862–64 average), a 54 percent drop. Of the 1862–64 consumption, about 27 percent was American and 53 percent was East Indian (see Table 10.8).

Table 10.8. United States, Great Britain, and European Consumption of
Raw Cotton, by Source

(in millions of pounds*) Years	USA	Brazil	West Indies	East Indies	Egypt	Total
1831–35	408.0	31.6	8.2	33.3	27.6	508.9
1836–40	583.6	25.4	15.4	57.0	30.1	711.6
1841–45	795.3	19.3	11.9	72.6	24.7	923.9
1846–50	950.9	24.0	6.3	88.1	30.7	1,099.8
1851–55	1,274.7	27.1	6.5	132.5	57.6	1,498.3
1856–60	1,642.6	26.9	7.7	201.1	56.8	1,935.2
1861	1,618.2	15.2	8.4	297.0	75.0	2,013.8
1862	363.5@	23.5	16.0	413.9	77.8	894.7
1863	220.3	29.2	27.2	546.5	145.1	968.2
1864	206.1	44.9	29.6	582.8	195.1	1,058.6
1865	318.4	57.7	71.6	661.3	257.8	1,366.8
1866	967.9	82.0	65.2	639.4	153.4	1,907.8

* Dividing the weight data by Ellison's number of bales gave the average weight per bale by
origin. Although this was for bales imported into the United Kingdom, there is no reason to
believe that bales imported into Europe differed appreciably in average weight. The average
weight per bale by origin was then applied to the number of bales by origin consumed by the
United States, United Kingdom, and Europe to get the weight of consumption by origin.

Some of this was Surat cotton that had been reexported to America; see Atkinson (1863), 5.

Sources: Donnell (1872) for number of bales consumed in Europe by origin.
    Hammond (1897) for United States consumption of US cotton.
    Mann (1860) and Great Britain, *Statistical Abstract for the United Kingdom* ([1867] 1965)
    for United Kingdom raw cotton imports weight data.
    Ellison ([1886] 1968) for number of bales imported into United Kingdom.

Econometric evidence suggests that long-run elasticities of supply by
rival non-American cotton producers during the antebellum era were relatively low. In other words, increases in the prices of raw cotton triggered
relatively small increases in the quantity supplied by rival producers.
Wright estimated elasticities of supply for India, Brazil, and Egypt for the
antebellum era. India and Brazil had elasticities of supply of roughly 0.3 to
0.4, while Egypt's supply possessed somewhat greater elasticity. The elasticities of supply for India and Egypt most likely reflect long-run supply, as
these estimates were based on lagged prices. Bent Hansen and Karim
Nashashibi found short- and long-term elasticities of acreage with respect
to price in Egypt during 1913 to 1961 of 0.25 and 0.30 respectively. British
import data support the notion of low price responsiveness by rival producers. Brazilian cotton exports to Great Britain had fluctuated between
40,000 and 80,000 400–pound bales between 1849 and 1861. Although
prices of Pernambuco cotton in Great Britain were high during 1857–61,

Table 10.9. Imports of Raw Cotton into Great Britain (in thousands of 400-pound bales)

Calendar Year	USA	W. Ind.	Originating Source Egypt	Brazil	E. Ind.	Other	Total
1856	1,950.1	1.5	86.5	54.6	451.2	15.8	2,559.7
1857	1,639.7	1.4	62.2	74.8	625.9	19.4	2,423.3
1858	2,083.1	1.1	95.6	46.5	331.8	27.7	2,585.9
1859	2,404.3	1.5	95.3	56.2	480.8	26.9	3,065.0
1860	2,791.2	1.7	110.1	43.2	510.4	20.8	3,477.3
1861	2,048.8	1.6	103.7	43.2	922.6	22.6	3,142.5
1862	55.1	4.7	163.1	58.3	986.1	42.6	1,309.9
1863	138.6	13.0	268.4	56.5	1,165.0	32.5	1,674.0
1864	204.5	19.3	367.7	95.0	1,505.2	41.5	2,233.3
1865	475.7	41.9	510.0	138.5	1,212.0	66.9	2,444.9
1866	1,303.1	36.8	324.4	171.3	1,553.0	54.2	3,442.8
1867	1,323.4	33.3	332.4	176.1	1,247.1	44.0	3,156.3
1868	1,436.3	18.6	339.7	247.0	1,234.3	44.2	3,320.2
1869	1,144.6	24.3	434.9	198.5	1,203.4	46.4	3,052.0
1870	1,791.9	16.4	388.0	160.5	853.7	135.2	3,345.8

Note: USA contains Bahamas and Mexico (during the war USA cotton was smuggled through these regions).
West Indies includes British West India Islands, New Granada, and Venezuela.
Egypt contains cotton from other Mediterranean ports.
East India includes China and Japan (mostly for 1862–66).
Source: Great Britain. *Statistical Abstract for the United Kingdom* ([1867] 1965, 58–59).

the average export to Great Britain was only 53,000 bales during this period (see Table 10.9). While the price of Pernambuco cotton roughly doubled in Great Britain between 1861 and 1862 and continued to climb in 1863, only a modest increase in imports of Brazilian cotton occurred—roughly 57,500 bales were imported per year. Egypt and the Mediterranean, too, had shown little responsiveness to the improved cotton prices of 1858–61, as their exports to Great Britain hovered around 100,000 bales. Between 1861 and 1862, exports from this region rose from 104,000 to 163,000 bales. Surprisingly, by 1865, Egypt's increase in cotton exports rivaled India's:

Year	Egypt	India[23]
1861	102,200	922,600
1865	442,100	1,114,900

The West Indies, New Granada and Venezuela were minor producers. Although their exports rose from fewer than 2,000 to 42,000 bales, this area was of little importance. "Other Countries" (outside East India, China, and the aforementioned regions) increased their exports to Great Britain from fewer than 22,600 to 66,900 bales during the Civil War. Thus, sources other than East India/China were able to provide roughly 586,000 bales more to Great Britain in 1865 than in 1861. But imports of United States-grown cotton had fallen from 2,400,000 bales (1859–61 average) to 340,000 bales in 1864–65 (and much of this was imported after the lifting of the blockade).

It was, then, to East India that Great Britain and Europe looked for relief. An average of 440,000 bales had been exported from India to Great Britain during 1853–60. The persistently high prices of 1858–61 had finally spurred India to export more. In 1861, 922,600 bales had arrived in Great Britain from India, compared with 510,000 bales in 1860. However, much of this increased export was the result of diverting trade from China and also sending the dregs of Indian cotton.

Unfortunately for the textile manufacturers, this increase between 1860 and 1861 of Indian exports to Great Britain was *larger* than the subsequent increase between 1861 and 1864. Cotton exports from India crept from 922,600 to 981,600 to 1,086,000 bales between 1861–63, before jumping to 1,266,000 bales in 1864. East Indian cotton producers were hesitant to increase their acreage early in the Civil War. Harnetty's acreage figures show only a 3.65 percent increase in acreage between 1860–61 and 1861–62. The acreage increased 15.4 percent between 1861–62 and 1862–63 and 25.3 percent in the subsequent year.[24]

During the antebellum era, India sent raw cotton to China, but China began to export cotton to Great Britain in 1862. China had exported fewer than four tons of cotton to Great Britain between 1856 and 1861. Beginning in 1862, but particularly during 1863–65, Chinese exports of raw cotton reached a peak of 215,000 bales. The exports disappeared almost immediately after the Civil War, with only 14,600 bales being exported in 1866 and fewer than 1,400 bales in 1867.[25]

Thus, the three-fold or larger increases in the prices of raw cotton failed to elicit more than a moderate and lagging supply response from the Confederacy's cotton-producing rivals. This sluggish response stemmed from two sources. First, it was risky to increase acreage in the face of volatile prices, especially in the early part of the war. Rival producers feared that, after the war, Great Britain and the rest of Europe would resume their dependence upon American-grown raw cotton. Indeed, the Cotton Supply Association of Manchester acknowledged this fear: "It would be said, 'What prospects do you hold out? You ask us to direct the industry and capital of our respective countries to the growth of cotton. But how is it that you have relied upon America for no less than 85 per cent. of your cotton supply; and what guarantee can you give us that America won't resume her old position and drive us out of the markets of the world?'" Second, there was the fear that the South had huge stockpiles of raw cotton waiting to inundate the market at the conclusion of the war. Mr. Mason, a director of the Cotton Supply Association of Manchester, tried to allay such fears at a conference of the association and representatives of various cotton producing countries: "It was said that 4,000,000 bales of American cotton were shut up in the Southern States, and that when a peace was patched up these bales would be let loose upon Lancashire like a deluge, but he thought this was a bug-bear." Mr. Mason was seconded by another member of the association who believed that "there were hardly remained 2,000,000 bales in the Southern States."[26] The rival producers' hesitation was reasonable, as even 2 million would have sent raw cotton prices tumbling. Other impediments to augmenting the cotton supply included inadequate overland transportation and the need to transfer labor from other endeavors to growing cotton. These producers had not become relatively more efficient than the American growers, and they knew it. As Table 10.9 shows, although Brazil and Egypt continued to send much greater quantities of raw cotton after the Civil War than they had before it, East India's exports receded after the war. There is nothing to suggest that the rival producers of raw cotton had gained any lasting competitiveness compared to the Southern producers, and by 1870 over half the raw cotton produced in the world was American. The percentage rose to over 70 percent by 1880. The latter proportion was similar to that of the antebellum period.[27]

If there was a diminution in world demand for American-grown raw cotton, it was not because rival producers had become more efficient relative to American producers. The extreme price increases inspired only a moderate and lagging supply response from the South's cotton-producing rivals. Had the South reduced her exports, say, by a third, and caused prices to rise by 50 percent, the supply response of her rivals would likely have been modest. By threatening to expand her output, the South might have plausibly forestalled entry by her rivals and exercised her price-setting power to reap higher profits for even an extended period of time.

Although the price path, stocks of raw cotton, and responses of rival producers described above reveal little evidence of weakening demand for raw cotton, the quantity is needed to ascertain the change in demand for raw cotton. Table 10.10 shows the state of demand under the assumption of a constant elasticity of demand but allowing for three different levels of that elasticity. World demand for all cotton exhibited an elasticity between 0.5 and 0.6 throughout the antebellum period (presumably world demand for American-grown cotton would have had a somewhat higher elasticity). However, given the large change in the quantity supplied, the assumption that elasticity of demand remained at the antebellum level is suspect, and one should consult the discussion in Appendix 3. If the elasticity increased between 1861 and 1862, the negative growth-in-demand estimates would be exaggerated. If the elasticity of demand increased initially but stabilized during the Civil War, the columns with the higher elasticities might give a better idea of the movement in world demand for all raw cotton during 1863–65. Table 10.10 shows that there was growth in demand for raw cotton even in 1861. The drop in demand did not occur until 1862. Thereafter the market recovered and demand was probably closer to its 1861 level by 1863 or 1864 (especially if the elasticity increased during this period).

The information in Table 10.10 implies that the world market for raw cotton was unlikely to be destined for a severe short-run downturn in the absence of the war-induced cotton shortage. Instead, the drastic disloca-tions engendered by the Civil War drove the sharp contraction in demand for raw cotton.

III. Conclusions

The following salient facts are crucial in understanding the world market for raw cotton. First, stocks of raw cotton and British cotton textile goods were not inordinately large on the eve of the Civil War. The stocks were quickly depleted by the summer of 1862. Second, prices of raw cotton were increasing during the first half of 1861 and advanced even faster after the Battle of Bull Run, while cotton yarn prices remained stable. British cotton piece-good prices were modestly weaker in 1861. Third, the growth in world demand for raw cotton continued to be strong through August 1861, declining only in commercial year 1862 with the onset of the disruption in the supply of American raw cotton. The growth in world demand for raw cotton largely mirrored the world demand for British cotton textiles. Therefore, the world market for raw cotton and particularly American-grown raw cotton exhibited no signs of being destined for a sharp and pos-sibly protracted downturn through August 1861.

Nor is there any evidence that, prior to August 1861, rival producers of raw cotton had become more efficient and usurped some of the world demand for raw cotton from the American producers. Instead, rival pro-ducers of raw cotton reacted sluggishly to both antebellum and Civil War

Table 10.10. Estimates of Per Annum Growth in World Demand for Raw Cotton (from All Sources)

Year	Quantity (Bales)	New York Price $/Bale	Per Annum Growth in Demand (by %)		
			e=0.5	e=1.0	e=1.5
1859	5,950,332	$43.03			
1860	7,313,119	39.46	17.69%	12.71%	7.93%
1861	7,029,674	48.39	6.45	17.88	30.54
1862	2,502,387	106.19	−47.27	−21.88	15.72
1863	2,160,230	183.10	13.36	48.85	95.46
1864	2,763,907	197.14	32.76	37.76	42.94
1865	3,143,048	149.29	− 1.04	−13.88	−25.06
1866	5,797,636	81.70	36.46	0.95	−25.32
1860–66			2.22	8.61	15.40
1861–65			− 5.86	8.37	24.76

Year	Quantity (Bales)	Liverpool Price $/Bale	Per Annum Growth in Demand		
			e=0.5	e=1.0	e=1.5
1859	5,950,332	$55.60			
1860	7,313,119	47.71	13.85%	5.47%	−2.29
1861	7,029,674	68.92	15.52	38.84	66.86
1862	2,502,387	146.83	−48.04	−24.16	10.71
1863	2,160,230	176.06	−5.47	3.51	13.35
1864	2,763,907	214.78	41.31	56.08	72.39
1865	3,143,048	153.62	−3.82	−18.66	−31.21
1866	5,797,636	121.62	64.12	46.03	29.93
1860–66			4.00	12.44	21.56
1861–65			−9.61	−0.08	10.45

Year: commercial year ending August 31, i.e. 1858 is September 1, 1857, through August 31, 1858.

Quantity: world supply in 400-pound bales (includes beginning stocks in United States and Great Britain, but not continental Europe). Weighting the various raw cotton bales by their source (to account for quality differences) yielded similar results as the above table.

New York Price: annual Uplands price per 400-pound bale in New York (deflated by Warren-Pearson index).

Liverpool Price: annual Uplands price per 400-pound bale in Liverpool (deflated by Rousseaux price index). Converted into gold dollars at rate $4.8647 per £ (see Mitchell 1908, 252).

Sources: Donnell (1872) for beginning stock in Great Britain and supply to Europe.

Watkins (1908) for beginning stock in United States and supply to United States.

price increases, and they were able to replace only a part of the shortfall in Southern cotton production.

The above findings argue against the thesis that the world demand for American-grown raw cotton was destined for a severe downturn, whether temporary or permanent. Because the world demand for finished cotton goods appeared stable during 1860–61 and only significantly weakened after the prices for raw cotton jumped in late 1861, the world demand for raw cotton (especially American-grown raw cotton) probably would have remained stable and possibly even increased during 1862 in the absence of the disruptions in the American demand for cotton textiles and the supply of American-grown raw cotton. These findings lend credence to Hanson's finding of steady growth in the world demand for all raw cotton during the 1860s.

The drastic rise in the price of raw cotton due to the blockade-induced reduction in the supply of American-grown raw cotton led to increased prices for cotton textiles during 1862. The consumers of cotton textiles reacted in 1862 by sharply curtailing their demand for cotton goods, either because of the negative impact on their real incomes or by postponing purchases of cotton goods (perhaps in hopes of lower future prices or because the implicit price of continuing to wear existing clothing fell). The dramatic decrease in the demand for cotton textiles adversely affected the world demand for raw cotton during commercial year 1862 (as shown by Table 10.10). The demand for cotton textiles rebounded after 1862, and the world demand for all raw cotton displayed a similar rebound in 1863 and 1864.

Table 10.11 shows the world demand for American-grown raw cotton. It is important to note three caveats about the estimates during the Civil War years. First, the New York beginning stock was listed as "unavailable" by Watkins. Inclusion of the New York beginning stock would decrease the negative growth-in-demand figure of 1863. A more important caveat is the huge inventory of raw cotton that accumulated in the South during the Civil War and that hung over demand in key markets. Due to the embargo and the blockade, most of the American-grown raw cotton was not taken to the New York or European markets from late 1861 through early 1865. We have only a rough idea of the volume of raw cotton held within the South. The presence of perhaps 2 or 3 million additional bales within the Confederacy would have suppressed the increase in the price of raw cotton and would have significantly affected the growth-in-demand estimates of 1862–65 in both Tables 10.10 and 10.11. Third, given the changing proportion of American-grown raw cotton in the total supply of raw cotton and the sharply fluctuating prices, the assumption that the elas-

Table 10.11. Per Annum Growth in Demand for American-Grown Raw Cotton (in Percent)

Year	Quantity (Bales)	NY Price $	Liverpool Price $	New York Price			Liverpool Price		
				e=0.7	e=1.0	e=2.0	e=0.7	e=1.0	e=2.0
1859	5,227,284	43.03	55.60						
1860	6,391,177	39.46	47.71	15.1	12.1	2.8	9.9	4.9	-10.0
1861	5,897,555	48.39	68.92	6.4	13.2	38.8	19.4	33.3	92.5
1862	1,016,716	106.19	146.83	-70.1	-62.2	-17.0	-70.7	-63.3	-21.7
1863	448,981	183.10	176.06	-35.3	-23.9	31.3	-49.9	-47.0	-36.5
1864	736,260	197.14	214.78	72.7	76.6	90.1	88.5	100.0	144.0
1865	639,819	149.29	153.62	-28.5	-34.2	-50.2	-31.3	-37.8	-55.5
1866	2,810,755	81.70	121.62	188.1	140.4	31.6	273.0	247.8	175.3
1867	2,986,014	63.94	87.52	-10.5	-16.9	-34.9	-15.6	-23.5	-45.0
1868	3,240,173	52.40	85.76	-5.6	-11.1	-27.1	7.0	6.4	4.2
1869	2,863,461	63.57	104.54	1.2	7.2	30.1	1.5	7.7	31.2
1870	3,551,389	57.42	85.03	15.5	12.0	1.2	7.4	0.9	-17.9
1871	5,096,130	43.25	71.37	17.7	8.1	-18.6	26.9	20.4	1.0
1859 through 1869				-3.2	-2.1	1.8	-1.6	0.3	6.8
1860 through 1870				-3.2	-2.1	1.6	-1.8	-0.1	5.8
1861 through 1871				-2.2	-2.6	-3.6	-1.2	-1.1	-0.8

Year: year ending August 31.

Quantity: beginning stocks at New York and Liverpool plus crop, in 400-pound bales.

Price: New York nominal price deflated by Warren & Pearson index; Liverpool nominal price deflated by Rousseaux index and converted to gold dollars by multiplying £ by 4.8647 (Mitchell 1908, 252).

Sources: Watkins (1908) for all data except beginning stock at Liverpool.

Donnell (1872) for beginning stock at Liverpool.

ticity of demand remained constant during this period is most unlikely. As the price of raw cotton increased during commercial year 1862 and as rival raw cotton producers increased their market share, the elasticity of demand for American-grown raw cotton increased. The increased elasticity of demand for American-grown raw cotton caused the negative growth-in-demand estimates shown in Table 10.11 to be exaggerated (see Appendix 5). In fact, given the small negative growth-in-demand figures for 1860–70 using the endpoint method of estimation, we cannot rule out the possibility that world demand for American-grown raw cotton *increased* slightly during the decade. The best guess of the course of world demand for American-grown raw cotton was that such demand fell in tandem with world demand for all raw cotton during the commercial year ending August 31, 1862 (but not as precipitously as implied by Table 10.11). Rival producers supplied a little more raw cotton during the commercial year 1862 in response to the doubling in raw cotton prices; however, the higher prices for raw cotton eventually inspired non-American producers of raw cotton to significantly increase their supply, and this eventual increase in the supply of raw cotton by rival producers suppressed the world demand for American-grown raw cotton in subsequent years. Thus, the best explanation for the continued stagnation of the world demand for American raw cotton appears to be the increase in the supply of raw cotton produced by rivals in response to the high prices during the Civil War. The real price of cotton in Liverpool was essentially the same in calendar year 1865 as it had been in 1862. The amount of non-American raw cotton imported into Europe was more than 1,250,000 bales greater in 1865 than in 1862. In 1866 when prices slumped even further, the quantity of non-American raw cotton imported increased by an additional 500,000 bales. Thus, the Civil War period witnessed a significant rightward shift in the supply by other producers; this non-American supply receded only gradually during the postbellum period. The marked increase in the non-American supply during the 1860s explains why the world demand for American-grown raw cotton stagnated or decreased, even though world demand for all raw cotton increased.

However, in the absence of the Civil War shortage of American-grown cotton, there is nothing to suggest a significant temporary or permanent downturn in the demand for American-grown raw cotton.

King Cotton was not about to be deposed on the eve of the Civil War. The underlying demand for raw cotton and the long-term prospect for growth in that demand remained strong. Short-term demand also would have remained strong if the South had been able to assure Europe of a steady (even if somewhat curtailed) supply. The postwar period demonstrated that the South was king among cotton growers. Although the South fell just short of regaining her former share of the market for raw cotton after the war, she was still able to easily recapture her leading role.

Cotton revenues remained the Confederacy's best economic asset, but realization of that asset depended upon the South's ability to properly play its cotton card in the face of Northern naval superiority.

$$11$$

KING COTTON
DURING THE WAR

The autumn of 1861 should have been an effective time for the Confederacy to exploit the South's price-setting power in the world market for raw cotton. The South could reasonably hope to reap well over $200 million per annum in revenue from such exports. What happened to King Cotton during the war?

I. How Much Cotton Was Exported and the Revenue Generated

The first step is to determine how much cotton the South exported. Owsley estimated that between 1 and 1.25 million bales of cotton were smuggled through the blockade after the spring of 1862. While Lebergott considers Owsley's estimate high, our computations confirm them as reasonable. From September 3, 1861, through June 30, 1865, Donnell, using semi-weekly New York data, reported that almost 1,011,267 bales reached New York City (not all of which was Southern cotton). Receipts of Southern cotton in England amounted to 554,000 bales; continental Europe received 153,000 bales for the calendar years 1862 through 1864 (see Table 11.1).[1]

Undoubtedly the United States received more cotton than what New York reported (Owsley reports Boston receipts totaling 100,000 bales), but this was largely offset by the reexports of cotton. New York exported roughly 105,000 bales to Great Britain, while Great Britain exported 160,000 bales to New York. An upward-biased rough figure, then, is 1,900,000 bales between September 1, 1861 (very little was shipped during July and August 1861), and June 30, 1865.

These 1,900,000 bales were not all smuggled through the combined Federal naval blockade and land cordon, for Federal authorities permitted leaks in the blockade (see Table 11.2). With hardship from the dearth of cotton pressing upon the New England textile industry, Lincoln countenanced a flow of cotton from captured ports and inland towns such as New

Orleans, Beaufort, Key West, and Memphis. New Orleans, the busiest of the permitted entrepots, exported 310,931 bales to Northern cities between April 1862 and August 31, 1865. However, these are not "normalized" bales, and using Watkins's estimate of 477 pounds per bale, we would get 370,785 400-pound bales. Captured and "abandoned" cotton from land conquest or sea activity probably accounted for another 73,000 bales, and possibly up to 190,000 bales. Fifty-three thousand bales were obtained by purchases sanctioned under the Act of 1864. Thus, it is erroneous to conclude that 1,900,000 400-pound bales breached the blockade. A figure of 1 to 1.5 million 400-pound bales smuggled through the blockade or overland via illegal trade is reasonable. Surprisingly, Lebergott himself comes up with a figure of roughly 1,244,000 bales of smuggled cotton, comprising 464,000 bales to Europe; 172,000 to the North by sea; and 608,000 to the North by land. Since Lebergott often used 500-pound bales in his discussion, the "normalized" 400-pound bale figure nears 1.5 million.

I will compute a downward-biased estimate of the blockade's effectiveness. Suppose that *all* 1.9 million 400-pound bales received by Northern and European buyers were smuggled through the blockade; compared to the prewar sales figures, this is a minute total, indeed. The four years prior to the war saw a combined crop of over 18 million bales placed on the market and sold, so roughly one-tenth the volume of cotton was exported during the Civil War. Had the Southerners received ten times the prewar price per pound for their cotton, their revenues would not have been adversely affected. Such was not the case. In New York the real price of cotton quadrupled from 13.01 cents per pound in 1860–61 to 53 cents per pound in 1863–64 (see Table 11.3). The Liverpool real price per pound tripled during the same period. The drastic reduction in exports of American-grown raw cotton induced only three and four-fold price increases partly because the rapid increases eventually led to a doubling of exports from the major rival raw cotton growers and because of fears that millions of bales remained in the South. Rival cotton producers sent 428.4 million pounds to Great Britain in 1861; in 1865, they sent 760.9 million pounds. Thus, the price increases may have primarily benefited the rival producers.

We can estimate the maximum revenue from the cotton actually exported by using the real New York price and the quantities exported per commercial year. The results are shown in Table 11.4. Maximum revenue in 1861–62 was a paltry $27.5 million. As the war progressed and cotton prices rose outside the South, ever-greater rewards for successfully smuggling cotton through a tightening blockade increased the annual flow of cotton to roughly 500,000 bales per year (some of which was exported with

Table 11.1. Confederate Cotton Exports by Destination during the Civil War

(in 400-pound Bales)	Total	1861*	1862	1863	1864	1865#
New York	1,011,267	13,953	189,765	274,783	318,211	214,555
England	553,868	2,639	72,000	138,609	204,511	136,109
Rest of Europe	153,000	0	60,000	30,000	43,000	20,000
Subtotal	1,718,135	16,592	321,765	443,392	565,722	370,664
Other U.S.Ports	100,000					
Captures: Sea	23,000					
Land	50,000					
Subtotal	1,891,135					
Reexports:						
New York	(105,741)					
Great Britain	(160,000)					
Total	1,625,394					

* September 1, 1861 through December 31, 1861.

\# January 1, 1865 through June 30, 1865.

Sources for Table 11.1

New York: Donnell (848,022 actual bales multiplied by 477/400 to convert into 400-pound bales; 477 was the 1860–61 weight—see Watkins 1908). Using 477 pounds biases the number of bales upwards, since the bales shipped during the war were likely smaller due to the deterioration of baling equipment. This figure largely agrees with Owsley. *Hunt's Merchants' Magazine* listed receipts at New York for 1862–64 of 674,299 bales, converting these bales by 477/400 yields 804,102 "normalized" bales. Donnell lists 782,759 "normalized" bales for the same period (Donnell 1872). The *Hunt's* figures lists domestic cotton (424,107 bales) and "foreign" cotton (250,192 bales), but much of the "foreign" cotton may have been Southern cotton sent to the West Indies or Great Britain and then shipped to New York (1864, vol. 50, 136; 1865, vol. 52, 118).

England: All figures from Donnell except 1863 and 1864; the 1863 and 1864 figures are Great Britain Board of Trade figures (see Great Britain. *Statistical Abstract of the United Kingdom*). Ellison and Donnell's data are quite similar, but Donnell presents his in weekly format. Board of Trade figures are in pounds and differ by 6,000 four hundred-pound bales from Donnell/Ellison (in both 1863 and 1864); apparently Donnell's and Ellison bales were 400 pounds. Hammond's figures agree with Ellison's. Owsley claims 251,368 bales were exported to Great Britain in 1863 and that an undercount of 70,000 bales occurred in 1864 (Owsley 1931, 287 cited *Economist;* however, the issue cited did not contain these facts).

Rest of Europe: Hammond's figures (which are accepted by Owsley) are higher than Donnell's (whose figures for shipments to Europe are ambiguous) and are used to bias the figure upward in 1862–64 (Hammond 1897, 261). No solid estimates of September 1 through December 31, 1861, and January 1 through June 30, 1865, exist. Given the paucity of exports to Great Britain and the generally lower exports to continental Europe, the estimate of zero bales in late 1861 is reasonable. Hammond lists 68,000 bales for the year 1865, so we adjust by multiplying (Southern cotton exported into England for the first half of 1865/Southern cotton exported into England for 1865), or (136,109/462,000) x 68,000 = 20,000 bales.

Table 11.1 continued

Sources for Table 11.1 continued

Other U.S. Ports: Owsley claims 100,000 bales went to Boston during the war (Owsley 1931, 288). New Orleans shipped 35,617 bales to Northern cities besides New York from 1862 to 1864 (*Hunt's Merchants' Magazine* 53 [1865], 256; New Orleans *Price Current* 1865).

Captures: Lebergott (1981, 881) and Owsley (1931, 288). Lebergott apparently used 500-pound bales, but it's not clear that Owsley did. No adjustment was made.

Note: the official records list 11,187 abandoned and 156,387 captured bales of cotton (not counting sea captures). Much of this may be subsumed within the New York receipts (U.S. House of Representatives, 1866–67, 5–6). In order to bias downward the number of bales actually smuggled through the blockade, we use the lower (Lebergott/Owsley) figures.

Reexports: Reexports from New York (normalized bales) taken from Donnell. *Hunt's Merchants' Magazine* 52 (1865), 118, lists 65,110 bales (77,644 "normalized") exported from New York from 1862 through 1864. For reexports from Britain see the *Economist* (March 11, 1865) and Owsley (1931, 288).

Table 11.2. Lower Bound Estimate of Southern Cotton That Was Not Smuggled

Captures:	
Sea[1]	23,000
Land[2]	50,000
New Orleans to North Trade[3]	310,931
Purchased by Act of 1864[4]	60,164
Total	444,095

Sources

[1] See Lebergott (1981, 881) and Owsley (1931, 288–89).

[2] See Lebergott (1981, 881) and Owsley (1931, 288–89). The Congressional report, "Captured and Forfeited Cotton," (U.S. House of Representatives, 1866–67, 5–6), lists 11,187 bales as abandoned and 156,387 bales as captured (presumably on land). However, in order to bias upward the amount of cotton smuggled, we use the Lebergott/Owsley estimates.

[3] *Hunt's Merchants' Magazine* 53 (1865), 255 and New Orleans *Price Current* (Sept. 1865). These are not "normalized" to bias the amount of smuggled cotton upwards.

[4] Lebergott (1981, 881) listed 53,838 bales from this source. These bales were listed as weighing 447 pounds, so he converted them into 500-pound bales. We convert them into 400-pound bales, i.e 53,838 x (447/400) = 60,164.

Table 11.3. New York and Liverpool Prices for Southern Cotton

Year	Pence/lb.	Liverpool pence per pound (Uplands mid.) Weighted Average Price Index	Real Price	% Change
1860–61	8.50	100.0	8.50	
1861–62	18.37	101.4	18.12	113.18
1862–63	22.46	103.4	21.72	19.87
1863–64	27.17	102.6	26.48	21.92
1864–65	19.11	100.9	18.94	−28.47

Year	Cents/lb.	New York cents per pound (Uplands mid.) Weighted Average Price Index	Real Price	% Change
1860–61	13.01	100.0	13.01	
1861–62	31.29	109.6	28.55	119.45
1862–63	67.21	136.5	49.24	72.47
1863–64	101.50	191.5	53.00	7.64
1864–65	83.38	207.8	40.13	−24.28

Sources: Watkins (1908), Donnell (1872), and Warren and Pearson (1932) wholesale price index.

the tacit approval of Washington). Although the maximum revenue rose to $129.2 million in 1863–64, the maximum total revenue for the *four* commercial years was an unimpressive $327 million. This maximum wartime total revenue from exporting raw cotton pales besides the prewar Southern revenue from cotton, as the revenue was $211.3 million for 1860–61 alone. Compared to the hypothetical revenue earned by a South exercising its price-setting power (perhaps up to $250 million per year), the $327 million earnings for four years represented a shortfall in revenue easily exceeding $500 million.

The amounts shown in Table 11.4 portray the revenue accruing to Southerners had they received the New York price. However, Southern cotton sellers did not reap the New York price (and London prices were not as high as New York prices). For instance, we did not subtract the $6 per bale New Orleans-to-New York peacetime shipping costs that we used to adjust the hypothetical revenue streams. More importantly, we have not adjusted for the very significant blockade-induced transportation wedge. This wedge affects the estimate of revenue earned from smuggling cotton from blockaded ports. If the vessels were owned and manned by Southerners, more of the revenue might have remained in Southern pockets. However, many other people besides Southerners also smuggled cotton. If

Table 11.4. Maximum Revenue from Cotton Using New York Prices

(Revenue Amounts in Thousands of Dollars)			
Commercial Year	Number of 400-lb Bales	Real Price per Bale	Maximum Revenue
1861–62	240,736	$114.20	$27,492
1862–63	410,092	196.96	80,772
1863–64	609,527	212.00	129,220
1864–65	557,780	160.52	89,535
Total	1,818,135		327,018

Note: 73,000 bales of captured cotton are not included.

Source: See Table 3. Donnell (1872). Donnell's figures are used to compute commercial year (September 1 through August 31) number of bales.

they paid Southerners only the "on-farm" price plus the cost of transporting the cotton to Southern ports, then probably no more than a third of the total revenue went to Southerners.

Therefore, the amount of revenue accruing to Southerners is ambiguous. We are left making a rough guess that these factors served to reduce revenues accruing to Southerners (producers, handlers, and the government) by at least one-third and perhaps as much as two-thirds. The reduced revenue from these adjustments probably increased the overall revenue shortfall from $500 million to $700 million. Some of the revenue loss might have been offset by switching labor from producing raw cotton to other pursuits. However, as Lebergott points out, the amount of labor switched was not as dramatic as the reduction in exports. He estimates that 6,800,000 bales were produced during the war, but that much of this was burned or rotted away. At war's end, perhaps 1,800,000 bales remained in the South. Therefore, the South suffered a drastic economic loss from its reduced revenues and profits from exporting raw cotton, while wasting much manpower.[2]

II. The Main Impetus for the Reduction in Revenue from Exporting Raw Cotton

One could argue that even if the above is possible, not all the dire results were due to the blockade. First, Southerners initially believed that King Cotton's sovereignty lay in coercing foreign intervention via starving textile producers of cotton. Early in the war, the informal embargo on exporting raw cotton was probably a bigger cause of reduced Southern incomes than the blockade. However, by April 1862 the embargo had lost much of its appeal. Had there been no blockade, the basic effect of the embargo, then, would have been largely a postponement of revenue rather than a catastrophic loss in revenue.

A second argument concerns the effect of the seizure of Southern territory by the Union army. The loss of New Orleans in April 1862 was certain to alter trade patterns and raise transportation costs. However, cotton could have been rerouted to Mobile and the Texas ports and, without the blockade, would have introduced a more moderate increase in transportation costs. There were no significant captures of Southern cotton-producing territories until April 1862. Nor was there a shortage of raw cotton within the South. According to James Watkins, the cotton crop harvested in late 1861 was well over 4 million bales, so much more cotton could have been shipped. Why wasn't it shipped in spring 1862, if the blockade was tissue-thin as Owsley maintains? As the war ended with 1,800,000 bales remaining in the South (in addition to the large quantities that were destroyed during the war), it's clear that paucity of cotton cannot explain the trickle of cotton exports from the South.

Why didn't the Southern growers and the Confederacy benefit from the dramatically higher prices? The most important reason was that the export reduction was a result of an increasing transportation cost wedge. Instead of Southern growers withholding raw cotton exports to benefit from the higher prices, they were discouraged from shipping raw cotton because of the increased transatlantic shipping costs and because of higher internal transportation costs (because they had to ship through different ports than usual, especially after New Orleans fell). Indeed, Southern growers did not reap higher prices for their cotton. Specie prices for cotton in the South rose in 1862–63, but fell thereafter (when the bulk of the cotton was sold), finishing the war *below* the 1860 specie price. While prices of raw cotton at blockaded ports remained largely stagnant during the war, prices at New York and Liverpool trebled and quadrupled. Thus, Southern growers received very little of the increased price. We can attribute the rising price differential to the blockade, because when ports were captured and opened for trade (such as New Orleans and Memphis) the price differential narrowed. At New Orleans, the price difference with New York was much less than the usual forty-five to fifty cents found at blockaded Southern ports. Cotton exported from New Orleans after April 1862 presumably did not incur the full blockade-induced ocean transportation charges, but there still appears to have been a price differential of five to fifteen cents between New Orleans and New York. Cotton shipped from Texas via Mexico saw considerable siphoning of revenue to non-Southern hands, with only fourteen to fifteen cents of the New York gold price of fifty-six cents accruing to Southerners. And of this fourteen or fifteen cents, some was paid to Southern teamsters to haul the cotton more than two hundred miles to Mexico.[3]

While the Southerners could have attempted to mitigate the blockade's effect on total revenue from cotton exports, the blockade's main effects would still hold. The Confederate and state governments occasionally floated loans based on those institutions' holdings of raw cotton. Unfortunately for these governments, the blockade depressed the value of their cotton. The bonds were usually based on raw cotton held at Southern ports and were therefore valued at five or six pence per pound (which was below the 1860–61 price). Thus, while cotton fetched three times as great a price in London and Liverpool, the Confederate and state governments could only get loans based on the blockade-depressed price of cotton. Certainly, the Confederate government would have built better credit had it purchased more cotton and used this enlarged holding as a basis for European loans. Of course, any such loans would still be vulnerable to the Confederacy's military fortunes.[4]

The blockade was an effective constraint upon the flow of cotton. It not only prevented the Confederacy from exploiting any potential gains by exercising its price-setting power in the market for raw cotton, but it was primarily responsible for the dramatic reduction in revenue from exporting raw cotton.

III. The Ramifications of the Blockade's Suppression of Southern Revenues from Exports of Raw Cotton

Southern revenue from exporting raw cotton fell far short of prewar and hypothetical revenue levels. In 1861–62, when the importance of establishing sound credit in Europe was paramount, the South reaped less than $30 million from cotton. While it is true that the cotton embargo postponed cotton revenues for six or seven months, the blockade must have accounted for the meager flow of fewer than 250,000 bales during the middle of 1862.

Historians have cited several "missed opportunities" for the Confederacy. The Federal blockade probably didn't reach a high level of efficiency until 1862. One can imagine the difference in Confederate purchasing power in Great Britain and Europe had an optimal export of roughly 3 million bales have been shipped in late 1861 instead of the trickle actually sent. Note that this is a policy for late 1861 and not the controversial policy prescription for April 1861 touted by General Joseph Johnston after the war. Jefferson Davis' friends and other observers pointed out, correctly, that little cotton remained in the Confederacy by April 1861. Treasury Secretary Memminger's biographer, Henry Capers, mocked the April 1861 plan as resolving itself "in a fleet of phantom ships loaded with phantom cotton."[5] However, there was a new crop of Southern cotton by September 1861. Although Southerners did not possess an ocean-going fleet of cargo ships, given British and Northern shippers' willingness to use their vessels to run the blockade or to trade illegally with Confederates at Texas, the supply of cargo ships does not appear to present an insuperable problem. In any event, improved Confederate purchasing power might have been used to buy modern warships or materials to construct a Confederate navy domestically. Rolled iron and ship machinery were two of the items badly needed by the nascent Confederate navy, and an improved Southern economy could have increased the military's ability to obtain such needed inputs.

Second, the shipment of a near-optimal amount of raw cotton in 1861–62 would have prevented much of the dislocation in the Southern economy. Planters were unable to sell much cotton after the summer of 1861, creating a riptide throughout the Southern economy. The shortfall in revenue from exporting raw cotton during the war was at least $500 million and probably closer to $700 million. Goldin and Lewis estimated that the expenditures (discounted to June 30, 1861, dollars) by the Confederate government and auxiliary state and local governments during the war were a billion dollars (including military payrolls). Eventually, the teetering economy proved less and less able to support military efforts.[6]

By toppling King Cotton from his regal perch and dealing the South a catastrophic economic loss, the blockade won a victory that was surely as devastating as any particular battlefield defeat in fatally weakening the South's war-making capability.

12

THE BLOCKADE'S EFFECTS UPON THE INTERNAL MOVEMENT OF RAW COTTON

The Union navy's blockade drastically reduced the shipment of raw cotton from the Southern states to European and Northern textiles manufacturers. The blockade directly affected the transportation costs between Southern seaports and ports in the North or Europe, and the increased ocean transportation costs drove a larger wedge between prices at Southern ports and prices at New York and Liverpool. Prices at Southern ports were pressed downward from the increased ocean transportation cost.

The blockade also exerted a dramatic effect upon the movement of raw cotton within the Confederate states. The blockade had three key effects upon the internal movement of raw cotton within the Confederate states and those states' ability to use raw cotton as an economic and political weapon. First, the blockade affected internal transportation costs by inducing growers to ship raw cotton to ports that were less closely blockaded. Clearly, if New Orleans, Mobile, and Memphis were closely blockaded or interdicted by the non-intercourse edict (as in the case of Memphis), Mississippi valley growers would be forced to look for other outlets, such as ports in Texas, Florida, and along the Atlantic. Rerouting raw cotton internally to these ports could significantly increase costs, further eroding the gains from shipping raw cotton. For instance, the movement of raw cotton from central Texas to the Rio Grande was extraordinarily expensive, but the Federal navy's blockade was effective enough to reroute the raw cotton from Galveston to Brownsville. A state by state examination of the western Confederacy will reveal the deficiencies of alternative exporting sites. Second, the disruption of intraregional shipments of raw cotton adversely affected the Southern transportation system. Increased reliance upon railroad shipments to the Atlantic ports of Wilmington and Norfolk hampered attempts to supply civilian and military needs in Virginia and North

Carolina. Third, the deranged intraregional movement of raw cotton had political ramifications for the nascent Confederate states.

I. Antebellum Movement of Raw Cotton

1) General Shipping Patterns

New Orleans was the preeminent antebellum port for exports of raw cotton, while Mobile was but a distant second (see Table 12.1). Charleston and Savannah were lesser, but still significant, ports. Florida, North Carolina, and Virginia shipped relatively small amounts of cotton. Finally, Texas and Memphis were increasing their share of cotton exports. However, New Orleans accounted for 45 percent or more of the exports in the years just before the Civil War.

Of the bumper crop of 1859–60, New Orleans received 1,800,000 bales from Louisiana and Mississippi. (Except where noted, all bales have been converted into 400-pound bales.) Those two states produced 2 million bales, so some of eastern Mississippi's cotton was probably fed by rail into Mobile. New Orleans received 428,000 bales from northern Alabama and Tennessee (including raw cotton initially received at Memphis). More than 190,000 bales were received from Arkansas (leaving about 180,000 bales produced by that state to be exported through Memphis or Texas). Finally, about 115,000 bales were received coastwise from Texas, Florida, and Mobile.[1]

Mobile received eastern Mississippi's raw cotton and the balance of Alabama's crop. The remaining raw cotton in the eastern states was probably shipped through Savannah, Charleston, and various minor ports on the Atlantic.

Table 12.2 shows the amount of cotton shipped by rail into the major port cities on the Atlantic, Mobile, and at Memphis. New Orleans received most of its raw cotton by water: down the Mississippi or across the Gulf of Mexico. The main railroad leading into the city—the New Orleans, Jackson & Great Northern—did not convey much of the cotton received at the city. The other railroads leading into New Orleans were local lines that did not service major cotton-producing areas. Moreover, about 200,000 bales of raw cotton shipped into Memphis (mostly by rail) eventually reached New Orleans via the Mississippi. Memphis, Charleston, Savannah, and Wilmington received most of their raw cotton by rail. For instance, 89 percent of the cotton exported from Charleston arrived via rail. Antebellum Wilmington exported roughly 20,000 to 36,000 bales per year, and the port received its cotton via rail. Although the Tombigbee and Alabama rivers served Mobile, the city obtained an increasing proportion of its cotton by

Table 12.1. Exports of Raw Cotton from Southern Ports

(in 400-pound bales) Port	1857–58	1858–59	1859–60	1860–61
Memphis*	10,635	95,346	125,249	171,033
	(0.31%)	(2.22%)	(2.33%)	(3.92%)
Virginia	27,299	36,890	65,678	93,172
	(0.79%)	(0.86%)	(1.22%)	(2.14%)
North Carolina	26,519	41,886	47,476	67,132
	(0.77%)	(0.97%)	(0.88%)	(1.54%)
Charleston/Georgetown	448,907	537,130	587,901	401,084
	(13.05%)	(12.48%)	(10.92%)	(9.20%)
Savannah	312,685	531,693	605,315	569,519
	(9.09%)	(12.35%)	(11.25%)	(13.06%)
Florida	135,198	193,868	222,114	144,498
	(3.93%)	(4.50%)	(4.13%)	(3.31%)
Mobile	577,212	787,174	971,571	652,052
	(16.77%)	(18.29%)	(18.05%)	(14.96%)
New Orleans#	1,741,932	1,865,414	2,465,687	2,088,782
	(50.62%)	(43.34%)	(45.81%)	(47.91%)
Texas	160,541	214,629	290,919	172,611
	(4.67%)	(4.99%)	(5.41%)	(3.96%)
Total	3,440,928	4,304,030	5,381,910	4,359,883

Note: Number in parentheses is the percent of that year's total exports.

* Memphis received over twice as much as listed here, but much went to New Orleans (and is included in that city's total).

New Orleans actually received 200,000 additional bales, but these were transshipped from other Gulf ports (and are included in those city's totals).

Source: *Hunts' Merchants Magazine* 45 (1861), 497.

Converted into 400-pound bales using Watkins estimated bale weights:

1857–58: 442   1858–59: 447   1859–60: 461   1860–61: 477

Table 12.2. Shipments of Raw Cotton by Rail into Some Port Cities

(in 400-pound bales)

Port	1857–58	1858–59	1859–60
New Orleans	—	162,454	220,787
Wilmington	21,059	26,320	36,023
Charleston	—	476,968	523,953
Savannah	—	424,336	497,647
Mobile	119,299	153,578	262,431
Memphis	—	—	381,037

Note: Converted into 400-pound bales using Watkins estimated bale weights—
    1857–58: 442   1858–59: 447   1859–60: 461

Sources

New Orleans: *Hunts' Merchants Magazine* 43 (1860), 634. These are receipts on the New Orleans, Jackson, and Great Northern railroads. The other New Orleans railroads were local lines that did not serve major cotton-producing regions.

Wilmington: Shipped via Wilmington & Weldon Railroad (Dozier 1920, 169). Some was shipped via the Wilmington & Manchester Railroad (from daily reports in Wilmington *Daily Journal*).

Charleston: Compiled from daily reports in Charleston *Daily Courier;* data from *Hunts' Merchants Magazine* 44 (1861), 373, confirmed the accuracy of the figures.

Savannah: Compiled from weekly reports in Savannah *Daily Morning News*. July and August 1860 figures not available.

Mobile: *Hunts' Merchants Magazine* 43 (1860), 632, lists Mobile & Ohio Railroad's (the major railroad into Mobile) shipments of cotton. See also *DeBow's Review* 29 (1860), 665, for similar information.

Memphis: *DeBow's Review* 29 (1860), 668.

rail. All told, perhaps one-third of the raw cotton arrived at the port cities via rail.

The more than 3 million bales of raw cotton exported from New Orleans and Mobile in 1859–60 were easily transported in peacetime, but, in the event of a blockade of New Orleans, Mobile, and Memphis, the alternative routes to ports were not attractive.

2) Alternative Routes for Southern Cotton

Texans shipped their cotton through Galveston and other coastal ports or down the Red River to New Orleans. Two thirds of Texas cotton went through the Texas coastal ports, with the remainder going down the Red River. Railroads probably helped drain the region around Houston into Galveston. Aside from two tiny lines reaching the Red River, much of northeast Texas' cotton required a significant wagon haul to river ports such as Shreveport. A well-organized ox-drawn wagon network existed throughout the Texas coastal regions. According to historian S. G. Reed, the rates were typically one cent a mile per 100 pounds. If New Orleans, Mobile, and Memphis were prevented from exporting, cotton grown in northeast Texas was probably stranded or subjected to a lengthy wagon haul to the Houston area. If Galveston was invested, too, then northeastern Texas cotton may have been unmarketable.

The Rio Grande was not a raw cotton-exporting site during the antebellum era. Very little cotton was grown in the southern tiers of counties in Texas, so any raw cotton shipped through Brownsville required a wagon haul of two hundred miles or more. The amount that could be hauled to the Rio Grande was limited by the availability of forage and water en route.

Arkansas was the most isolated state in the Confederacy. Two short railroads existed in the state. One line ran from east central Arkansas to the Mississippi River opposite Memphis. The other was in central Arkansas, almost straddling the Arkansas and White rivers. Only a modest amount of cotton was grown in the region around the eastern railroad, so Memphis probably did not receive much of Arkansas' cotton. The Arkansas, White, and Red rivers carried most of the state's raw cotton to the Mississippi River and then to New Orleans. Historian Carl Moneyhon reports that shipping rates in Arkansas varied from $2 per bale for shipping down the White River to New Orleans, $1 per bale for shipping down the White River to Memphis, and 0.8 cents a mile per 100 pounds between Little Rock and a river landing (fifty miles). The latter rate translated into a $1.60 charge per 400-pound bale, and when the roads were muddy, the rate would double. It is hard to see any alternatives to Memphis and New Orleans for most of Arkansas' cotton. Shipping through Galveston would require the aforementioned wagon haul across north central Texas. Shipping through Mobile required a lengthy and circuitous railroad haul, and if that port were blockaded, the remaining outlets would have required a very long haul on several different railroads to Savannah or to other eastern ports. In any event, Arkansas cotton was unlikely to be exported if New Orleans, Mobile, and Memphis were closed off.

Louisiana's raw cotton was shipped down the Red and Mississippi Rivers to New Orleans. As mentioned, only a small fraction of the raw cotton received at the Crescent City came by rail. Very little raw cotton was grown in southwest Louisiana, and any movement of Louisiana raw cotton through Galveston (much less Brownsville) would have entailed either a wagon haul across southern Louisiana or up the Red River, and then down through central Texas. If Mobile was open, the raw cotton could be shipped either across Lake Pontchartrain and along the Mississippi coast; through Vicksburg, Meridian, and then to Mobile; or north from New

Orleans to Jackson and then via Meridian to Mobile. If Mobile, too, was cut off, then Louisiana raw cotton would be forced to use the circuitous route north through Mississippi, across northern Alabama, and then to Savannah and other eastern ports.

Mississippi's railroads formed an "H" with the lower two legs ending in New Orleans and Mobile and the upper two legs ending in Memphis and Corinth. The crossbar of the "H" ran from Vicksburg to Meridian (there was a gap between Meridian and east central Alabama). *Hunt's Merchants' Magazine* reported that "neither [Mississippi or Arkansas] has a seaport through which to export their crop to foreign countries and to domestic ports. Hence, it will be found that, ordinarily, all the cotton of Arkansas, and nearly all of the State of Mississippi, is distributed via New Orleans. Some portions of Mississippi's cotton are shipped to Mobile."[2] If New Orleans and Mobile were closed, the rail alternatives would have been north to Corinth and then through northern Alabama and down through Georgia to Savannah. Some of the cotton grown in the northern part of Mississippi may have been shipped through Memphis or shipped down the Tombigbee River to Mobile. Most of the cotton grown in the western part of the state used the Mississippi River to New Orleans. Some of Mississippi's cotton may have used the New Orleans, Jackson & Great Northern railroad.

It is clear that the raw cotton grown in the western Confederacy would face greatly increased internal transportation costs if New Orleans, Mobile, and Galveston were blockaded. The costs might have increased enough to cause growers to keep raw cotton on the plantation. These four states grew half the cotton produced in the South.

Alabama's cotton probably went to three or four outlets. Northern Alabama had rail access to Memphis, Kentucky, and Virginia (although Memphis was the primary outlet). The western part of the state had the Tombigbee River that flowed into Mobile. The Mobile & Ohio railroad had been completed just prior to the war. The railroad ran from Mobile through the southwest region of Alabama before heading north through Mississippi. Eventually, over 250,000 bales were shipped by rail into Mobile during 1859–60 (see Table 12.2). The Mobile & Ohio's only connection with an east-west railroad did not occur until near the Tennessee/Mississippi border. The central section of the state relied upon the Alabama River, although there was a railroad in this part of the state that connected Selma to points in the north central part of the state. There was a railroad from the Florida panhandle and through the southeastern part of the state that eventually meandered through Georgia to Savannah. Eventually a rail link to Tensas (on the Alabama River emptying into Mobile Bay) was built, and from Tensas, cotton could be shipped across Mobile Bay to Mobile. The Chattahoochee River formed the southern Alabama/Georgia border and ended at Apalachicola, Florida (a minor seaport).

Most of Alabama's cotton was grown in a belt south of present-day Birmingham and to within fifty miles of the Florida border. Mobile probably received over half of the state's output. Certainly the western portion of the state would have difficulty shipping cotton to Europe if New Orleans, Mobile and Memphis were sealed off. The eastern part of the state would find it difficult to export cotton if Savannah was also blockaded. The next best outlet then would have been Charleston, but this would have required shipment over several different railroads.

Georgia and South Carolina were relatively well endowed with rivers and railroads. The ports of Savannah and Charleston ranked below New Orleans and Mobile with a combined export of roughly 1 million bales per annum, or 23 percent of the raw cotton exported from the South. Most of Charleston's receipts of raw cotton were shipped along the South Carolina Railroad. The South Carolina Railroad linked Augusta, Georgia and Charleston (Augusta was connected with Atlanta via another railroad). Savannah was linked by rail to various points in Georgia, as well as by the Savannah and Ogeechee rivers. In addition, railroads extended from Georgia to Charleston. The closure of New Orleans, Memphis, and Mobile probably had minimal effect upon Georgia's exports of raw cotton, except for the effect that increased demand for Georgia's railroads might have exerted on rail freights. However, if the Federals closed Savannah, then Georgia would have been forced to seek outlets at Charleston, Wilmington, and Norfolk—all requiring significant railroad shipments.

The antebellum transportation system was adequate for shipping millions of bales of cotton to the various ports. However, a handful of warships properly stationed could derange the flow of most of the raw cotton. The transportation system was not well equipped to handle significant changes in the flow of raw cotton. Just how poorly the system would work when the flow was disrupted would be painfully demonstrated.

II. Wartime Exports of Raw Cotton

The Civil War wrought major shifts in the flow of raw cotton. Fewer than 2 million bales were shipped out of the South during the war, against over 17 million bales during the four years preceding the war. New Orleans and Mobile, once the most important export centers, became almost completely shut off from the export market for periods of time because of the Union navy's blockade. Four cities that had either a minor or a non-existent trade in raw cotton during the antebellum era were destined to become major entrepots for raw cotton: Memphis, Norfolk, Brownsville/Matamoros, and Wilmington.

The experiences of the four largest raw cotton export centers during the antebellum era—New Orleans, Mobile, Savannah, and Charleston—are described first; these four ports suffered absolute and relative reductions in the exports of raw cotton. The experiences of four ports that gained importance in the export of raw cotton are discussed subsequently.

1) New Orleans

Union blockaders, Northern interdiction of river trade, and the Confederate embargo on exports of raw cotton combined to reduce activity at the port of New Orleans. The blockade did not deter all trade, as some 300 vessels ran through the blockade during the ten months prior to Federal occupation. This number of arrivals was a sixth of the normal number. Arrivals of steamboats from the upper Mississippi River were also dramatically reduced. Cotton receipts were minimal, largely due to the voluntary cotton embargo, but probably also because the blockade constricted the outlet. Growers and their factors in the city were also fearful of a Union attack upon the city, so relatively little raw cotton was stored there.[3]

New Orleans surrendered in late April 1862. Upon his arrival in New Orleans, Federal General Benjamin Butler immediately sought to revive river trade. He issued safe conduct passes to steamboats bringing cotton and other staple products and food to New Orleans, offered Federal currency or specie in payment, and even promised salt in payment for Southern produce. The trade resulted in more than 300,000 bales being shipped from the city between May 1862 and the end of the war. Certainly this volume paled against the antebellum shipments of more than two million 400-pound bales per year.

2) Mobile

Mobile was relatively easy to blockade. The port possessed a main ship channel and two shallower outlets, all of which were easy to watch. Very little sea trade transpired during the summer of 1861. The initial proclamation of a blockade may have immediately discouraged foreign vessels from entering Mobile, even though the Federal blockade did not become stringent until late 1861 (due to a lack of ships). However, the summer months were usually months of sluggish trade anyway. When the cotton

Table 12.3. Estimated Number of Bales Smuggled through the Blockade

(Calendar Year)

Number of 400-pound Bales Smuggled by Steamers

Year	Wilmington	Charleston	Georgia/ E.Florida	W.Florida	Mobile	Texas	Total
1862	4,155	21,388	2,771	693	11,080	3,463	43,550
1863	74,790	31,713	2,078	8,311	13,850	1,385	132,127
1864	112,878	22,864	0	693	11,773	11,080	159,288
1865*	1,385	8,113	0	0	693	18,006	28,197
Total	193,208	84,078	4,849	9,697	37,396	33,934	363,162

(Calendar Year)

Number of 400-pound Bales Smuggled by Sailing Vessels

Year	Carolina Ports	Georgia/ E.Florida Ports	Gulf Ports	Total
1862	13,163	1,950	33,800	48,913
1863	3,738	1,625	21,125	26,488
1864	975	1,625	10,075	12,675
1865*	163	0	1,138	1,301
Total	18,039	5,200	66,138	89,377

Note: Mobile contains 9,000 bales run from Louisiana ports during early 1862. Texas does not include raw cotton shipped from the Rio Grande.

* 1865 includes first quarter for all ports, except Texas (through May).

Sources: Lebergott (1981, 880) for average cargo.

      Wise (1988, Appendices) for number of successful clearances by steamers.

      Price (1948, 1951–52, 1955) for number of clearances by sailing vessels.

crop of late 1861 was harvested, the informal Confederate embargo on exporting cotton combined with the blockade to throttle trade. Confederate impressment of steamers for military purposes and the blockade contributed to the diminished coastal trade, leading to food shortages and rising prices. What trade that transpired between New Orleans and Mobile was routed through Mississippi Sound. General Butler encouraged trade between Mobile and the Crescent City. Butler was willing to ship bacon, army supplies, medicine, and, most importantly, salt to Mobile in exchange for cotton and flour. At one time three pounds of cotton were exchanged for one pound of bacon.[4]

Using data from Lebergott, Price, and Wise, we can estimate how much raw cotton was smuggled through the blockade at Mobile. The results are shown in Table 12.3. Wise shows that forty steamers cleared Mobile after 1861 until the end of the war. The number of sailing vessels clearing Mobile is difficult to ascertain, as Price's data combines the clearances for all Gulf ports: 264 from January 1, 1862, to the end of the war. However, since the sailing vessels carried less than one-fourth as many bales as the steam vessels, the overall number of bales shipped from the Gulf on sailing vessels was only 66,000. In addition, the forty steam vessels clearing Mobile carried an additional 30,000 bales. Therefore, even if we assume that all of the sailing vessels cleared from Mobile (and they most assuredly did not), fewer than 100,000 bales of raw cotton were smuggled from Mobile after 1861. Between 50,00 and 70,000 bales is a more likely estimate.[5]

Since the interior of Alabama was the most immune from Federal attacks, a considerable stock of Confederate-owned cotton was stored there. In November 1864, the Confederate government had more than 100,000 bales in Alabama. As the Confederacy collapsed, Federal raiders and Confederate authorities burned thousands of bales of cotton. On his raid through Alabama and Georgia, General James H. Wilson burned 275,000 bales, including 125,000 in Alabama. Confederate authorities destroyed an additional 80,000 bales. Presumably, Mobile was so tightly blockaded that this cotton could not be profitably smuggled from there, and the internal transportation costs to alternative ports were too high for the cotton to be smuggled elsewhere. Historian Arthur Bergeron argues that the Confederacy should have concentrated more effort in running supplies into Mobile to help sustain the war effort, but it is difficult to see how more runners could have been coaxed into running the blockade there. Between the greater hazards in running in and out of Mobile and the greater distance from Nassau, Bermuda, and Havana (the key staging ports), blockade runners naturally preferred Wilmington. Stephen Wise, too, argues that Mobile should have been used to relieve the transportation bottleneck arising from the over-dependence upon Wilmington to supply the armies in Virginia and along the Tennessee front. Under his reasoning, Mobile should have been the entrepot for supplying the armies in Tennessee, Mississippi, Georgia, and Alabama, while Wilmington supplied the Atlantic states. He believes that the government either should have provided incentives or enacted and enforced regulations directing more blockaders towards Mobile; otherwise, as noted above, the blockade runners would continue to run into Wilmington instead of Mobile.[6]

3) Charleston and Savannah

Initially, Charleston was the center of the blockade running on the Atlantic coast, although such efforts resulted in only twenty-nine clearances of steam vessels from the port in 1862 and forty-three in 1863. However, the blockade and Federal land operations around the port succeeded in reducing blockade-running activity around Charleston, and only fourteen steamers arrived between July 1863 and July 1864. From January 1, 1862, to the end of the war, only 114 steam vessels cleared Charleston.

From Table 12.3, we see that fewer than 85,000 bales left Charleston on steam vessels after January 1, 1862. The number of bales leaving Charleston via sailing vessels is more ambiguous. Price's data shows the number of sailing vessels arriving and leaving at all North and South Carolina ports combined: 220 after 1861. Therefore, the number of clearances from Carolina ports must have been roughly 110. The sailing vessels tended to be small craft, and Lebergott estimated that the ones leaving Charleston carried only 95 400-pound bales, while sailing vessels leaving other ports carried 162.5 bales. Even if we apply the 162.5 bales to all sailing vessels leaving Carolina ports, the shipments total only 18,000 bales. Thus, probably fewer than 100,000 bales left Charleston after 1861.[7]

Savannah was even more constricted. Wise shows that only four steamers successfully cleared Savannah after 1861. All told, only seven steamers and thirty-two sailing vessels exited all Georgia and East Florida ports. Given the average cargoes estimated by Lebergott, these ports shipped perhaps 11,000 bales of cotton.

The difficulty in evading the blockading warships at Charleston and Savannah drastically reduced the exports of raw cotton from these major ports. When Charleston became besieged in 1863, the blockade-running efforts were shifted to Wilmington, North Carolina, a heretofore sleepy port.

4) Norfolk

Antebellum Norfolk was not a major cotton exporting port. In 1859, Norfolk exported almost 18,000 bales, a large increase from its exports of 1858. Norfolk was primarily the site of a considerable grain and flour trade. Soon after the war began, Federal ships blockaded the city.

After its occupation by Union troops in early 1862, Norfolk became a major center of trade between the belligerents. Ostensibly the trade was sanctioned by the Federal government to relieve the needs of "loyal" residents of Norfolk and adjacent areas, as Federal Generals John Dix and Egbert Viele believed that "We must either let them [Norfolk residents] feed themselves or we must feed them."[8] However, the volume of cotton being received by the Federal officials far surpassed the amount raised in the district. In the words of General George Gordon, testifying before Congress: "There is now, and has been for many years past, little or no cotton produced in the six counties east of Chowan river for export, and the quantity produced there the last three years has been extremely small, nor was there any surplus there at the beginning of that period." Gordon concluded that "all the cotton that passes across the Blackwater and Chowan rivers is the property of the rebel government, and passes only by their permission."[9]

General Dix pressed for permission to sanction trade through a system of permits. Although the blockade had not been lifted against Norfolk, the Lincoln government countenanced trade with Norfolk residents. Dix was hoping to monopolize the trade via the use of the permits, even though such activities violated international trade: A country could not simultaneously blockade and trade with a port, specifically because of the potential abuse of monopolizing trade. Dix permitted so much trade that one observer believed that 4,000 tons of badly needed bacon flowed through the Norfolk region during Dix's reign. A cotton trader, Thomas Hobday, testified that bacon was traded for cotton on a pound-for-pound basis and that three pounds of cotton was traded for one pound of coffee. Salt was another commodity greatly desired by the Confederates, and General Gordon commented that the salt was being used to preserve meat for the Confederate armies. The trade was carried from Norfolk by canal to Albemarle Sound and then up the Chowan River to the Seaboard Railroad. Reputedly 10,000 pounds of bacon was delivered daily up this route. At this time, Confederate meat rations in the Army of Northern Virginia had been reduced to four ounces per day from the standard twelve ounces and that army was in danger of being forced to disband. As Ludwell Johnson pithily put it, "Truly, Dix had saved Lee's bacon." The rascally General Butler eventually replaced Dix. Allegedly wherever Butler went, corruption was sure to follow. Butler requested permits for up to $100,000 worth of supplies per month, but the Treasury Department more than complied with his request by issuing permits for $400,000 per month. The blockade was removed against Norfolk in November 1864.[10]

Testimony before the congressional committee investigating trade with the enemy revealed why the trade permit system failed. The treasury agents in charge of the system were lax in ascertaining the loyalty of the petitioners, and the agents also failed to certify whether the petitioners actually owned any raw cotton or whether they were adhering to a policy of getting the permit first, the cotton later. In the words of one witness, Treasury Department desire to get as much cotton shipped north as possible made the agents less than diligent in choosing with whom they issued the permits: "He [a Treasury official] claimed that it did not make any difference under this law who brought out the cotton—that Jeff. Davis might bring out cotton under this law." Others testified that the cotton was not of local origins: "I think a portion of it was Gulf cotton, from its staple, and a portion in North Carolina, also from its staple."[11] Thus, the trade permit system in the Norfolk region failed to prevent Confederate cotton from being exchanged for badly needed supplies, nor did it provide much relief for Norfolk residents.

5) Memphis

Memphis had grown into the most important inland cotton market in the United States. New railroads, planked roads, river traffic, and increased cotton acreage in the Yazoo Delta contributed to Memphis's ascendancy. The Civil War and the early prohibitions against trade curtailed Memphis's cotton trade. Although some cotton continued to seep into Memphis, in disregard of the Confederate government's request that cotton be stored on the plantation, it didn't benefit the planters or the Confederacy. Much of the cotton was burned prior to the Federal occupation of the city in June 1862. With the cotton trade stagnant because of the interdiction of trade from Northern states, Memphis began to experience shortages of necessities.

Perhaps fortunately for Memphis, Federal troops occupied the city in June 1862. Shortly thereafter, the U.S. Treasury Department opened trade with Memphis. Originally General William T. Sherman acquiesced (on humanitarian grounds) in limited trade by small farmers. However, Sherman quickly grew cynical about the trade and tried to prevent purchases of raw cotton for specie or Federal treasury notes (believing instead that payment for cotton should be withheld until the end of the war). He also prohibited shipments of salt through the lines, claiming that enough salt had gone through the lines to cure meat for the two Confederate armies in Mississippi. Sherman was overruled and the trade was thrown open with few limitations; before departing Memphis, Sherman retorted, "if trade be opened, Memphis is better to our enemy than before it was taken." Sherman's eventual successor, General Cadwallader Washburn, agreed with Sherman's assessment and favored suspension of all commercial intercourse. By August 1864, trade through Memphis was authorized for up to $2 million per month, an amount greater than those allowed for Nashville, eastern Virginia, and North Carolina, and Senator Zachariah Chandler claimed that $20 million to $32 million worth of supplies had passed through Memphis between June 1862 and June 1864. Federal General Washburn ordered the prohibition of trade on May 15, 1864, and he informed Secretary of War Edwin Stanton of his reasons: Most of the

commerce went into disloyal hands and not into the hands of the Unionists. The volume of the trade at Memphis exceeded the amount needed to
assist Unionists in western Tennessee (who were probably a minority of the
populace), nor was it likely that much of the cotton reached England or
France to thereby dissuade their intervention. Although an exact number
of bales of raw cotton shipped through Memphis during the war is not
available, the city may have come close to matching the 400,000 bales it
shipped north in the four years prior to the war.[12]

6) Texas

Blockade runners had an easier time running materiel into the Rio Grande
area. With Mexico's neutrality and international jurisdiction over the river,
Federal blockaders were unable to interdict trade as effectively as at other
ports. While a significant amount of cotton (probably 300,000 or more
bales) crossed the Rio Grande at Brownsville before being exported out of
Matamoros and Bagdad, Mexico, it is unlikely that the Confederacy benefited much. The Confederates had to expend much effort in transporting
cotton to the Rio Grande and then to move the imported materiel back into
the interior, greatly reducing the profits from cotton. In addition, the Mexican authorities levied import and export taxes on the cotton, further sap-
ping cotton's vitality as an economic asset. The loss of oxen and wagons en
route to Matamoros was great. Since the South possessed few wagon manufacturers, the Texans often were unable to make good the loss of wagons.
The materiel obtained in return quite likely was required to sustain the
rag-tag trans-Mississippi Confederate forces, even though these forces
were essentially of minor importance to the war's outcome. Since Confederate troops in the trans-Mississippi were chronically short of arms and
other supplies, probably only a fraction of the goods entering Matamoros
ever helped main Confederate effort east of the Mississippi. Historian
James Irby believes that different Confederate policies might have made better use of the Rio Grande as a supply source for the Confederacy as a whole,
but in light of the transportation difficulties, he may be too optimistic.[13]

There were five additional disadvantages to the Texas cotton trade with
Matamoros. First, there was a shortage of rope and bagging to bale the cotton, so rope and bagging were high on the list of goods shipped to Matamoros. Cotton trader Benjamin Camp testified that "in Texas they have
not a yard of bagging or a pound of rope, except what is sent from England
or Europe; and that for bagging and rope for one thousand bales of cotton
I can bring out one thousand bales and pay for it all in greenbacks except,
probably, as to the first cargo, when I should have to take in about five

thousand dollars' worth of goods, to induce the rebel government to allow the cotton to come out."[14] Second, Matamoros was ill-equipped to handle the volume of trade, as lighters had to be employed because of the shallowness of the harbor. Not very many lighters were available, nor could they operate when the water was low. Thus, many ocean vessels were forced to wait for cotton, sometimes for a few months. Third, the long overland haul gradually exhausted the forage en route, and occasional droughts also disrupted the trade. Fourth, the volatile political situation in Mexico occasionally disrupted the trade. Finally, the Confederate officials were on tenuous ground. Texas contained a significant number of Unionists and lukewarm secessionists. Government action in impressing or regulating the cotton trade was constrained by its possible effect upon the citizenry. Eventually, the Richmond government exercised less and less control over the trans-Mississippi. The area became known as Kirby Smithdom, after General Kirby Smith who commanded the trans-Mississippi. Camp's testimony to the congressional committee alluded to this autonomy of the trans-Mississippi: "Kirby Smith has full control there [trans-Mississippi], and he cares no more about Jeff. Davis than we do. There, individuals do own cotton [instead of the Confederate government], and that is the only place where you can trade to any extent with individuals."[15] If anything, the Matamoros trade exemplified the desperate lengths that cotton traders were willing to go in the face of the Federal blockade.

These factors combined to create a huge wedge between the price of raw cotton in Texas and in Liverpool and New York. In 1864, raw cotton sold for six cents in Texas, but almost fifty-six cents (in gold) in New York. In 1981, historian Stanley Lebergott broke down the fifty cent per pound difference in price. The cost of transportation to the Rio Grande accounted for three cents, while the smuggling costs amounted to almost thirteen cents. The Mexicans levied taxes in excess of seven cents per pound. The final transportation costs from Cuba to Liverpool were twenty cents. Presumably, shipping from Galveston to Cuba instead of smuggling across the Rio Grande would have avoided the twenty-three cents incurred in transporting raw cotton across the river and the Mexican duties. We can deduce, then, that people who opted for the Rio Grande faced blockade-running costs (from Galveston) in excess of twenty-three cents.

If Secretary of State Seward had desired an outlet for Southern cotton, the Rio Grande must have been pleasing. Seward could convince himself that the trade was not particularly harmful to the Union cause, while providing some cotton to help curb the foreign appetite for the staple. Although foreign shippers participated in the Matamoros trade, a large proportion of the cotton ended up in New York City. Ships were allowed to clear from New York for Matamoros. Charles Stillman, a prominent antebellum businessman and Southern sympathizer, received clearance for his ships to ply between New York and Matamoros.[16]

According to the Board of Trade figures listed in the *Statistical Abstract for the United Kingdom,* the United Kingdom imported 211,000 400-pound bales of raw cotton from Mexico during 1862–65 (some of which left Mexico after the blockade was removed). Prior to 1862, Great Britain imported no cotton from Mexico, and, in 1866, the volume dwindled to fewer than 1,000 bales before evaporating completely. Like the Bermuda/Bahamas trade, it was completely war-induced. How much went North is unclear, but James Daddysman believes another additional 100,000 to 150,000 bales went North or to other points. If 350,000 bales were shipped through Matamoros, the port would rival New Orleans in volume. Thus, roughly 20 percent of all cotton shipped from the South came through Matamoros.[17]

Because specie was scarce in the Confederacy, some blockade runners were hesitant to ship cargo on the inward trip, but Confederate legislation made it mandatory that materiel be brought in. However, much of the materiel received at Matamoros was of Mexican origin. The northeastern states of Mexico supplied metal, blankets, shoes, coffee, percussion caps, cloth, and other goods. Due to the volatile political situation in Mexico, Mexicans did not supply arms. The Federal consuls in Matamoros and Monterey complained about the trade to the Treasury Department, with the vice consul in Monterey claiming that the Confederates had an order for 600,000 blankets pending as well as contracts for wheat and flour.[18]

Federal Secretary of the Navy Gideon Welles had pressed for an attack and occupation of Brownsville in order to stanch the flow of materiel and cotton. Since he recognized the difficulty of blockading international waters, Welles ordered his commanders to stop capturing blockade runners unless such vessels were explicitly heading for the Texas side of the river. The Federal government finally sent a force to capture and occupy Brownsville in late 1863. This discomfited the Matamoros trade and caused the price of raw cotton to fall. Although initially disruptive, the trade quickly adjusted by moving the river crossing westward to Laredo and Eagle Pass, outside the control of the Union forces. Although this imposed additional expense, it did not curtail the trade. Eventually the Union forces evacuated Brownsville (July 1864), and trade resumed its previous flow.

The blockade curbed Galveston's exports of raw cotton during the war. The port could have exported more, but Union troops occupied the city during 1863 and 1864. Forty-nine steam blockade runners successfully cleared Galveston and other Texas ports during the war, as well as perhaps two or three times as many sailing vessels. The steam vessels probably carried 34,000 bales from Galveston; as we've seen in the discussion regarding Mobile, roughly 66,000 bales were shipped by sailing vessels from all the Gulf ports. Therefore, perhaps up to 70,000 total bales were shipped from Texas ports north of the Rio Grande.

7) Wilmington

With Charleston and Savannah tightly blockaded, the onus of supplying the eastern Confederacy fell upon Wilmington, North Carolina. Railroads connected Wilmington to interior points in North Carolina and northward into Virginia. As the war wore on, the port became the "lifeline" for Lee's army; arms, munitions, meat, and materiel flowed through the blockade. Wilmington's usefulness as a supply conduit can be seen from some figures. From November 1, 1863, to October 25, 1864, over 3,000 tons of meat, 420,000 pairs of boots and shoes, and 137,000 shoulder arms were imported through Wilmington.[19]

Wilmington had two advantages as a blockade-running port. First, next to Norfolk, it was the nearest major port with rail connections to Richmond and the armies fighting in Virginia. Second, because of its geography, there were *two* outlets, twenty-five miles apart, to be guarded.[20]

Wilmington's main drawback was its distance from major cotton-producing areas. Cotton had to be shipped via railroad into the city. As the city's importance in the raw cotton trade grew, so did demands upon the railroads. Shipments of raw cotton from the main cotton-producing regions clogged the rail arteries leading into Wilmington. Within two years of the war's inception, Southern railroads had deteriorated. Assistant Adjutant-General William Wadley provided estimates of the freight capacity of the key railroads in the Confederacy in the spring of 1863; the two major railroads leading into Wilmington, the Wilmington & Weldon and the Wilmington & Manchester, had the capacity to carry 150 tons of freight per day. The Wilmington & Weldon was estimated to be able to run half a train per day in each direction, while the Wilmington & Manchester was reckoned to be able to run one train per day in each direction. If these two railroads conveyed all of the raw cotton received at Wilmington during the period January 1, 1862, through January 1, 1865, then shipping the roughly 70,000 400-pound bales per year would have tied up over 25 percent of the total freight-carrying capacity of the two major rail lines around Wilmington. Thus, the shipments of raw cotton clogged inbound freight to Wilmington, lessening the ability of Wilmington to forward supplies from the Deep South to the armies in Virginia and North Carolina.[21]

Eventually Confederate generals in the Tennessee theater began to complain of the use of railroads to ship raw cotton rather than military supplies. Of course, without the raw cotton shipments from Wilmington, much-needed military materiel from Europe would not have been obtained. Still, the derangement of the pattern of raw cotton shipments added to the burdens of the Southern railroads.[22]

Two other factors hindered blockade running out of Wilmington. First, the Wilmington trade was interrupted in September 1862 by an outbreak of yellow fever. The fever also affected Nassau and Bermuda, and trade was rerouted to Halifax. Quarantines delayed the movement of vessels between Nassau and Bermuda with the south Atlantic ports. Second, Wilmington was not prepared to become a major exporter of raw cotton. Antebellum Wilmington was a minor cotton shipping port; in the four years, 1857–60, Wilmington exported fewer than 25,000 bales per annum. Naval stores, timber, and some foodstuffs were the port's main exports. Sailing vessels typically conveyed these commodities northward, and steam vessels only began stopping at Wilmington in 1860. In addition to the disruptions created by larger railroad shipments of cotton, baling the increased amount of raw cotton proved difficult. These factors delayed the loading of blockade runners. Steamers that entered Wilmington in the first nine months of 1863 remained for an average of more than three weeks. For the next nine months through June 1864, the duration of stay at Wilmington was reduced to about two weeks. The wait increased again over the summer of 1864 (three weeks), while decreasing to two weeks again in the final quarter of 1864. Part of the delay in the summer of 1864 may have been the result of the yellow fever in Nassau and Bermuda.[23]

Despite these drawbacks, between January 1, 1862, and January 3, 1865, steamers cleared Wilmington 304 times for Nassau, Bermuda, and Halifax. Federal blockading vessels captured or destroyed twenty-five vessels. Lebergott estimates that steamers carried an average of 692.5 400-pound bales. Since 279 steamers successfully cleared Wilmington, we get 193,200 bales via steamer. Sailing vessels were of minor importance. As shown in the discussion of Charleston, the sailing vessels carried fewer than 20,000 bales from all Carolina ports after 1861. Including the number of bales on all the sailing vessels we get a maximum of nearly 215,000 bales from Wilmington over three years. Compared to antebellum volume, Wilmington was now shipping perhaps 150 to 200 percent more bales.

8) The Disrupted Movement of Raw Cotton

New Orleans, Memphis, Texas, and Wilmington/Charleston each shipped roughly 300,000 bales during the war. The remaining 600,000 bales (more or less) were shipped through Norfolk, Savannah, and Florida, traded between the lines on various military frontiers, or captured by Federal warships and troops. Aside from the amounts shipped through Memphis and New Orleans after Federal occupation of those cities, the growers in the Mississippi valley probably were forced to hold their raw cotton on the plantations or trade with Northerners. Indeed, some of the Mississippi valley growers called upon the Confederate or state governments to relieve them by purchasing the crops.[24]

Growers in most of eastern Louisiana, Arkansas, Mississippi, and western Alabama lacked economically viable alternative routes to New Orleans and Mobile because of the deficiencies of the railroads. The railroads leading into Wilmington were incapable of transporting much of the Mississippi valley's raw cotton. In addition, Wilmington lacked the requisite number of cotton presses to handle large quantities. Charleston and Savannah were better equipped to handle increases in cotton shipments, but planters in Mississippi, Louisiana, Arkansas, and western Alabama would have had to depend upon a circuitous shipment by rail to reach these ports. The east-west railroad "system" running through northern Mississippi and Tennessee was inadequate to meet the needs of shipping almost 3 million bales annually from the Mississippi valley region, as well as the foodstuffs required by the army, to south Atlantic ports.

Wagon transportation was unlikely to offer much relief to the hard-pressed railroads. The army required large numbers of wagons, and the South possessed relatively limited wagon-producing capacity. Before the war was even a year old, military commanders were complaining about the lack of wagons. Had most of the Mississippi valley's cotton been shipped east by wagon to railheads, the wagon shortage would have been even worse than what the military claimed. In 1907, the Department of Agriculture surveyed cotton growers on the length and costs of wagon hauling. Although the cash costs are not directly applicable (due to the forty-five year time gap), the physical requirements are of use. Cotton growers in Mississippi reported hauling eleven miles on average to their river or railroad shipping points, so the round-trip (twenty-two miles) usually took 1.1 days. Growers in Louisiana, Arkansas, and Alabama reported similar hauls. The wagons carried an average of four or five 400-pound bales. Unless they floated cotton to Vicksburg or New Orleans, growers along the Mississippi probably faced about a forty mile one-way trip to the railroad running north-south through Jackson. Such a trip at 1907 rates of speed would have taken at least four days (and perhaps longer if the roads were worse in 1861). Assuming that the planters in this region originally faced a one-day trip to the Mississippi River, the new route entailed three extra days to the railroads.

Therefore, if the Mississippi River outlets were cut off, the demand for alternative transportation would have increased. The huge increase in demand for wagon and rail transport would have ignited transportation costs. Increasing internal transportation costs should have been manifested by diverging prices between inland towns and port towns. In 1954, Eugene Lerner compiled prices for four Southern towns: Richmond, Fayetteville (North Carolina), Augusta (Georgia), and Wilmington. As we've seen, Wilmington became a major blockade-running port. Augusta was an inland town with railroad connections to Charleston and Wilmington. Prior to Fort Sumter, raw cotton prices at Wilmington were at most a cent or two above those at Richmond and Fayetteville (unfortunately, raw cotton prices at Augusta were not reported until February 1862). By 1862, real cotton prices at Wilmington were five to ten cents above those of Augusta and Fayetteville. The gap narrowed throughout 1862 and 1863, but in December 1863, Wilmington's cotton prices again accelerated much faster than Augusta's and somewhat faster than Fayetteville's. For most of the war, the real price differentials (using the respective city price indices) between Wilmington and Augusta exceeded three cents. Ideally, we would like to compare raw cotton prices in the Mississippi valley, but no similar time series of prices have been found.

III. Political Ramifications of the Disrupted Internal Movement of Raw Cotton

If the Mississippi valley planters couldn't economically export their raw cotton, what would have been their options? The planters might have switched to growing foodstuffs. Assuming that the Mississippi was open from Memphis to New Orleans, the valley growers could have shipped their food to these cities. New Orleans was an attractive market for foodstuffs, as that city had lost much of its grain and packed meat supplies from the upper Mississippi valley after the passage of the non-intercourse edicts. Memphis could have been used as a supply depot for the Confederate troops in Tennessee. Sending foodstuffs all the way to troops and citizens in Virginia might have been possible, too, depending upon the carrying capacity of the railroads. However, it is unlikely that the increased production of foodstuffs would have completely offset the loss of the lucra-tive raw cotton market. According to the September 1, 1860, New Orelans *Price Current* annual report, for the commercial year 1859–60, the raw cotton received at New Orleans was valued at $109 million; the total receipts of all other products at New Orleans totaled $76 million. In any event, the inability to export raw cotton cheaply from New Orleans, Mobile, and Memphis created significant dislocations for Mississippi valley growers.

Would the dislocations caused by the blockade alone have created polit-ical discord within the Confederacy?[25] Many of the planters along the Mis-sissippi River and residents of New Orleans were initially wary of secession. The opposition to secession in Mississippi, for instance, came from, "the Piney woods, the Tennessee River hills, and the Mississippi River counties." In Arkansas, the Bell-Douglas voters in 1860 possessed a majority in the two tiers of counties closest to the Mississippi, as these vot-ers were apparently worried about the ramifications of a Breckinridge vic-tory. Many of the large Arkansas planters also voted for Bell. These people recognized the possibility that New Orleans would be blockaded or attacked, preventing access to the Gulf of Mexico. Thus, they had much to lose economically. When their states seceded, most of the planters gave secession their support, but the specter of economic losses shadowed their support. In Arkansas, the secessionists gained the upper hand only after Lincoln's call for volunteers to suppress the seceded states. Even then, the yeomanry of northwest Arkansas never truly embraced secession, and recruiting was largely unsuccessful in this region.[26]

Unionist sentiment persisted throughout the South. Although some organized "peace societies" existed, such sentiment probably wouldn't have presented a serious threat to the Confederacy as long as the war went well. Military reverses, economic hardship, and unpopular government edicts combined to erode support for the war. By late 1862, Louisiana's governor advised Jefferson Davis to return Louisiana troops to maintain the state's allegiance to the Confederacy. Many citizens evaded the draft, with some moving to Texas. Arkansas was wracked by food shortages, internal dis-sension, and non-compliance with conscription. The German community in Texas opposed secession and conscription. Residents of the state also com-plained about the Confederate government's inability to halt depredations by native Americans. Mississippi, too, eventually displayed many signs of unrest. The fall of New Orleans created great economic hardship for peo-ple on the Gulf coast of Mississippi, so many opted either to enter Union lines or to trade with Northerners. Confederate military leaders sent gloomy reports about the growing numbers of residents in the northern part of the state who signed Federal loyalty oaths. A judge wrote in 1864: "Mississippi is in a most deplorable condition, and is rapidly tending to the most deplorable disgrace. Very many of the middle class, a large number of the more intelligent, and nearly all of the lower class of her people are drifting to the Yankees." Mississippi Senator James Phelan warned Davis that "the infernal hydra of reconstruction is again stirring its envenomed heads in our State."[25]

During the Civil War, many cotton planters along the Mississippi River chose self-interest over nationalism. Trade resumed at New Orleans and Memphis, as well as smaller towns. More than 600,000 bales of cotton were exported from Memphis and New Orleans. Many Confederate authorities were chagrined at the "disloyalty" of the valley growers. Cavalry units patrolled regions to interdict the between-the-lines trading. Citizens and military leaders bemoaned the cotton trade's adverse effects upon morale: "The soldiers, I am sorry to say, are deserting and going home and to the enemy in consequence of the cotton speculation that is now going on [along] the Mississippi River." General Richard Taylor, commanding in Louisiana and along the Mississippi River, lamented the illicit trading: "The illegal traffic with the enemy has certainly caused much of the demoralization found to exist in Mississippi and East Louisiana, and is attributable in my opinion to the license granted by chiefs of bureaux [sic] at Richmond."[28] However, not all of the Confederate military leaders were against civilians trading with the enemy. One general believed that the demoralization issue could be turned to the Confederacy's purpose: "I now believe that our people on the border who have been compelled to trade with the enemy for subsistence are more patriotic and more liberal to our soldiers than those in the interior, and that they have been greatly misrepresented by those who did not understand their condition. . . . I believe that a trade should be opened. . . . I have reason to believe that we could . . . have corrupted the Yankee army and fed and clothed our own by a judicious use of cotton."[29] Some of those who favored between-the-lines trading did so only if the government monopolized the trade. Some of these military leaders believed that the government should even impress raw cotton in threatened areas. However, some military leaders believed that even government involvement in the trade created demoralization:

> The very heavy movements of Government cotton by the authorized agents in the district were upon such a scale that every man, woman, and child, whose inclinations prompted them, immediately set out with their wagons . . . . The loyal element of the citizens becoming exasperated at what they

fancied to be a huge speculation of Government agents, held meetings and threatened to burn every bale of cotton in the district. . . . It is proper also to add that my own troops become infected with the fever against the contractors and government agents, and disaffected about orders to permit the authorized agent to pass by with large quantities, while those who really needed goods for family use were not allowed to carry in their petty loads of one or two bales.[30]

Would the same pressures that drove planters to denounce their loyalty to the Confederacy have occurred in the face of a strict blockade or perhaps occupation of Mobile, New Orleans, and Memphis without interbelligerent trading? Even if New Orleans, Memphis, and Mobile were only blockaded and not occupied by Federal troops or even if there was no interbelligerent trade, the Confederate government would have had to address the issue of economic dislocation. A Confederate administration that was unable to raise a Federal blockade of these ports would face rising discontent. Would the planters have viewed the administration as incompetent? Would the planters have continued to honor an embargo? Would the economic dislocation alone have created disaffection for secession?

IV. Conclusions

The Mississippi valley was particularly vulnerable to the effects of a Union blockade of New Orleans, Mobile, and Memphis. The remaining ports simply were not feasible alternatives for the bulk of Mississippi valley-grown raw cotton and other products. The blockade and later occupation of New Orleans and Memphis severely disrupted the valley's economy. Patriotism probably muted discontent through 1861 and into 1862, but the planters might have become very impatient by the time of a second crop of raw cotton in late 1862, even without the battlefield disasters of early 1862.

The psychological effects of seeing perhaps twenty strategically-placed Union warships completely stifling the valley economy, even in the face of large and possibly victorious Confederate armies, would have been a demoralizing experience. Unless the Confederacy built or purchased enough warships to raise the blockade, the South's economy would be humbled by the Union navy alone. Few governments would have been able to withstand the criticism generated by this sort of situation, and the Davis government was testy to begin with. One can imagine that valley growers might have again chosen self-interest and sought some separate reconciliation with the Union in the absence of effective Confederate responses to the blockade. Thus, the blockade alone might have rendered asunder the nascent Confederacy. The Union's early captures of New Orleans and Memphis and later triumph at Vicksburg were dramatic successes for the North and probably facilitated the burgeoning interbelligerent trade and accompanying demoralization. However, the blockade alone may have generated similar outcomes, albeit more slowly.

13

Putting King Cotton
to Work for the
Federal Government

Federal Policies toward Cotton during the Civil War

Confederate hopes for independence rested partially upon the region's dominance in the world market for raw cotton. However, the region's dominance was rapidly being thwarted. By the end of April 1862, the Federal navy had implemented its blockade and had also captured several important Confederate positions: Roanoke Island and Fort Macon in North Carolina, Norfolk, New Orleans, and Memphis. These triumphs gave the Federal government a unique opportunity: The Union might usurp the Confederacy's potential economic gains from exporting raw cotton. In other words, the Federal government might have exercised a form of economic jujitsu against the Confederacy by placing an export tax on raw cotton at New Orleans, Norfolk, and Memphis. Federal gains from taxing raw cotton exports might have offset much of the cost of maintaining the blockade.

This opportunity arose because the Federal occupation of New Orleans and Memphis and its navy's tight blockade of Mobile closed the entrepots for 70 percent of the South's raw cotton crop (see Table 12.1). The Federal control of these ports confronted the Mississippi valley planters with some unenviable choices. They could try to trade with the Federals at Memphis or New Orleans, ship their raw cotton outside the valley via circuitous routes (by wagon and railroad to south Atlantic ports or by wagon to the Rio Grande), or simply store their raw cotton. The rickety Southern railroads made shipping large amounts of raw cotton from the Mississippi valley to Charleston, Wilmington, and Savannah unlikely. Even if Mississippi valley growers succeeded in shipping their cotton overland to Wilmington, Charleston, or Galveston, they faced another obstacle. The Federal navy's blockade dramatically increased the difference between the price received by producers of raw cotton and the price paid in the North and Europe. Thus, the Federal navy's control of Memphis and New Orleans and its blockade of Mobile effectively sealed off the bulk of the Mississippi valley cotton crop.

How could the Federal government have exploited its ability to control the Mississippi valley cotton trade? What were the potential benefits to the Federal government from setting an optimal export duty? However, an optimal duty might not be the tax revenue-maximizing duty, as other political and economic factors could affect the optimal level of an export duty. Therefore, Federal officials considered alternatives to using an export duty, including capturing raw cotton and capturing the ports of Wilmington, Charleston, and Savannah.

I. Setting an Optimal Export Duty

President Abraham Lincoln decided to resume trade at New Orleans, Memphis, and Norfolk almost immediately after occupying them. While the Federal authorities never explicitly stated the proposition, they had reason to hope to defray part of the cost of the blockade/occupation. The simplest way for the Federal government to have gained revenue would have been to place an export duty on raw cotton. To avoid tax evasion, the tax would be placed on all raw cotton shipped from Memphis, New Orleans, Norfolk, and any other captured ports, regardless of the avowed destination. Since the naval blockade created a large transportation cost wedge between the prices at blockaded Southern ports and Northern or European ports, a fairly large export duty could be levied without inducing growers to opt for the blockaded Atlantic and Texas ports or to the Rio Grande. The blockade increased the difference in prices between blockaded Southern ports and European or Northern ports from one or two cents per pound to almost fifty cents per pound. However, even at Federal-occupied New Orleans, the price differential reached fifteen to twenty cents per pound, as Confederate commerce-raiding had increased the transportation costs for Northern shippers. The optimal rate of taxation was constrained by this factor, as too high a tax and Southern growers would avoid the occupied ports and take the risks of shipping through a blockaded port. These considerations probably limited an export duty to perhaps thirty cents per pound. Placing an export duty on raw cotton at Memphis, New Orleans, and Norfolk offered the promise of raising Federal tax revenues, while minimizing the gains accruing to Southern producers of raw cotton.

Figure 13.1. The Market for Southern-Grown Raw Cotton

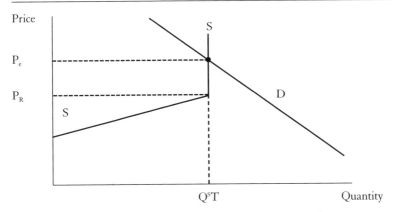

The total supply of Southern-grown raw cotton is Q^s_T. SS is the supply curve by growers to cotton textile manufacturers. For prices above P_R, the growers do not wish to hold any inventories, and the supply to manufacturers is perfectly inelastic and equal to the total supply. Below P_R, the growers wish to hold some of the raw cotton as inventory on the plantation. The intersection of the manufacturers' demand and the growers' supply curve gives the equilibrium price.

The potential export duty revenue depended upon the elasticities of demand and supply. The demand for raw cotton tended to be slightly inelastic (for moderate changes in prices) during the antebellum period, but the elasticity was likely to increase for significant price changes (such as a doubling or tripling of prices). In the short-run, for moderate changes in price, the elasticity of supply was likely to be quite low. In Figure 13.1, for any price above P_R, the supply of raw cotton is perfectly inelastic; one can think of P_R as the "reservation" price that induces the producers not to hold any inventories on the plantation (i.e. all raw cotton is taken to market). The reservation price roughly corresponds to a price where the planters recoup their variable costs (including transportation costs to Southern ports). For prices below P_R, the supply of raw cotton is not perfectly inelastic, and some of the cotton would be held as stock on the plantation. The supply curve was apparently pretty elastic below the reservation price. Despite the huge run-up in transportation costs caused by the blockade, the real price of raw cotton at Southern ports remained essentially stable throughout the Civil War. Thus, a rough approximation of the supply curve is that it was perfectly elastic (i.e. horizontal) at the reservation price and perfectly inelastic (i.e. vertical) for all prices above the reservation price. Assuming a perfectly elastic supply at the reservation price will also create a downward bias for the tax revenue estimates.[1]

In 1860–61, the crop consisted of 4.59 million 400-pound bales; the average New Orleans price per pound was 11.1 cents (or $44.40 per 400-pound bale). Historian Lewis Gray shows that cotton prices at New Orleans had varied from 5.8 cents in 1848–49 to 12.4 cents in 1856–57 during the last fifteen years of the antebellum period. The 5.8 cents figure was considerably lower than the next lowest figures (7.4 and 8.4 in 1851–52 and 1854–55 respectively). A conservative guess is that eight cents would have been close to the reservation price. If the Federal government had assessed a three cents per pound tax or $12.00 per 400-pound bale (in 1861 dollars), Southerners might have continued to ship out the same amount of raw cotton as in 1860–61. A three cents per pound tax (plus the added internal transportation cost of shipping from Georgia, east Alabama, and other eastern Confederate states to New Orleans or Memphis) might have been preferable to facing the much larger transportation costs involved in running the blockade. At $12.00 per bale, the Federal government might have realized over $30 million just on the cotton produced in the Mississippi valley. Since the Federal government spent roughly $100 million per year on its navy during the Civil War, the potential for financing a significant part of its naval endeavors through a tax on cotton was real enough. Even this understates the potential to finance the cost of implementing the blockade, as the tax revenues are in 1861 dollars while the spending figures are in inflated 1862–65 dollars. Depending upon the elasticity of demand, a higher tax rate might have netted even greater revenues. Therefore, establishing an even larger tax might accomplish two desirable goals (from the Federal point of view): increased Federal tax revenue and decreased Southern producer surplus (gains from selling their cotton). Given an initial price elasticity of demand of 0.8, an export duty of more than $12.00 per bale might have brought in tax revenues approaching $60 million (in prewar dollars) per year while simultaneously reducing producer surplus. Of course, the growers' long-run response to a tax might have reduced the revenue in subsequent years. In addition, if the tax was perceived to be temporary, the demand and supply of raw cotton might have fallen off temporarily as manufacturers and growers postponed transactions in expectation of either a reduction in or a rescinding of the tax. Still, the conclusion must be that a successful export duty could have netted the Federal government significant tax revenues and perhaps even have made the blockade a paying proposition.

Was the tax on cotton set properly? Cotton shipped out of Memphis and New Orleans was assessed with various duties: an internal revenue tax of two cents a pound, a Treasury Department-imposed tax of four cents a pound, a hospital tax of unspecified amounts, a warehouse tax of $5 per bale, and a mandated tax of 25 percent of the New York price. One trader complained that the various taxes amounted to, "41.5 cents per pound paid to the government, on the basis of $1 a pound in the market." These amounts are in greenbacks and not gold. However, a 40 percent tax was a reasonable amount. In September 1864, Secretary of the Treasury William Fessenden instructed his agents to make only three deductions on cotton sales: the two cents per pound internal revenue tax, the Treasury fee of four cents per pound, and expenses incurred in purchasing, storing, and shipping the cotton to New York (New Orleans and Memphis were exempted from the last deduction). These charges were probably too low. The combined financial gain to the Federal government from captured, abandoned, and purchased cotton under the Act of 1864 was less than $22 million in current dollars (perhaps $10 million in 1861 dollars).[2]

While it is unrealistic to assume that the Federal government knew the relevant demand and supply elasticities, they could have come tolerably close to the revenue-maximizing duty. However, these rough calculations based purely on tax revenue may be unsatisfactory as they neglect political, economic, and military consequences of any such trade. These factors might have caused the Federal government to set an export duty at a rate other than the revenue-maximizing one.

II. The Export Duty and the Confederacy

A Federal policy of combining non-intercourse with a tight blockade theoretically denied the Southern growers and the Confederacy any producer surplus from exporting staple goods. An export tax of less than thirty cents per pound (in greenbacks) would allow some additional producer surplus to seep into the Confederacy (assuming that supply was not perfectly elastic at the reservation price). What would have been the ramifications of allowing the South to gain producer surplus from selling raw cotton? The Federal government needed to weigh the tax revenue it received against the benefits to Southerners. Unfortunately, the tax rate that optimized tax revenue might be significantly lower than the transportation cost wedge and raise producer surplus to unacceptable levels. A different strategy might have been to set the tax where the marginal benefit to the North from an export duty was driven to equality with the marginal benefit to the Confederates. A simple proxy for such a procedure might have been to maximize the difference between the tax revenue going to the Federal government and the producer surplus going to Southern producers of raw cotton (and indirectly to the Confederacy).

However, there were several ostensible political reasons to loosen the restrictions on trade with the Confederacy. For instance, Lincoln initially exercised discretion regarding Kentucky, as he believed that keeping Kentucky in the Union was crucial. He allowed trade through Kentucky during the first summer of the war, despite criticism from many Northerners. The Confederates eventually violated Kentucky's "neutrality" and the state swung, more or less securely, into the Union camp.

The interbelligerent trade shifted to Memphis, Norfolk, and New Orleans in mid-1862. The Federal policy was to allow trade in rebellious regions that came under Federal military control, or as the secretary of the treasury, Salmon Chase, put it, "Let commerce follow the flag."[3] Initially, Federal generals at Memphis approved limited trade in order for local residents to subsist. General William Tecumseh Sherman wrote: "A great deal of cotton has come in of late in small parcels. . . . and I have somewhat relaxed the rules as to internal trade. . . . Though in some cases the privilege has been and will be abused, I think it good policy to encourage it, and that the farmers and property holders may realize their dependence on other parts of our country, and also realize that a state of war long continued will reduce them to a state of absolute ruin."[4] Sherman later recanted his belief in the efficacy of trade in fostering Unionism.

Southerners were hesitant, at first, to trade with the Yankees at New Orleans. Even though Federal General Benjamin Butler zealously sought cotton while in command at the Crescent City, Confederate and Louisiana authorities discouraged citizens from trading. Less reticence occurred at Memphis, where a brisk trade was conducted. Confederate military leaders in the Mississippi valley were quick to see the desirability of such trade, and a Confederate quartermaster provided a good explanation of the gains from trading with the Yankees: "[Cotton] . . . badly put up, now exposed to the weather, and liable to be destroyed by the enemy— might be utilized before it becomes utterly worthless. No draft would then have to be made upon the supplies accumulating at Richmond, which could be devoted exclusively to General Lee's army. Large expense in transportation would be saved, both from and to the seaboard, and to that extent the overburdened railroad facilities relieved."[5] While the North obtained more than 500,000 bales of raw cotton at New Orleans and Memphis during the war, it was disappointed with the results.

Norfolk was the first major port to be blockaded by the Federal navy. After the Union army occupied the town in 1862, the port became a trading center. Federal Generals John A. Dix and Benjamin Butler enthusiastically pressed for between-the-lines trading, and some Federal authorities were willing to trade packed meat and salt for raw cotton. Much of the packed meat eventually fed the Confederate Army of Northern Virginia, so the trade was particularly deleterious to the Union war effort. General Ulysses S. Grant disliked the trade, but had to tolerate it until January 1865. After his suspension of the trade, General Lee's food supply collapsed and the Confederates had to abandon the defenses around Petersburg and Richmond.

Ironically, some Confederate leaders bemoaned the interbelligerent trade. General Robert E. Lee stated: "I have inquired into the evils alleged to proceed from the contraband trade in North Carolina. . . . I find that traffic is carried on to a large extent without authority, and that the effects are so demoralizing in their tendency."[6] Lee was painfully aware of the need to trade with either the Federal authorities or Northern cotton speculators, as his army needed the supplies obtained in return for raw cotton. However, Lee believed that the trade should be under government control:

> I also think it would be advisable to forbid cotton being brought east of the Roanoke, except by Government agents. I have issued an order forbidding the transportation of contraband articles across our lines, but the force available to compel the observance of the order and the slow forms of proceeding under the law to condemn such property when seized, render all efforts to restrain the illicit trade nearly abortive. . . . I fear it can not be repressed. In view of the loss of the port of Wilmington for obtaining supplies, we should endeavor to make the traffic across the lines as productive as possible, and this illegal trade is very injurious to that conducted on Government account, besides its other bad effects.[7]

Jefferson Davis never reconciled himself to the necessity of such trade, unlike some of his secretaries of war. Secretary of War George Randolph advised Davis that the Confederate government (but not private citizens) could legally trade with Northerners. Indeed, he claimed that such trade was necessary to sustain the Confederate army. Other Confederate authorities recognized the efficiency of trading with the Yankees, as blockade running could be very expensive. Secretary of the Treasury George Trenholm described one such venture:

> The Collie contract alone will furnish supplies to the extent of £200,000, and this amount and all others of like character should be deducted from the estimates. Two steamers under this contract have already arrived. By the terms of this agreement 50 per cent is to be added to the value of the goods, so that the sum to be allowed for these supplies in reduction of the estimates

is in fact £300,000. And as payment is to be made in cotton at 6 pence, it will require 30,000 bales of cotton for this single contract. As 5,000 bales at present prices in England would have yielded £200,000, this unfortunate arrangement entails a positive loss of 25,000 bales of cotton, and places in a conspicuous point of view the necessity that existed for abandoning this mode of obtaining supplies.

Because of the expenses involved in using private shippers, Trenholm wanted the government to operate a fleet of blockade runners. The Confederate government arranged to buy fourteen of the newest and best blockade-running steamers. The government would pay for these vessels from the proceeds of blockade running.[8]

Despite these arguments for interbelligerent trade, Davis feared that trade would demoralize the populace. His fears were not without foundation. Residents of the Mississippi valley had been somewhat wary of secession, viewing, accurately as it turned out, the act as disruptive to trade along the river. Although Mississippi valley planters gave secession their support once the act was a fait accompli, they were constantly haunted by the likelihood of an interruption to trade. Thus, when New Orleans was captured and Mobile was tightly blockaded, many Southerners opted to enter Union lines and trade with the Northerners. Some of the residents even opted to sign Federal loyalty oaths. The *Official Records* contain many complaints about the "disloyalty" of the valley growers, and cavalry patrols were organized to deter between-the-lines trading. However, the soldiers were not immune to the trade's charms, and their commanders often bemoaned the demoralizing effects of involvement with the cotton trade. Other military and political leaders were less pessimistic, and perhaps General Leonidas Polk's cynical attitude best sums up the practicality of the trade: "I suggest that you use these cotton purchases for the purpose of controlling the enemy's movements and keeping him quiet. I believe it can be done if managed skillfully. It is important for us at least as long as active operations are in progress in front of Dalton. Use these gentlemen so as to prolong their operations and give all the time you may. See that the Yankees get cotton now and then, but not faster than suits our purposes."[9]

Certainly, Jefferson Davis's and other Confederate authorities' fears concerning the potential demoralization of Southern citizens were not unfounded. Lincoln hoped to create demoralization among Southerners. Historians Lawrence Powell and Michael Wayne believe that Lincoln adroitly used trade and other privileges to cultivate latent Unionism and to "detach Southern allegiances from the Confederate government and reattach them to the Federal government" via magnanimity and appeals to self-interest.[10]

These factors reveal the complexity involved in ascertaining an optimal export duty. The cotton trade created a clash between the Union's hopes of fostering Unionism and exploiting raw cotton and the despair of increasing the Confederate government's ability to obtain supplies.

III. The Federal Policy and Northern Interests

Aside from tax revenue considerations, there were several reasons for the North to acquire some raw cotton from the South. First, the Lincoln administration believed that Northern textile manufacturers needed Southern raw cotton to survive, so Lincoln was willing to loosen the blockade to alleviate the distress of the textiles manufacturers. Second, military leaders believed that raw cotton was necessary to produce tents and sails for the army and the navy. A third factor was the possibility of selling cotton to Europe for badly needed specie. Edward Atkinson, a cotton manufacturer, advised the president that although the Confederates were able to ship only a fraction of their normal volume of cotton, the prices were so remunerative that their revenue was nearly the same as that prior to the war. Therefore, the president should allow more cotton to come through the lines, thereby reducing prices and presumably Confederate revenues. Apparently Atkinson's idea influenced Lincoln, as the president incorporated the thought in his discussion of the trade with General Edward Canby in late 1864:

> As to cotton, by the external blockade, the price is made certainly six times as great as it was. And yet the enemy gets through at least one-sixth part as much in a given period, say a year, as if there were no blockade, and receives as much for it as he would for a full crop in time of peace. The effect, in substance, is, that we give him six ordinary crops without the trouble of producing any but the first; and at the same time leave his fields and his laborers free to produce provisions. You know how this keeps up his armies at home and procures supplies from abroad. For other reasons we cannot give up the blockade, and hence it becomes immensely important to use it to get the cotton away from him. Better give him guns for it than let him, as now, get both guns and ammunition for it. But even this only presents part of the public interest to get out cotton. Our finances are greatly involved in the matter. The way cotton goes now carries so much gold out of the country as to leave us paper currency only, and that so far depreciated as that for every

hard dollar's worth of supplies we obtain, we contract to pay two and a half dollars hereafter. This is much to be regretted; and while I believe we can live through it, at all events it demands an earnest effort on the part of all to correct it. And if pecuniary greed can be made to aid us in such effort, let us be thankful that so much good can be got out of pecuniary greed.[11]

Lincoln's argument rings hollow on several counts. First, the Confederacy was unable to reap six times the prewar real price for its raw cotton, as the real price in New York during 1864 averaged four times the prewar price. When Lincoln wrote to Canby, the price of raw cotton had skidded 30 percent from the August 1864 peak. Most of the higher prices for raw cotton resulted from the blockade-induced transportation costs and did not directly benefit the Confederacy, and the volume of raw cotton exports was not one-sixth but closer to one-eighth (during 1864). Thus, Confederate revenue from raw cotton was being depressed by the blockade-induced transportation wedge. Second, the terms of trade from between-the-lines activity were much better for the Confederacy than shipping through the blockade, especially when the trade consisted of goods rather than greenbacks or gold for cotton. The shifts in relative prices indicated the blockade's effectiveness. By trading a pound of bacon for a pound of raw cotton, the Federal authorities were allowing the Confederates to negate the effects of the blockade. Of course, the price of raw cotton in the North had risen much faster than coffee, meat, or salt, and, by trading through the lines, Northern *traders* received improved terms of trade. If anything, Lincoln was giving up "guns and ammunition" for raw cotton, while the Europeans gave up only guns.

The goal of obtaining enough cotton to sustain Northern textile manufacturers was a partial success. Atkinson claimed that the cotton famine had passed without ever having been reached. Northern textile manufacturers, receiving word that the 1860–61 crop was smaller than the 1859–60 crop, had accumulated large stocks prior to Fort Sumter, and the large stocks helped mitigate the disruption from the war. However, as the war continued into its second year, the Northern manufacturers felt the disruption of the supply of raw cotton and eventually had to reduce production of textiles. More than one million 400-pound bales of Southern cotton reached the North during the Civil War. The Northern states consumed roughly 800,000 bales per annum during the last five years of the antebellum period, but only a little more than 300,000 annually during the war. A small proportion of these were obtained from captures or abandonment, but the rest were either run through the blockade or came through the lines (mostly through Union-occupied cities).[12]

These factors complicated the choice of an export duty. The overall well-being of the Federal government and the Northern population might not be maximized by establishing an export duty that maximized tax revenue. Assuming that the supply of raw cotton was not perfectly inelastic for all prices, Northern textile manufacturers and their customers (including the Federal government) could bear some of the burden from taxes on raw cotton. During 1865–66, a House of Representatives committee heard recommendations from textile manufacturers that they needed a drawback on excise taxes paid on raw cotton in order to compete with foreign manufacturers. A peacetime cotton tax would have fallen primarily upon foreign manufacturers and their customers (some of whom were Americans), since the Northern textile manufacturers consumed less than a quarter of the total Southern cotton supply during the antebellum period. However, a wartime cotton tax might have fallen more heavily upon Northerners (assuming they acquired the bulk of the cotton exported from New Orleans and Memphis).[13]

In addition to the economic factors, the cotton trade held a potential danger: demoralization of the military. Charles Dana, an observer for Secretary of War Edwin Stanton, reported, "The mania for sudden fortunes made in cotton . . . has to an alarming extent corrupted and demoralized the army. Every colonel, captain, or quartermaster is in secret partnership with some operator in cotton; every soldier dreams of adding a bale of cotton to his monthly pay." While Dana's observations were exaggerated, he was not alone in his belief that the trade demoralized the troops. Secretary of the Treasury Salmon Chase admitted that the trade, as conducted, led to demoralization: "These frauds upon the public treasury, and the demoralizing effects of the system, are evidenced by many letters to this department from its own officers, from officers of the army and navy, and from many others who have observed them, including some of the traders themselves."[14] Eventually, other Union leaders believed that the government should monopolize the cotton trade to minimize the corrupting influences.

IV. The Federal Policy and Foreign Interests

The international repercussions of a cutoff in the export of Southern-grown cotton haunted Secretary of State William Seward and other Northerners. British and French textile manufacturers worried about their dependence upon American-grown raw cotton. A London writer described the possible effects of losing the supply of American-grown cotton: "It is impossible to reflect seriously upon the nature of our cotton supply, without evoking a phantom that no exorcism will banish." The writer painted a deserted mill town with "voiceless misery and death" and the epitaph, "'The cotton supply from America has ceased.'" However, not all British observers were so pessimistic. Perhaps the Southern envoys would have been less sanguine had they known that Lord Lyons, British ambassador to the United States, observed that "the very exaggerated and very false ideas they have in the South about cotton will lead to very foolish conduct. It is true that cotton is almost a necessity to us, but it is still more necessary for them to sell it than it is for us to buy it." Should the South actually withhold its great staple commodity from export to England, it seemed evident to the British minister, "that other cotton would be got elsewhere or a substitute found."[15] Other British writers thought that the Southerners would eventually exploit their price-setting power to increase revenues: "It is certain that, should the South establish its political independence, the Government of Richmond will impose an export duty upon cotton in order to create a revenue; in such case, with a reduced supply from America, and that burdened with an export duty, there seems no good reason why India should not compete with the trans-Atlantic states."[16]

Aside from the potential dearth of cotton, some British observers saw potential for the North to use the blockade to either assuage the disruption to its own cotton manufacturing or even to usurp the South's power from cotton:

> We do not anticipate any *corrupt* [italics theirs] connivance on the part of the Federal cruisers, which would allow cotton vessels to slip through the blockade; but we do anticipate a *cunning* [italics theirs] connivance of this sort—and on a very extensive scale. It must never be forgotten that the North want cotton even more imperiously than we do. By preventing any cotton being exported, the Northern cruisers are stopping the mills and ruining the trade of their own manufacturers: they are cutting their own throats. They will soon begin to reflect that they will injure and impoverish their antagonists quite as effectively by capturing their cotton at sea as by preventing it from putting to sea at all,—while they will benefit themselves incomparably more.[17]

To forestall any European intervention because of a shortage of cotton, Seward hoped that Federal forces would seize a Southern port and open a flow of cotton. Seward also advocated loosening the blockade, refused to press Mexico to stop the contraband trade at Matamoros, and promoted trade between the lines. His policies were opposed by other cabinet members, particularly Secretary of the Navy Gideon Welles. However, historian David Crook defends Seward's actions, characterizing them as being "commonly underestimated." Crook describes Seward's promises of getting raw cotton from occupied ports as "tantalizingly vague," and he believed that Seward's policies helped keep France and Great Britain divided on the feasibility and advisability of intervening.[18]

Since very little Southern raw cotton reached Europe during the period September 1, 1861, to September 31, 1862 (a period considered as posing the most danger of foreign intervention), either Seward was a diplomat of extreme ability (using fewer than 50,000 bales of Southern cotton to satisfy Europe's voracious appetite for raw cotton and to deter intervention) or there were other, more compelling, reasons for the British and French non-intervention.

Did Seward need to exhort Federal officers to procure raw cotton by almost any means necessary? Did the opening of New Orleans, Norfolk, and Memphis, with their attendant dribble of raw cotton to Europe, forestall intervention? The British and French did not intervene and there have been several theories as to why. Louis Schmidt attributed British reticence to intervene upon their need for United States grain. E. D. Adams and Frank Owsley dismissed Schmidt's thesis. Eli Ginzburg presented a more balanced assessment and concluded that, although losing Northern wheat would have imposed some dislocation in the British economy, such dislocation would have been moderate. Therefore, Northern wheat was not a major determinant of British neutrality. Norman Ferris reached a different conclusion on the wheat issue. He believed that Adams and Owsley went too far in dismissing Schmidt's thesis, and he demonstrates that British statesmen were concerned about Northern wheat. Ferris concluded that while Northern wheat was not the primary determinant of non-intervention, it was a factor.[19] Other factors cited as deterring British intervention include British dislike of slavery, risk of war with the North, profitability of neutrality from selling arms and munitions to both sides, fears for Canada, and fears about instability on the European continent. In addition, the British recognized potential future benefits from the Federal interpretations of maritime laws. Factors that made intervention attractive included a desire to see the United States permanently divided, desire to maintain free trade, and irritation over perceived Northern arrogance and slights. Probably no one factor by itself deterred intervention. Instead, British and French leaders weighed the different factors. Since all the factors arguing against intervention outweighed the perceived benefits, no intervention occurred. However, removing any one or a combination of the factors arguing against intervention might have tipped the balance, with the key being the removal of any one of several arguments. Together the arguments were compelling, but individually they were not. Finally, there is the question of whether intervention implied support for the Confederacy. Some Federal authorities believed that British interests (freeing up an adequate flow of cotton, for instance) would have been better served by allying with the North. Regardless of why Britain and France did not intervene, the temptation is to say that they never would have intervened, so Seward's policies were clearly injurious. While there may be strong reasons to suspect that intervention was unlikely, one cannot dismiss the possibility. The prospects of foreign intervention seemed real enough during 1861–62. Seward's caution during the first eighteen months of the war was justified. However, his obsession with supplying cotton to forestall intervention should have ended by the middle of 1863 when Union victories at Gettysburg, Vicksburg, and Port Hudson and advances in middle Tennessee doused the last embers of possible foreign intervention. But Seward continued to be mesmerized by the intervention bogeyman and continued to press for trade.

The North also faced international law considerations that argued against Seward's policy of loosening the blockade and promoting trade. The blockade was in danger of being disputed by the European powers. Attorney General Edward Bates explained to his fellow cabinet members in November 1862 that the policy of blockading an occupied port was illegal. Such a situation occurred at Norfolk where Federal General Dix wanted to issue trade permits and create a monopoly of the trade. The policy of loosening the blockade for the convenience of certain European powers was also certain to breed contempt for the blockade. These policies ran the risk of invalidating the blockade's legality in the eyes of foreign powers.[20]

Aside from the danger of having foreign powers declare the blockade illegal, the setting of an export duty should not have been significantly affected by international considerations after 1862, when the threat of foreign intervention to get raw cotton dissipated. Indeed, there was another option available to Europeans, as Lincoln had argued that if the Europeans wanted a quick reopening of trade they should help the North suppress the Confederacy.[21]

V. Other Policies

Lincoln faced an early decision whether to implement a blockade or to close the ports. On March 18, 1861, he queried Bates, Chase, and Welles on whether the executive had the power to collect duties on shipboard, offshore from rebel-held ports and how many naval vessels were available to collect the duties. The blockade was chosen for legal and international reasons. A tight blockade would theoretically prevent the North from getting any cotton from trade.[22]

With a close blockade, the North could have tried to rely upon confiscated cotton to supply its textile manufacturers. Obviously, the Northern government gained from the sale of every bale confiscated (or stolen, depending upon one's perspective), while the Confederacy lost from such confiscation. Although the actual captures were inadequate to meet the factories' needs, more effort might have been exerted in finding cotton to confiscate. Some military operations were designed to capture cotton. Even as late as 1864 Federal military policy was affected by the desire to procure cotton. For instance, General Nathaniel Banks's army was directed towards the Red River instead of pressing towards Mobile. To be sure, Banks was not an unwilling participant in this venture, and the lure of cotton proved a siren song for this Massachusetts politician with presidential aspirations. Unfortunately for Banks, he didn't lash himself to one of Rear-Admiral David Porter's gunboat masts (or put cotton in his ears) and ignore the Red River. Instead his inept handling of the campaign effectively ended his military career. Meanwhile, Porter and his sailors obtained considerable quantities of cotton, often fraudulently labeled C.S.A. (initials that were derisively referred to as the Cotton Stealing Association).[23]

Another strategy was to promote "abandoned cotton." Treasury agent William Mellen hoped that Southerners would voluntarily "abandon" sufficient quantities of cotton. Abandoned cotton would be sold on Federal account; the owners could then file proofs of loyalty and hope to receive compensation. However, Mellen believed that the presence of speculators made the "abandonment" policy less effective. The quantities of abandoned cotton around Memphis were limited to a few thousand bales.[24]

The policies of relying upon captured and abandoned raw cotton would not have insured an adequate supply of raw cotton to meet the North's needs. Indeed, these policies netted fewer than 170,000 bales during the war.[25] Conversely, these policies and the blockade helped prevent the Confederacy from reaping even more benefit from its raw cotton. After the threat of foreign intervention dwindled in 1862, variations of these policies may have been more practical alternatives to that of regulating the trade.

Federal trade regulations evolved throughout the war. The method of payment for cotton was a nettlesome question. Initially, no restrictions were placed on the mode of payment. Mellen advised Chase to prohibit the use of gold in the trade, and he believed that even allowing trading goods for cotton was preferable to trading gold for cotton. However, trading goods for cotton dissipated most of the transportation wedge created by the blockade and raised Confederate gains from the trade to deleterious levels. As the trade burgeoned in the middle of 1862, especially around Memphis, Federal General Sherman suspended payment by gold, silver, and treasury notes, declaring them contraband of war. Sherman preferred a system of deferred payment, similar in intent to the program implemented in 1864. Treasury Secretary Chase had been favorably disposed to adopt a similar plan in September 1862.[26]

Sherman's orders were countermanded by the War Department. Chase believed that Seward was behind the countermanded order. Critics of Sherman declared that using treasury notes would discourage Southern growers from bringing in their cotton, but the Treasury Department eventually formulated regulations prohibiting transportation of coin or bullion into the states or sections formerly declared to be in insurrection. By 1864, new regulations stipulated that owners of cotton could sell their product to treasury agents by pledging allegiance to the Union and receiving one fourth of the net proceeds immediately and the remainder, upon adhering to their oath of allegiance, after the war. The hope was that the regulation would foster increased trade and Unionism. Edward Bates assessed the merits of Secretary of the Treasury William Fessenden's plan to the cabinet. Bates thought the plan was workable only, "by refusing permits to all of our people, to go into the enemy country, to get cotton." He believed that the treasury agents should be passive. Local people should bring their cotton to the agents rather than giving permits to traders to go and fetch the cotton, a situation, "leading to corrupt speculation and odious monopoly." Not everyone agreed with a passive role for the agents.[27]

Fessenden's policy created consternation in the cotton trade. One Confederate general stated that the policy of allowing only one-third of the value of cotton to be paid in supplies (and the rest in greenbacks) now made trading with the Yankees unprofitable. Because of the Confederates' disgruntlement, the July 2, 1864, purchasing act resulted in the purchase of fewer than 55,000 bales. Some Northern leaders called for the Federal government to monopolize the trade. However, Lincoln apparently disliked this method, believing that the trade should be open to all.[28]

Would capturing the major ports earlier in the war have been a better policy? Occupying Wilmington and Charleston would have increased the North's ability to control the Southern cotton crop, and the North might have hoped for even more revenue from an export duty. At worst, Confederate gains from smuggling cotton would dwindle with the loss of these ports. However, historians Richard Beringer, et al., doubt the feasibility of early captures. The North was not prepared to launch seaborne assaults upon the South, and the Confederates could have used their railroads and telegraphs to rapidly respond to Union attacks. In addition, the Confederates had placed a higher proportion of their troops in the port cities early in the war than they maintained later.[29]

VI. Conclusions

Some commentators believe that Lincoln's policy towards the cotton trade was misguided and deleterious to the Northern war effort. However, historian Thomas O'Conner offers an interesting interpretation of Lincoln's actions. To O'Conner, the key to understanding Lincoln's actions was his willingness to be flexible until the circumstances made themselves clear, or as Lincoln told his secretary, John Hay, "My policy is to have no policy." O'Conner compared Lincoln's strategy to that of an "option" quarterback in football, reacting to and trying to exploit the new developments: "Lincoln seems to have considered it mandatory that his cotton policy conform to the practical dangers which faced the Union at the time." Thus, Lincoln sought to encourage border state Unionists and to deter Europeans from intervening. He countenanced trade until the foreign threat disappeared. O'Conner's thesis is intriguing, but it overstates Lincoln's ability to match policy to events. After the threat of foreign intervention receded in late 1862 (and practically disappeared after mid-1863), Lincoln still countenanced an increasing flow of cotton.[30]

Lincoln's contemporaries were less charitable about the results of his various policies. A House of Representatives committee conducted an investigation titled *Trade with Rebellious States* and concluded:

> It is the judgment of your committee that the trade . . . has been of no real benefit to our government; but, on the other hand, has inflicted very great injury upon the public service. It has induced a spirit of speculation and plunder among the people, who have entered into a disgraceful scramble for wealth during a time of war, waged to save the life of the nation, and has fed that greed of gain which must wound the public morals. It has tended to the demoralization and corruption of the army and navy by the exhibition of the vast rewards which have accrued from this trade and from the temptation and bribery with which they have been constantly assailed. It is believed to have led to the prolongation of the war, and to have cost the country thousands of lives and millions upon millions of treasure.[31]

Historian James Ford Rhodes echoed the committee's assessment: "For the South it [commercial intercourse] was a necessary evil; for the North it was an evil and not a necessary one."[32] Lincoln, himself, may have pointed out a flaw with the various policies designed to get raw cotton, as on occasion he emphasized to European powers that the quickest way to restore a steady flow of raw cotton was to crush the rebellion as quickly as possible. His argument also applied to Northern textile manufacturers: Cutting off trade might have led to a quicker Confederate collapse. Grant's decision to stop the Norfolk trade revealed the promise inherent in ending commercial intercourse.[33]

What are we to make of these policies? The need to acquire raw cotton from the South was probably greatest during the first eighteen months of the war. Seward's plan of reassuring European powers that the North was trying to open a flow of raw cotton could have plausibly contributed to those powers' decision not to intervene. The Federal government needed to acquire cotton in order to clothe and equip its burgeoning army. The hope that widespread latent Unionism existed also demanded some hesitation in completely cutting off trade. Minimizing economic upheaval in the textiles industry was also a worthwhile goal. Ironically, when the need was the greatest, the flow of cotton obtained was meager. As the need to deter European powers dwindled and the hope of widespread Unionism faded, the North obtained ever increasing amounts of raw cotton, often on terms that negated the effects of the blockade.

Clearly, the Norfolk trade was the most damaging to the North, while the cotton carted to the Rio Grande did not seriously hurt Northern interests. The Confederacy obtained some supplies from the Rio Grande trade, but most of the supplies remained in the strategic backwater of the trans-Mississippi. If the blockade was going to leak, Brownsville/Matamoros was a far better place than Norfolk. In addition, the North allowed the Southerners much better terms of trade at Norfolk than at Brownsville. The New Orleans and Memphis trade hurt the North more than the Brownsville trade, but probably less than the Norfolk trade. Finally, the use of Wilmington as the major blockade-running port, despite its inability to handle a large volume of raw cotton and long distance from the main cotton growing regions, bears testimony to the stringency imposed by the blockade.

Given the usefulness to the Confederacy of the supplies obtained for raw cotton, the North probably needed both to have set a higher tax on cotton and to have made greater efforts to collect the tax, especially after 1862. In addition, allowing goods to be traded directly for raw cotton should have been prohibited. While this might have resulted in less cotton being traded, such a policy would have seriously eroded the Confederacy's benefits from trading cotton.

The North did not gain as much from the cotton trade as it could have; the South did not gain as much from the cotton trade as it could have. Given the complexity of the situation, it would be unfair to expect that either government would have maximized the potential gains from raw cotton, but Lincoln displayed more flexibility than Jefferson Davis did in the battle over cotton. Davis's belief that withholding cotton might induce the Europeans to intervene, while unfulfilled, was not foolish, and he was one of the first to see that the policy wasn't going to work. However, he was slow in accepting the value of trading cotton with Northerners for badly needed supplies. Lincoln attempted to use cotton whenever possible, and, although he waited too long, he eventually gave Grant the authority to stop the Norfolk trade. Lincoln's mistakes regarding trade perhaps sufficed to prolong the war and heighten the risk of Northern war-weariness, while Davis's mistakes may have forfeited the Confederacy's best economic asset.

14

CONCLUSION:

Was the Blockade Worthwhile?

The United States Navy eventually commissioned almost 700 vessels. The government spent $567 million in navy-related expenses (calculated in 1879). In comparison, the gross expenditure on the war was $6.8 billion. Thus, naval expenditures represented about one-twelfth of the total expenditures. According to William Fox, there were 132,500 men in naval service during the war (compared to Livermore's estimate of 2.8 million in the army). Although blockade duty was dreadfully dull, it was not particularly dangerous, as only 4,800 men died in action or from other causes during the war. Fox noted that "unlike the army, the mortality from disease was, apparently, not in excess of the normal death rate of civil life." Of course, some of these deaths and expenditures were incurred by naval actions not directly related to the blockade. While blockade duty was often uncomfortable, the sailors might hope for a share of prize money.[1]

Although the number of vessels appears formidable, many of them were converted merchantmen armed with a few guns. These vessels might be best thought of as pickets, whose duty was to sound the alarm. Steamers, captured blockade runners, and regular warships would then do the pursuing. To maintain such a large number of vessels, especially the many steamers, the Federal navy had to perform small miracles of logistics. The resupply of coal and food required intermediate ports on the Southern coast, which the navy already possessed or captured early in the war. Still, the number of support vessels was impressive and added to the costs.

Was the blockade a good use of Northerners' money? We've seen the various effects that it had upon the Southern war effort. The blockade was comprehensive enough to act as a lever against the Southern economy. It depressed the prices of and revenues from staples such as cotton, tobacco, and sugar within the South while simultaneously raising the prices of imported products such as manufactured goods, some food commodities, and other items; therefore, the blockade diminished the purchasing power of Southern staples. The shortfall in Southern revenues from exporting raw cotton rivaled, if not exceeded, the Federal government's expenditures on its navy during the war. Given that the Northern economy was richer than the Southern economy, the lost export revenue certainly hurt the Confederacy more than the expended resources taxed the North. The blockade also contributed to the collapse of the Southern logistical system, leading to the surrender of the main Confederate army in Virginia. The blockade forced Southerners to rely more upon their frail railroad network, especially in the Atlantic states. In addition to forcing an over-reliance upon the railroads, the blockade deprived those railroads of necessary supplies of railroad iron, machinery, and supplies.

Despite these achievements, a question remains whether the blockade needed to be as tightly conducted as it was. The Federal government's policy of loosening the blockade to foster Unionism and to sustain Northern textile manufacturers, among other reasons, yielded dubious benefits at high costs. The between-the-lines trade often restored cotton's purchasing power to almost its antebellum level (adjusting for the intraregional movement of cotton to the front lines and moving goods received back into the "interior"). The Federal government faced other options, such as capturing the major ports and possibly not even blockading some minor ports. Certainly the blockade of the Mississippi River and Mobile caused most of the effects on exports of raw cotton. Blockading these two points did not require large numbers of warships. What would have happened if the blockade had only been maintained at these two points?

Blockading only two points on the Southern coastline might have caused international law controversies. Did a blockade of only two points fall short of the definition of a "binding blockade?" If so, then the Federal government probably needed to either capture New Orleans and Mobile, thereby potentially ending trade there while not relying upon a "blockade," or the government needed to make a sufficient show of force at the remaining ports. Fortunately for the Federal government, the number of crucial Southern ports remaining was limited: Richmond/Norfolk, Wilmington, Charleston, Savannah, and Galveston. For strategic reasons, the Federal navy was certain to be involved in attacking, occupying, or blockading Richmond and Norfolk. Charleston, Wilmington, and Savannah were larger ports equipped to handle and distribute exports and imports. Each had rail connections to Virginia and also with the Deep South, albeit over several different rail lines. Savannah and Charleston were better located to receive cotton from Georgia and eastern Alabama. However, these two cities' ability to succor Virginia was less certain, as witness even Wilmington's difficulties in forwarding supplies to Virginia. Still, for international law considerations and to keep the cost of importing war materiel high, the Federal navy also needed to blockade or capture these ports.

The potential of some of the minor ports was blunted by inadequate transportation. The small Florida ports of St. Marks, Cedar Key, and Fernandina lacked railroad and river connections to Georgia, much less the rest of the Confederacy. Apalachicola, Florida, at least had river connections to Columbus, Georgia, making the small port potentially useful in supplying troops in northern Georgia, Tennessee, and perhaps Savannah. Transporting goods from Columbus to the Virginia front was possible but required lengthy railroad shipment.[2] Brunswick, Georgia, lacked railroad connections to the interior until a connection was made with the Atlantic & Gulf Railroad during the war. The smaller Carolina ports—Georgetown, New Bern, Morehead City, Edenton, Elizabeth City, Beaufort, and Plymouth—were far from the major cotton-producing regions, but most had river connections inland. These ports might have been useful in ferrying imports to the Virginia front while lessening the burden on railroads bringing goods from the Deep South. As long as the rivers were navigable, these ports could have supplied Richmond and troops throughout Virginia. Being able to freely import meat, manufactured goods, war materiel, and consumer goods through these ports would have mitigated the reduction in the purchasing power of raw cotton. While there would have been greater transportation costs in sending cotton from Georgia or Alabama to the Carolina ports, at least this cotton would not face the ruinous costs associated with blockade running. However, these ports' minor roles in the antebellum economy made expanding their capacity for handling exports and imports questionable. The Federal navy needed to seal off these minor ports, if the effort did not require too many resources. That navy, via captures and blockades, largely succeeded in negating whatever usefulness the minor Carolina ports possessed. Sealing off Galveston and the other small Texas ports further diminished the Confederacy's access to Texas beef. Given the Rio Grande's isolation, the Federal attempts to blockade the river might have been a questionable use of resources, aside from fulfilling the international law definition of a binding blockade.

Should the Federal government have devoted more resources to its navy? Additional resources might have been devoted to making the blockade more stringent at Wilmington, for instance, or to capturing that port. Capturing the port earlier in the war might have hastened the final outcome, unless the Confederates could regain some of the North Carolina inlets. While Charleston resumed blockade-running activity in 1864, the city's distance from the Virginia front reduced its usefulness as a site for war material and reduced its substitutability for Wilmington.

In summary, the Federal navy's efforts appear to have been judicious, allowing for the inevitable mistakes and learning required in making the blockade effective. For the resources expended, the blockade appears to have been a worthwhile investment.

Appendix 1

CALCULATING
SUPPLIES OF MEAT

While the census reports large holdings of livestock in the South, several factors curb the optimistic outlook for the Southern meat supply. First, the cattle and swine were unevenly distributed. More than a third of the South's cattle were concentrated in Texas, and two other states with high per capita holdings of cattle, Arkansas and Florida, lay on the periphery of the Confederacy. Without Texas, Southern per-capita cattle holdings fall to 0.823. Without Texas, Arkansas and Florida, the per-capita figure was 0.762 head, a figure that was only slightly larger than the Northern states' holdings. The distribution of swine within the South was not as skewed as cattle. While Arkansas and Texas again had higher per capita holdings than the rest of the Southern states, the difference was not nearly as pronounced. Louisiana, South Carolina, and Virginia had the lowest per capita holdings of swine, but these states had reasonable access to the large holdings of Tennessee, Kentucky, Missouri, and the upper Mississippi valley during peacetime. Still, the relative isolation of significant portions of Southern livestock holdings boded ill for the Confederacy.

Converting Southern livestock holdings into potential meat supplies provides further reason to be less enthusiastic about the South's outlook for meat. Attempts to estimate the South's meat supply revolve around three key questions:

1. What were the average live weights of cattle and swine?
2. What were the ratios of net-to-live weight of cattle and swine?
3. What were the slaughter ratios for cattle and swine?

The South's higher per capita holdings of livestock were partially offset by the lower quality of Southern livestock. Southern livestock tended to feed off the countryside, and, compared to Northern livestock, received relatively small amounts of corn and other feed. The result was that Northern livestock were significantly larger than their Southern counterparts. Battalio and Kagel estimated that Southern livestock weighed 70 percent of Northern livestock, or an average of 149 pounds for swine, 800 pounds for oxen, and 450 pounds for other cattle, but this percentage may understate the actual weight of Southern livestock. Cattle delivered at New York in 1860 averaged roughly 800 pounds. During the same period in Chicago, the cattle weighed around 600 pounds. In addition, the commissioner of agriculture stated, "There can be no doubt that the average of western beef cattle, when marketed, is as high as 750 pounds." Texas cattle varied greatly in weight, and historian Dobie believes the longhorns matured slowly and attained an average weight of 800 pounds only after several years. Allen cites two small herds of Texas cattle seen just after the Civil War. One group averaged 1,008 pounds and the other group 1,200 pounds. However, Allen believed that these cattle provided tough, stringy meat, and the poor quality helped account for the Texas cattle receiving prices 20 percent less than western cattle. McCoy chronicles an 1868 sale of select Texas cattle in Kansas; the cattle averaged over 1,200 pounds each. Still, since Texas cattle were rarely grain-fed, the likelihood is that they were smaller or leaner than grain-fed Northern cattle. At New Orleans, the "Western" cattle sold at a premium of $10 to $15 per head over the Texas cattle. *Hunt's Merchant's Magazine* showed that the average weight per hog in the northwest states was between 206 and 234 pounds during the 1860–61 packing season, with Iowa, Wisconsin, and Ohio having the heaviest swine. Kentucky and Missouri had the smallest hogs of the group listed. Unfortunately, no average weights were listed for any of the Confederate states. During the Civil War, Confederate Commissary-General Lucius B. Northrop estimated that the hogs purchased in the upper South weighed, on average, 180 pounds in 1861 and 150 pounds in 1862. Northrop did not provide any reason why the hogs that the Commissary Department purchased in 1862 were lighter than those purchased in 1861, nor did he account for the low dressed-to-live weight ratio. The low net-to-live weight ratio may have been the result of contracts allowing the packers to retain a fraction of the hog for private use. Commissary officer Frank Ruffin explained the practice: "The compensation [for the meat contractors] has been the fifth quarter, as it is called, which was the usual butcher's profit from time immemorial."[1]

If Southern swine and beeves were smaller than their Northern counterparts, would the ratios of dressed weight-to-live weight of Southern livestock have been similar to those of Northern livestock? Is it possible that smaller animals have a lower dressed weight-to-live weight ratio? The head and bones might weigh the same, regardless of the overall weight of a mature animal. One Virginia respondent to a commissioner of patents survey implied as much: "To obtain the net from the gross weight [of hogs], deduct 25 pounds from the first 100 pounds, 12.5 pounds from the second." The commissioner of agriculture reported, "A common steer, weighing 1,200 pounds live weight, will scarcely make 600 pounds of beef, while a steer of good blood and in ripe condition, weighing 1,700 pounds, will produce 1,000 pounds of meat." However, Gallman believed the variability in net-to-live weight was of minor importance. In a livestock feed manual, the author discussed the importance of fattening, which increased the proportion of dressed carcass to live-weight. In cattle, a lean ox would provide 47 percent dressed weight-to-live weight, while a fattened ox produced 60 percent. For swine, the dressed weight-to-live weight ratios ranged from 73 to 82 percent. Morrison estimates the dressed weight-to-live weight ratios as 65 to 80 percent for swine and 50 to 60 percent for cattle. Swine slaughtered during 1923–29 averaged 225.2 pounds live weight and 167.8 pounds dressed weight, an average dressed weight-to-live weight ratio of 74.5 percent.[2]

Tables 1.7 and 1.8 use census data and various assumptions by economic historians Gallman, Fogel, Engerman, Towne, Rasmussen, and Grossman. The lower bound estimate uses the most conservative estimates of live-weight of cattle, dressed-to-live weight ratio of cattle, live-weight of calves, slaughter ratios, live-weight of swine, and dressed-to-live weight ratio of swine, while the upper bound uses the largest estimate of these variables.

Appendix 2

ESTIMATING POTENTIAL
TOTAL REVENUE FROM
RAW COTTON

In order to estimate potential total revenue from exporting raw cotton, the first step is to estimate the world demand for American-grown raw cotton. For this purpose, the world demand for American-grown raw cotton is typically assumed to have a constant elasticity: $Q^D = DP^{-e}$ (with e in absolute value). In this equation, D is a shift parameter encapsulating all other factors affecting the quantity demanded except for price. Unfortunately, such an equation does not enable us to discuss maximizing total revenue. After all, if $|e| < 1.0$, total revenue is maximized as Q goes to zero; while for $|e| > 1.0$, total revenue is maximized at Q = +oo. Instead, a quadratic equation shall be used to generate revenue estimates.

A quadratic approximation can be fitted using a Taylor Expansion about the observed 1860–61 price and quantity combination: P = $52.04 per 400-pound bale and Q = 5,897.555 bales. Like all quadratic combinations where $Q = a - bP + cP^2$ (where a, b, c > 0), the demand curve eventually becomes positively-sloped—there is a minimum Q^D (in this case, at P = $80.94). Moreover, the Taylor Expansion version also has the unlikely result of less elastic demand for prices both greater than as well as less than P = $52.04; therefore, total revenue is maximized only at very high (infinite) prices. These drawbacks make the Taylor Expansion insufficient for our purposes.

Another approach is to derive a quadratic approximation based on two assumptions:

(i) 5,897.555 (000's of bales) = $a - bP + cP^2$ when P = 52.04 (i.e., the observed 1860–61 price per 400-pound bale in New York).

(ii) $-e = (dQ/dP)(P/Q) = -0.8$ at P = $52.04 and Q = 5,897.555.

Equation (ii) becomes:

(–b + 2cP)(52.04/5897.555) = –0.8 or –b + 2cP = –90.661875.

Solving the two equations:

(i) 5897.555 = a – 52.04b + 2708.1616c
(ii) –90.661875 = –b + 104.08c

yields:

$$c = (a/2708.1616) – 3.9198543$$

Thus, our coefficients depend upon the value we choose for the intercept (the quantity demanded when P = 0). If a = 14,861.839, we get the Taylor Expansion equation discussed above. If a = 10,615.599, we get a linear equation. As discussed earlier, for a = 14,861.39 (the Taylor Expansion), the demand curve starts to slope upward at a relatively low P. Using a > 14,861.39 creates upward-sloping demand curves at even lower prices than $80.94 (the price at which the Taylor Expansion begins to curve upward). Thus, we should select a < 14,861.39 to keep the demand curve from becoming upward-sloping at too low a price. Obviously Q^D > 5897.555 at P = 0, so a > 5,897.555 and 5897.555 < a < 14,861.39. This creates a relatively wide range of equations and results. The range for a is probably between the intercept of the linear demand function and the Taylor Expansion function:

$$10,615.599 < a < 14,861.39.$$

Choosing a = 12,000 generated the demand function:

Q^D = 12,000 – 143.86714P + 0.5111959P^2 (Q^D in 000's of 400-pound bales and P in dollars per bale).

Aside from the importance of the elasticity of demand, the growth in demand also would affect the South's gains from restricting its output of raw cotton. The antebellum world demand for American-grown raw cotton was growing at roughly 5 percent per annum. On the eve of the Civil War, there was no reason to anticipate a permanent change in the rate of growth in demand, although short-term fluctuations occurred. The growth in demand implied that the same output would reap a higher price or that more could be sold at the original 1860–61 price. Primarily, the growth in demand meant that revenue equal to that earned in 1860–61 could be obtained from a smaller output.

Given an estimated demand function, calculating a total revenue function is a simple matter. However, two adjustments must be made to such a total revenue function. First, the equations and elasticities estimated used the New York price of raw cotton. The South was more interested in the price received at New Orleans (a truer reflection of the amount received by planters, rail and river shippers, warehousemen, etc., in other words, the revenue accruing to Southerners). The New York–New Orleans prices generally differed by one-and-a-half cents per pound, or perhaps $6 per 400-pound bale. Thus, the South received $($P_{NY}$ – 6)$. Second, the demand estimates assumed a fixed supply of American-grown raw cotton. This assumption avoided the simultaneity problem in estimating demand. The fixed supply, however, included the beginning stocks of raw cotton in Great Britain and America (New York). The beginning stock could well be a function of the price or expected price, but it will be treated as exogenous. The South faced "competition" from existing stocks of raw cotton. The existence of stocks diluted the effectiveness of the South's price-setting power, and any attempt to raise raw cotton prices would also benefit the third party holders of stocks.

The total revenue function for the South, then, would be:

$$TR = \$ (P_{NY} - 6)[Q^D(P) - BS] \text{ where BS = Beginning Stock}$$[1]

If the beginning 1861–62 stock of American-grown raw cotton dropped to 900,000 bales from the large beginning 1860–61 stock of 1,307,000 and if the demand grew by 5 percent, then the maximum possible total revenue accruing to the South would be $247 million (based on a slightly larger crop of 4,651,000 bales and P = $59.06).[2]

Appendix 3

A MODEL OF
THE WORLD DEMAND
FOR AMERICAN-GROWN
RAW COTTON

The world demand for American-grown raw cotton was the residual of total world demand for raw cotton less the supply of raw cotton by rival producers (see Figure A-3.1). The world demand for raw cotton is denoted by Q_T. The short-run supply of raw cotton by producers other than American producers is $S_o P^a$, with "a" being the elasticity of supply. The demand

Figure A-3.1. The World Market for Raw Cotton

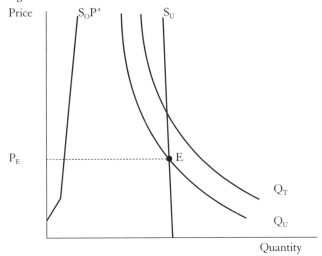

The world demand for raw cotton is Q_T. The short-run supply of raw cotton by producers other than American producers is $S_O P^a$, with "a" being the elasticity of supply. The demand for American-grown cotton, Q_U, is the residual of $Q_T - S_O P^a$. The supply of American-grown cotton is S_U; the intersection of Q_U and S_U (at point E) gives the market price of raw cotton, P_E.

for American-grown cotton, Q_U, is the residual of the world demand for cotton, Q_T, and $S_o P^a$, i.e.

$$(1) \quad Q_U = Q_T - S_o P^a$$

The short-run supply of American-grown cotton is S_U, and the intersection of Q_U and S_U gives the market price of raw cotton. We can replace Q_T with $D_T P^{-e}$ (the explicit function for world demand for raw cotton, with e = elasticity of world demand for all raw cotton in absolute value). Thus:

$$(2) \quad Q_U = D_T P^{-e} - S_o P^a$$

Figure A-3.1 can be used to examine Hanson's paradox of rising world demand for all raw cotton concurrent with falling world demand for American-grown raw cotton. World demand for American-grown raw cotton could have fallen for three reasons. First, the world demand for all raw cotton could have fallen (perhaps because of a fall in the demand for cotton textiles), shifting both Q_T and Q_U to the left. Of course, such an event would resolve only one half of Hanson's paradox (falling world demand for American-grown raw cotton). Second, the rival producers of raw cotton might have become more efficient and increased their supply, shifting $S_o P^a$ to the right. Since the world demand for American-grown raw cotton was the residual of total world demand for raw cotton less the supply of raw cotton by rival producers, an increase in the supply by rival producers would have exerted a downward pressure upon the world demand for American-grown raw cotton. Thus, if world demand for all raw cotton remained stationary or even increased somewhat, the world demand for American-grown raw cotton *could* simultaneously decrease. The price of raw cotton would decrease, and the quantity demanded of all raw cotton would increase. The share of raw cotton supplied by non-American producers would increase (and persist if the increased relative efficiency was not ephemeral). Therefore, a long-term increase in the share of raw cotton supplied by non-American producers combined with falling prices would be compelling evidence that rival producers became relatively more efficient in producing raw cotton, and that such increased efficiency retarded the world demand for American-grown raw cotton. The increased share of raw cotton supplied by non-American producers would also affect the elasticity of world demand for American-grown raw cotton, as will be discussed below.

There is a third possible solution to Hanson's puzzling findings: the Civil War–induced reduction of the supply of American-grown raw cotton. Did the disruption of the flow of raw cotton from the Southern states affect the demand for American-grown raw cotton? During the war, the

Union navy's blockade induced a large increase in the cost of transporting raw cotton from Southern ports to European ports; Lebergott cited price differences of 45 to 50 cents per pound between Southern ports and Liverpool. The increase in shipping costs shifted the supply of American-grown raw cotton (facing European buyers) to the left, and this shift raised the price of raw cotton and decreased the quantity sold.[1]

When the supply of raw cotton from the Southern states shifted to the left, two new factors would affect the world demand for American-grown raw cotton and, hence, the growth-in-demand estimates. First, as the supply of American-grown raw cotton decreased and the price of raw cotton increased, there would be a *movement along* the supply curve of non-American raw cotton suppliers and the quantity supplied by these rival producers would increase. Presumably the quantity supplied would initially be augmented by diverting shipments to Europe instead of China and Japan or by reducing domestic usage of raw cotton (in other rival cotton-producing regions). If the higher prices were expected to persist, existing producers would subsequently expand their supply and less efficient producers would enter the market. If the high prices created by the reduced supply of American-grown raw cotton were expected to persist, the supply curve of non-American producers would become more elastic over time, causing this supply curve to flatten and perhaps shift to the right. If these new producers of raw cotton incurred relatively large fixed costs in clearing and preparing land for cultivation of raw cotton, then they could continue to produce cotton even when the price of raw cotton fell. The supply by non-American producers could remain to the right of the original supply curve for an extended period. Such a situation would exert a downward pressure upon the demand for American-grown raw cotton. When the supply curve of these producers flattened, the demand for American-grown raw cotton would flatten and perhaps shift to the left, resulting in a negative growth in demand. While such an increased supply by rivals creates a situation much like the case discussed above where rival producers became more efficient, it is important to emphasize the difference between the two cases. Where the rival suppliers became relatively more efficient, the price of raw cotton falls; in the other case, the reduction in the supply of American-grown raw cotton and the attendant increase in the price of raw cotton *caused* the rightward shift in the supply by rival raw cotton producers.

The second new factor relates to the elasticity of world demand for American-grown raw cotton. Wright and Hanson calculated the growth rates for demand for American-grown cotton assuming constant elasticity of demand. By totally differentiating equation 2, we get:

$$* \qquad * \quad * \qquad\qquad * \quad *$$

(3) $Q_U = (1/\emptyset)(D_T - eP) - ((1-\emptyset)/\emptyset)(S_o + aP),$

where $\emptyset = Q_U/Q_T$, i.e. the proportion of Southern-produced raw cotton to the total world supply. Rearranging terms, one obtains:

$$* \qquad\qquad * \qquad\qquad * \qquad\qquad\qquad *$$

(4) $Q_U = [(1/\emptyset)D_T - ((1-\emptyset)/\emptyset)S_o] - [(1/\emptyset)e + ((1-\emptyset)/\emptyset)a]P$

Equation (4) can be rewritten as:

$$* \quad * \quad *$$

(5) $Q_U = D_U - e_U P$

$$* \qquad\qquad * \qquad\qquad *$$

Where $D_U = (1/\emptyset)D_T - ((1-\emptyset)/\emptyset)S_o$ and $e_U = (1/\emptyset)e + ((1-\emptyset)/\emptyset)a$

This specification immediately calls into question the assumption of constant elasticity of world demand for American-grown cotton that has been used for growth-in-demand estimates. If the proportion of Southern-grown raw cotton to the total world consumption changes significantly, the shifting proportions would alter the elasticity of demand for Southern-grown raw cotton. Specifically, as Wright recognized, if the elasticity of supply of raw cotton produced by non-Southern producers is less than the elasticity of world demand for all cotton, then as the US share diminishes, the elasticity of demand for Southern-grown cotton will increase (in absolute value). While Wright discussed the ramifications of this finding upon his estimates of the postwar rate of growth in demand, he did not demonstrate how such a change in elasticity would affect the wartime rates of growth in demand. Hanson, too, pointed out that the assumption of constant elasticity may be unrealistic when applied to the 1860s, but he dealt with this situation by estimating the growth-in-demand figures under two separate but constant elasticities. However, this provision of two separate sets of estimates does not demonstrate the effects of *changing* elasticities upon the growth-in-demand estimates.[2]

During the Civil War, the large decrease in the supply of American-grown raw cotton between 1861 and 1862 probably raised prices into a more elastic region of demand. How would a change in the price elasticity of demand affect the estimate of growth in demand? Figure A-3.2 shows what might happen by dropping the assumption of constant price elasticity of demand. From an initial Q* and P* combination, we show two possible demand curves, both having equal price elasticity of demand at Q* and P*. The non-linear demand curve has constant elasticity. The linear

Figure A-3.2. Growth in Demand If the Elasticity Is Not Constant

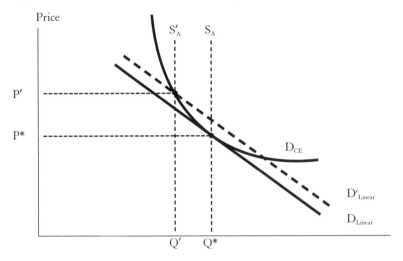

D_{CE} has constant elasticity of e^* (all elasticities are assumed to be in absolute value). D_{Linear} has elasticity of e^* at (Q^*,P^*), but at any other point, the elasticity is different (specifically, for $Q > Q^*$, $e < e^*$ and for $Q < Q^*$, $e > e^*$).

If the supply decreases from S_A to S'_A, then the price increases from P^* to P'. The new quantity demanded is Q'. If we had assumed that demand has constant elasticity, then we would have estimated zero growth in demand, i.e. stationary demand. If, instead, we had assumed linear demand, we then would have estimated a positive growth in demand (demand shifting to D'_{Linear}).

demand curve has varying elasticity; specifically, as Q gets smaller, the demand becomes more elastic. Suppose that the price increases to P′ when the supply of American-grown raw cotton shifts to the left, and the quantity demanded is Q′. If we initially assumed that demand had constant elasticity when we observed Q′, then the growth-in-demand estimate would be zero. If, instead, the true demand was linear, then there would have been an increase in demand and the growth in demand would have been positive. Hence, if demand becomes more elastic as price increases, then the assumption of constant elasticity will reduce a positive growth-in-demand estimate or exaggerate any negative growth in demand. The extent of the exaggeration is difficult to ascertain. The change in demand between periods can be represented by:

$$(D_1/D_0) = (Q_1/Q_0)/(P_0^{e0}/P_1^{e1})$$

If the elasticity of demand is constant, then $e_0 = e_1$, and units of measure are irrelevant. However, with changing elasticity of demand, units of measurement matter. Although (Q_1/Q_0) does not depend upon the units of measurement, the price ratio depends on e_0 and e_i; therefore, we cannot compute the absolute change in demand when the elasticity shifts. As an example, the 1860 real price of Uplands raw cotton in New York was $39.46 per 400-pound bale and $197.30 per ton. In 1861, the New York price was $48.39 per 400-pound bale and $241.95 per ton. Suppose the elasticity in 1860 was 0.8 and in 1861 was 1.5.

In bales: $(P_{1860}{}^{0.8}/P_{1861}{}^{1.5}) = (\$18.92/\$336.51) = 17.79.$
In tons: $(P_{1860}{}^{0.8}/P_{1861}{}^{1.5}) = (\$68.56/\$3763.47) = 54.89.$

After the Civil War ended and as the Southern states gradually resumed their antebellum level of raw cotton output, the price of raw cotton fell. As it fell, the price elasticity of world demand for American-grown raw cotton might fall (affecting the estimate of growth in demand under the assumption of constant elasticity of demand). However, the elasticity of demand for American-grown cotton might remain higher than the antebellum elasticity because of the increased supply of non-American producers (who might only gradually reduce their supply of raw cotton in the face of declining raw cotton prices) that reduced the American-grown raw cotton's proportional share of the total world supply.

The above discussion demonstrates that the large shocks to the market for raw cotton during the 1860s require that any estimates of growth in demand need to be carefully interpreted. The explanation provided for Hanson's striking result (growing world demand for all raw cotton concurrent with falling or stagnant world demand for American-grown raw cotton) points up the danger of confusing secular stagnation with the unusual and largely temporary circumstances created by the war.

Appendix 4

Estimating the Growth in Demand for British Cotton Textile Exports

Tables 10.4 and 10.5 present estimates of the changes in an index of demand for British cotton textile exports under different plausible elasticities of demand. The change in demand is calculated from the equation:

$$\overset{*}{D} = (1 + \overset{*}{P_c})^{e+a}(1 + \overset{*}{S}) - 1$$

Where P_c = British price of the specific cotton good

e = elasticity of demand
a = elasticity of supply
D = the shift term of the demand curve for cotton goods
S = the shift term of the supply curve for cotton goods
* = the rate of change in the variable

Since we don't have an estimate for the elasticity of supply, the tables are constructed under the assumption that the elasticity of supply is zero, so the equation simplifies to:

$$\overset{*}{D} = (1 + \overset{*}{P_c})^{e}(1 + \overset{*}{S}) - 1$$

If the elasticity of supply is non-zero, then the tables can be used to estimate the change in demand for e+a = 0.5, 1.0 or 1.5. It must be emphasized that these are crude estimates.

Unfortunately, the estimates are based on the declared value and not upon the actual retail price. Ideally we would like to estimate $Q^D = DP_R^{-e}$, where P_R = retail price. The retail price would be approximated by:

$$P_R = P + T + t,$$

where P = declared value or wholesale price in Manchester

T = transportation costs from Manchester to the final destination
t = tariff charges

Transportation charges from Liverpool to the United States averaged about 0.3 pence per pound of raw cotton during the main shipping months of October through April. The freight rates for a pound of cotton cloth were probably similar. However, the Liverpool to United States freight rates were stable during the war, rising by 10 percent in the first two years, before falling thereafter. Because freight rates comprised a minor proportion of the wholesale price for raw cotton (and presumably cotton goods) and were relatively stable, the main effect on the estimates of demand would be to moderately mute the changes in prices (since the numerator and denominator of the price change would both be slightly larger).

Even adding three pence per pound of cotton yarn for transportation during the Civil War period only created secondary changes in the estimate of demand. Compare these results with those of Table 10.5 (Yarn Exports):

Calendar Year	e = 0.5	e = 1.5
1861	− 6.66%	− 0.12%
1862	−43.08%	−32.90%
1863	− 1.69%	49.21%
1864	7.32%	19.48%
1865	26.91%	9.21%
1866	31.81%	27.42%

The change in transportation costs to Confederate ports and the change wrought by the Morrill Tariff, of course, are exceptions to the generally modest effects of adjusting the estimate of demand figures for transportation and tariff costs. In both cases, the drastic divergence between the price of cotton goods in Manchester and the retail price in either Northern or Southern cities may significantly affect the estimates of demand.

No freight rate series for the Liverpool to East India trade have been discovered by the author. Cassels quotes two authors in the 1860s who estimated the cost of shipping raw cotton from the fields in East India to England at 2.5 pence per pound. Of this amount, between 0.75 and 1.0 pence was for the shipping from India to Great Britain. Silver believes the cost was 1.5 pence per pound.[1]

The growth-of-demand figures for 1862 that are presented in Tables 10.4 and 10.5 are crude estimates because of possible shifts in the price elasticity of demand. These estimates are also sensitive to quality changes in the goods and other factors, so the figures should be adjusted for changes in the quality of the cotton goods. The mix of goods may have shifted towards the coarser classes of cloths; moreover, within the classes of cloth, the quality of goods shipped in 1862 was lower than in previous years. For instance, the *Economist* stated that grey shirtings differed in price by 3d. per pound depending upon whether the material was made of American or East Indian raw cotton. The difference in using American or East Indian raw cotton would represent a 19 percent differential in the April price of grey shirtings. These changes suppressed the price increases, and the failure of the computations to take account of the reduction in quality biases the estimated rate of growth downward. Table A-4.1 shows an adjustment to the growth in demand for white/plain cloth exports under the assumption that the prices are understated because of the deteriorating quality. The prices are assumed to be understated by 10 percent in 1862, 16 percent in 1863 and 1864, and 10 percent in 1865. The price adjustment reduces the 1862 negative growth-in-demand rates by one-tenth to over one-half (the larger the elasticity, the larger the reduction). The growth-in-demand rebound of 1863 is increased by up to 21 percent (in the case of e = 1.5). Conversely, the 1865 and 1866 growth-in-demand figures are reduced. Thus, the price adjustments to correct for quality changes serve to moderate the estimates of changes in demand in 1862 and 1866. Regardless of the quality changes or the elasticity of demand, the 1861–66 white/plain cloth growth-in-demand figures show strong growth during the period.

Table A-4.1. Growth in Demand for Great Britain Plain Cloth Exports, Adjusted for the Effects of Quality Changes on Price

Prices Unadjusted for Quality

Calendar Year	Quantity (000s Yds)	Real Price($)	Price Elasticity of Demand e=0.5	e=1.0	e=1.5
1861	1,734,585	3.16	−2.80%	−1.67%	−0.54%
1862	1,033,324	3.76	−35.04	−29.16	−22.75
1863	1,110,645	5.00	23.93	42.89	64.85
1864	1,101,566	5.88	7.56	16.65	26.50
1865	1,308,606	5.22	11.95	5.49	−0.59
1866	1,677,873	5.12	26.98	25.75	24.53
1861–66					
Per Annum			4.25%	9.40%	14.81%

Prices Adjusted for Quality

Calendar Year	Quantity (000s Yds)	Real Price($)	Price Elasticity of Demand e=0.5	e=1.0	e=1.5
1861	1,734,585	3.16	− 2.80%	−1.67%	−0.54%
1862	1,033,324	4.14	−31.85	−22.03	−10.80
1863	1,110,645	5.80	27.28	50.73	78.49
1864	1,101,566	6.82	7.56	16.65	26.50
1865	1,308,606	5.74	9.00	0.01	−8.24
1866	1,677,873	5.12	21.07	14.33	7.96
1861–66					
Per Annum			4.25%	9.40%	14.81%

Sources: Ellison ([1886] 1968, Table 2) and Rousseaux (1860=100).

Note: *Economist* quote of May 22, 1862, states that shirtings differed by 3d. per shirt because of quality differences (the quotations for shirtings in May, 1862 were listed at 13–14d., so perhaps shirtings ranged in price from 12 to 15d.); thus the difference in quality could result in a 20 to 25 percent difference in price. In 1862, perhaps half of the cotton cloth was poorer quality (there still was a significant amount of American cotton in the textiles), and the real price is adjusted by 10 percent. By 1863 and 1864 the proportion of East Indian cotton and sizing probably increased, reducing the quality further; the real price for 1863 and 1864 is adjusted by 16 percent. In 1865, reemergence of American cotton probably improved quality, and the real price is adjusted by 10 percent. By 1866, the quality probably approximated that of antebellum levels. If the price adjustment is increased, the negative 1862 growth in demand figures are further reduced.

Appendix 5

ESTIMATING THE GROWTH IN
DEMAND FOR AMERICAN-GROWN
RAW COTTON

I begin by reestimating the growth in world demand for American-grown raw cotton. The total supply of American-grown raw cotton is assumed to be fixed at the beginning of each commercial year (September 1 through August 31). The supply consists of the beginning stocks held in Great Britain and the United States and the crop harvested in the fall and winter. Wright and Hanson's total supply data is similar, except that they did not include beginning stocks held in Great Britain. Ideally, we would like to include beginning stocks held in France and the other European countries, but stock figures for these countries are for December 31 instead of September 1. The estimates listed in Table 10.11 use New York and Liverpool real prices per 400-pound bale of Uplands raw cotton.

Over the period covered by Table 10.11, the Liverpool prices had higher average rates of growth than the New York prices. Generally, there was not much difference between using 1859–69, 1860–70 or 1861–71 as endpoints for ten-year periods. The largest difference was that the estimate for 1861–71 using an elasticity of 2.0 revealed a negative rather than a positive average rate of growth as shown by similar estimates for 1859–69 and 1860–70. Hanson and Wright assumed a constant elasticity of 1.0, but the table shows other elasticities for comparison. The estimates in Table 10.11 bracket Hanson's findings of an annual growth of roughly –1.0 percent over 1860–70; the New York prices (as used by Hanson and Wright) showed about a 2.0 percent per annum decrease in demand, while the Liverpool prices generated a stagnant demand.[1]

As mentioned earlier, the assumption of constant elasticity of demand during the Civil War requires more scrutiny. There are two reasons to doubt the validity of this assumption. First, the initial dramatic price increase from the reduction in the supply of American-grown cotton during the Civil War probably moved the supply curve into a more elastic region of the world demand curve for all raw cotton. Second, the Civil War period was marked by a sharp decline in the proportion of American-grown raw cotton in the total world supply. As shown in Appendix 3, a decrease in the proportion of raw cotton supplied by American growers would increase the elasticity of world demand for American-grown raw cotton. If the price elasticity increased significantly during the Civil War, then the growth-in-demand estimates presented in Table 10.11 need to be reexamined.

Figure A-3.1 suggested a way to "decompose" the decrease in the quantity demanded between the effects of a change in elasticity and the effects of a decrease in demand (movement of the demand curve). Suppose we examine the changes in price and quantity between commercial years 1861 and 1862. In 1861, the real New York price was $48.39 and the quantity of American-grown raw cotton was 5,897,555 bales; in 1862, the price rose to $106.19 and the quantity in New York and Europe was 1,016,716 bales. These points are plotted in Figure A-5.1 (Point A for 1861 and Point B for 1862).

Suppose the elasticity of demand (in absolute value) at Point A is 0.7. If demand had constant elasticity (CES), then at P = $106.19, the quantity demanded would have been 3,402,000 (Point C). We would have concluded that demand had fallen (negative growth in demand). If demand had been linear, the quantity demanded would have been 966,000 (Point D), and we would have concluded that demand had increased. The linear demand case is a striking result. The demand between commercial years 1861 and 1862 is estimated in Table 10.11 to have sharply *decreased* (70 percent for e = 0.7); the linear demand implies that world demand for American-grown raw cotton *increased* between commercial years 1861 and 1862. While a reduced world demand for British cotton textiles would have exerted a downward pressure on the world demand for raw cotton (both American and non-American), the 70 percent drop in demand implied by the CES function (with e = 0.7) appears to be much too high. However, there is little reason to believe that world demand for cotton textiles and, by extension, the demand for raw cotton increased between 1861 and 1862.

Given the range of plausible estimates of the initial elasticity of demand and of the specifications of the demand equation, determining the exact effect of changing elasticity of demand upon the growth-in-demand estimates is problematical. However, if there was a significant change in the elasticity of demand between 1861 and 1862 because of the dramatic

Figure A-5.1. The Effects of Changing Elasticity upon Growth in Demand between 1861 and 1862

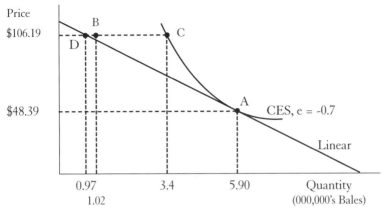

In 1861, the New York price of American-grown raw cotton was $48.39 per 400-pound bale, while the quantity was 5,897,555 bales (Point A). In 1862, the New York price of American-grown raw cotton was $106.19 per bale, while the quantity was 1,016,716 bales (Point B). At Point A, there are two possible demand curves: a constant elasticity demand curve (with elasticity = –0.7) and a linear demand curve with changing elasticity. When the price increased to $106.19, the quantity demanded on the linear demand curve is 966,500 bales (Point D), while the quantity demanded on the CES demand curve is 3,402,000 bales (Point C). Thus, the growth in demand is negative for the CES demand curve, but positive for the linear demand curve.

increase in the price of raw cotton, then there would be significant distortions in any estimate of the growth in demand using constant elasticity.

The growth-in-demand estimates are very sensitive to the missing data on the beginning stock of American-grown raw cotton held in New York; to the effect on prices of the existence of two or three million bales of cotton held within the Confederacy during the Civil War; to the estimate of the initial elasticity of demand; and to the specifications of the demand equation. Do the available price and quantity data enable us to narrow the range of plausible estimates of the initial elasticity of demand or to choose a specification for the demand curve?

The total supply of American-grown raw cotton is assumed to be fixed at the beginning of each commercial year. Because of the problems discussed above regarding the lack of data concerning the beginning New York stocks and the significant amounts of raw cotton held within the Confederacy during the Civil War years, the extent of the supply is unknown and the assumption of a fixed supply is untenable during this period. Therefore, regression equations including the Civil War years are unlikely to be reliable.

Given that the supply of American-grown raw cotton is predetermined, the regressions are run using supply as an independent variable. To capture the shift in demand, a time trend is used. However, the quantity of American-grown raw cotton and the time trend are strongly correlated and may create a multicollinearity problem.

Taking the natural logs of the New York and Liverpool uplands raw cotton prices, the natural logs of the quantities of American-grown raw cotton, and employing a trend variable generated constant elasticity equations for the antebellum period (1831–61) that are very similar to Wright's equations (even though the total supply figure differs because of my inclusion of beginning stocks in Britain). The world demand for American-grown raw cotton displayed more than a 5 percent annual growth rate and had elasticity roughly equal to one (although this elasticity may be biased upwards because of errors in the quantity variable).[2]

(6) Ln(New York Price) = 17.70 − 1.01Ln(US Supply) + 0.056(Trend).
     (5.746)   (−4.579)   (4.389)
     Adjusted R^2 = 0.4198[3]

Linear equations using the same data possessed much lower adjusted R^2's. However, a non-CES equation had only a slightly lower adjusted R^2 than did the CES equation (6):

(7) NY Price = 549.03 − 36.50Ln(US Supply) + 2.011(Trend)[4]
     (4.431)   (−4.129)   (3.920)
     Adjusted R^2 = 0.3674

Thus, the CES equation appears to explain slightly better the relatively moderate changes in the prices of American-grown raw cotton during the antebellum period than the semi-log equation; however, the closeness of the adjusted R^2's suggests that the semi-log function cannot be rejected in favor of the CES function on statistical grounds. As explained above, there also are theoretical reasons to favor a non-CES functional form over a CES function. Nor can we assume that the CES equation would do a better job than the semi-log equation in explaining the drastic changes in price that occurred during the Civil War.

How well did equations (6) and (7) "predict" the 1862 price and quantity? Plugging in the observed 1862 US Supply of 1,016,716 bales, the CES function predicts a price of $246.70, while the semi-log function predicts a price of $106.51. The actual 1862 price was $106.19. The CES function implies a reduction in the world demand for American-grown raw cotton, while the semi-log function implies that such demand had *increased* by the amount of the trend variable. However, before one anoints the semi-log regression equation as a great predictor, two caveats must be borne. First, if the errors in the quantity variable bias the elasticity upward, then both equations may underestimate the price associated with a quantity equal to 1,016,716. Second, these equations ignore the existence of two or three million bales of raw cotton held within the Confederacy in 1862. If this raw cotton dampened the increase in the price of raw cotton between 1861 and 1862, then the semi-log's estimate of $106.51 is an *underestimate* and is close to the observed price only by coincidence. Conversely, the CES's prediction of $246.70, while probably too high even if no additional raw cotton existed within the Confederacy, may not be as erroneous as it appears at first glance.

Given that the existing supply of raw cotton within the Confederacy exerted a downward pressure on the price, it is probable that the CES function overstates the decrease in world demand for American-grown raw cotton, while the semi-log function overstates the increase in demand. Somewhere between these poles lies the true story of the direction of world demand for American-grown raw cotton in commercial year 1862, and we need to recall our discussion of the cotton textile market to narrow the range.

NOTES

Notes to Introduction

1. McCoy [1874] 1940, 94.
2. Luraghi 1978, 137.
3. Beringer, et al. 1986, 139, 201.
4. Owsley 1931, 290.
5. Coddington 1949, 299–300, 304.
6. Anderson 1962, 232, 303.
7. U.S. Department of State 1934, 441; see also Seward to C. F. Adams, ibid., 440.
8. Lebergott 1981, 896; Fremantle 1864, 10.
9. Wise 1988, 226; Price 1955, 98–99.
10. *Congressional Globe* 1858, 961.
11. Davis 1992, vol. 7, 23.

Notes to Chapter 1

1. U.S. Department of the Treasury 1860, 316–51. Charleston exports are also listed in the Charleston *Daily Courier* (various annual reports in early September); Savannah and Wilmington exports are from *DeBow's Review* 1860, vol. 29, 669–70; 1861, vol. 30, 369.
2. U.S. Department of the Treasury 1860, 408–517.
3. Lonn [1933] 1965, 13–17; U.S. Bureau of the Census 1865, cciv; U.S. Department of the Treasury 1860, 489.
4. *DeBow's Review* 1862, vol. 7, 122–23; *Hunt's Merchants' Magazine* 1861, vol. 44, 352.
5. Hutchison and Williamson 1971, 591–612. Hutchison and Williamson assumed a slaughter ratio of 0.3 instead of 0.16666 and 0.2 used in Tables 1.7 and 1.8 (the higher ratio being applied to "other cattle" while the lower ratio pertained to oxen and milch cows); partially offsetting their use of a higher slaughter ratio, Hutchison and Williamson chose a lower average live weight (500 pounds) than Fogel and Engerman.
6. U.S. War Department 1880–1901. *War of the Rebellion: A Compilation of the Official Records of the Union and Confederate Armies,* ser. 4, vol. 1, 872 (hereafter denoted as OR); Fishlow 1964, 354; *DeBow's Review* 1860, vol. 29, 529–30, 665.
7. New York Chamber of Commerce 1862, vol. 4, 287; Genovese [1961] 1965, 107.

8. Philadelphia Board of Trade 1863, 60; Baltimore *American and Commercial Advertiser,* January 2, 1860; January 1, 1861; New York *Shipping and Commercial List, and Price Current* and Philadelphia *Price Current,* daily compilation of manifests of vessels arriving at New York and Philadelphia.

9. Kohlmeier 1938, 248–49; *Hunt's Merchants' Magazine* 1861, vol. 44, 37. The South Carolina Railroad ran from Camden, in the center of the state, to Charleston.

10. If the actual annual consumption level was closer to 200 pounds, an additional 65,000 tons would be needed to supply the 6.5 million adult male equivalents in the Confederacy.

11. McCoy [1874] 1940, 24–25. Bieber and Gard quote a resident of Beaumont, Texas, who estimated that 40,000 head crossed the Neches River there en route to Louisiana. A resident of Liberty recorded the number of drives and head of cattle that used the Trinity River ferry. In 1855 twenty-five droves with a total of 5,843 head used the ferry, while in 1856 the numbers were thirty-one and 6,869. Both authors cited a Galveston *Weekly News* report that 32,412 beeves from western Texas had crossed the Sabine into Louisiana during the first ten months of 1856 (Gard 1954, 25; McCoy [1874] 1940, 24–25).

12. Brayer and Brayer 1952, 29. The northward movement of cattle appears to have been between 20,000–80,000 per year (U.S. Department of Agriculture 1862, 330). The 80,000 figure may have been a typographical error as the Chicago Board of Trade listed only 8,000 head (*Annual Report* 1859, 56). Census official Clarence Gordon estimated that 876,500 head of cattle had been driven out of Texas to all points prior to 1866 (U.S. Bureau of the Census 1883, 966). Unfortunately, he did not divulge the basis of this estimate. Exports to foreign ports were minimal; the customs districts reported that only 80 head were exported in 1859 and 335 in 1860 (ibid., 976).

13. Haney 1910, 267; U.S. Department of Agriculture 1870, 251.

14. Hayes [1879] 1974, 749, 754; *Texas Almanac* 1859, 150; Galveston *Weekly News,* September 10, 1857.

15. Mobile *Daily Register,* daily accounts of arrivals. Unfortunately, the existing issues have many gaps. There were almost complete issues for January and February 1858 and less complete issues for March 1859 through June 1860. Table 1.13 shows both the shipments of cattle listed and an estimated amount that accounts for the missing days.

16. U.S. Bureau of the Census 1883, 976–77; Galenson 1977, 5.

17. U.S. Patent Office 1851, vol. 2, 189; *DeBow's Review* 1859, vol. 26, 117.

18. Buker 1993, 146.

19. U.S. Department of the Navy 1894–1922, *Official Records of the Union and Confederate Navies in the War of Rebellion,* ser. 2, vol. 2, 67. Subsequent references to the *Official Records- Navy* will be abbreviated as ORN.

20. U.S. Naval History Department 1971, vol. 1, 30. While Welles's hesitation in commissioning ironclads may seem unfathomable, at least one historian

believes Welles was prudent. The United States had commissioned the building of an iron-armored vessel in 1852 but, after a $500,000 expenditure, had nothing to show for it (Silverstone 1989, 15). Thus Welles decided to let Congress make the initial push for ironclads. A panel was formed during the summer of 1861 and approved three prototypes. Admiral David Porter recalled the skepticism by several prominent naval architects regarding ironclad vessels, including the Federal navy's own chief constructor, John Lenthall. So doubtful was the board appointed to examine prototype vessels that it gave Welles little definitive advice (Porter 1886, 358). In the course of investigating a technical problem with John Ericsson, one of the prototype builders stumbled across Ericsson's *Monitor* design. The now familiar story of the rush to get the *Monitor* to Hampton Roads to duel with the *Virginia* followed. Still, the *Monitor* was an untried vessel, and Porter explained Welles's hesitance: "It would have been a bold man, indeed, who, as Secretary of the Navy, would have taken the responsibility of building any number of untried 'Monitors' without something to justify him in doing so (Porter 1886, 357)." In addition, Welles was savvy enough to recognize the potential political disaster from any large mistake in the acquisition of ironclads. T. Harry Williams believes that the radical Republicans avidly searched for ways to persecute Welles, a prewar Democrat, and found their casus belli when an entire class of ironclads (20 vessels) proved defective, costing the national treasury over $10 million (Williams [1941] 1969, 359–60). A Congressional committee issued a report discussing the brouhaha (U.S. Congress 1865, "Light-Draught Monitors"). Senator Benjamin Wade, a Radical Republican, chaired the committee (*Congressional Globe* 1865, 824–25). Ironically, the War Department ordered seven ironclads for river service from Eads, a St. Louis firm, before the Navy Department even convened a panel to consider the merits of ironclads.

21. U.S. Bureau of the Census 1862, 107; 1865, 698; ORN, ser. 2, vol. 1, 503–4, 507; vol. 2, 67–69; Still 1971, 11. A New Orleans shipbuilder, James Martin, testified in 1862 that he did not believe that any ocean-going steamers or warships had been built in New Orleans prior to 1861. He thought that antebellum New Orleans produced only river craft (ORN, ser. 2, vol. 1, 507). Historian Louis C. Hunter also believes New Orleans shipbuilders primarily built smaller vessels (Hunter 1949, 107). Mallory wrote that ships could be constructed in the Confederacy, although such ships might be more expensive than Northern-built vessels: "The estimates submitted to the department for constructing ships exhibit a difference of 80 per cent between the offers of builders who are familiar with and prepared for the construction of war vessels in Northern ports and those of our own ports" (ORN, ser. 2, vol. 2, 51).

22. U.S. Department of the Treasury 1862, 461; ORN, ser. 2, vol. 1, 581, 599, 606; vol. 2, 72–74, 77, 151–52, 183, 244; U.S. Bureau of the Census 1865, 716, 738; Still 1971, 144; Moore 1861–68, vol. 4, 59; U.S. Naval Academy 1974, vol. 1, 137, 163, 168.

23. Black 1952, 9.

24. *Hunt's Merchants' Magazine* 1861, vol. 44, 373; Savannah *Daily Morning News* 1860; Wilmington *Journal* 1857–60; *DeBow's Review* 1861, vol. 30, 369. North Carolina was not a major cotton exporting state, as all ports in North Carolina combined to export just 56,000 bales.

25. OR, ser. 4, vol. 1, 1094; Showalter 1975, 45.

26. Jones, A. 1992, 129. Henry Sharpe, a former Union commissary officer, wrote that an "ordinary Ohio River steamer" could carry 500 tons of supplies; such an amount would supply 40,000 men and 18,000 animals for two days (Sharpe 1899, 189).

27. Davis 1991, 304–6.

Notes to Chapter 2

1. U.S. Bureau of the Census 1864, 200.

2. U.S. Bureau of the Census 1864, 177.

3. Richmond *Daily Whig,* January 7, 1861; Philadelphia Board of Trade 1861, 75–79; U.S. Department of the Treasury 1859, 320–21, 344–45; 1860, 324–25, 348–49; 1862, 22–23, 46–47.

4. *DeBow's Review* 1860, vol. 28, 100–101.

5. *DeBow's Review* 1858, vol. 25, 467–68.

6. Baltimore *American and Commercial Advertiser,* "Annual Statement of the Trade and Commerce of Baltimore," January 1, 1861.

7. U.S. Senate 1864, 121; Boston Board of Trade 1857–61; Baltimore *American and Commercial Advertiser,* January 2, 1860; Lindstrom 1970, 107; Philadelphia Board of Trade 1859–60, 164; 1861, 75.

8. Charleston *Daily Courier,* "Charleston Market" reports, weekly recaps for 1859–61; *Hunt's Merchants' Magazine* 1861, vol. 44, 373; Lindstrom 1970, 102, 108–10.

9. Richmond *Daily Whig,* January 7, 1861; U.S. Bureau of Statistics 1886, 266; Baltimore *American and Commercial Advertiser,* January 1, 1858; New Orleans *Price Current,* "Review of the Market," first September issue, 1855–60; U.S. Department of the Treasury 1859, 304–5, 316–19, 330–31; 1860, 308–9, 320–23, 336–37; 1862, 6–7, 18–21, 34–35.

10. Huston 1966, 215–16, 219. Donald Engels cites ten pounds of fodder and ten pounds of grain per day for horses and mules (see 1978, 18–20). For amounts of actual feed while campaigning, see Adams (1920, vol. 2, 4).

11. Hilliard 1972, 137–38; U.S. Bureau of the Census 1864, 156, 160, 164, 204–5; Richmond *Daily Whig,* January 7, 1861; New Orleans *Price Current,* September 1, 1860.

Notes to Part 2

1. Wise 1988, 26–27.

1. New Orleans *Daily Picayune* weekly reports on cattle trade and New Orleans *Daily Crescent,* August 30, September 27–28, November 9, 1861; Winters 1963, 40; Dabney 1944, 492.

2. New Orleans *Daily Crescent,* October 8, 1861; March 24–25, April 5, 19, 1862. See also March 26, April 4, 1862, for a defense of the price control.

3. OR, ser. 1, vol. 53, 801–2; New Orleans *Daily Crescent,* February 21, 1862.

4. OR, ser. 1, vol. 6, 800, 878; see also 515, 566 for Lovell's testimony at a court of inquiry in April 1863. Federal General Benjamin Butler stated that less than thirty days provisions remained in the city when he arrived (Butler 1917, vol. 2, 365–66).

5. New Orleans *Daily Crescent,* July 17, September 25, October 2, 26, 1861, March 14, 1862; Winters 1963, 53; Scharf 1887, 249; *Hunt's Merchants' Magazine* 1865, vol. 53, 253.

6. New Orleans *Daily Crescent,* December 19, 1861.

7. New Orleans *Daily Crescent,* January 17, February 5, 6, 26, 1862.

8. Owens (1990), Wright (1981), Connelly (1971) offer good analyses of the importance of western rivers for Confederate logistics.

Notes to Chapter 4

1. Davis 1923, vol. 5, 127; OR, ser. 4, vol. 1, 870–71; ser. 1, vol. 25, pt. 2, 612–13. General Northrop became one of the most reviled men in the Confederate army. He even had the temerity to deny needed supplies to Robert E. Lee. Northrop at times seemed to relish his role as Cassandra. In fairness, the task of supplying the Confederate armies was daunting. For Northrop's early efforts to get meat from the border states, see Davis 1923, vol. 5, 124; OR, ser. 4, vol. 1, 757, 870. For a detailed account of Northrop's wartime experiences, see Moore (1996).

2. OR, ser. 4, vol. 1, 873.

3. OR, ser. 1, vol. 51, pt. 2, 738; ser. 4, vol. 1, 874–79.

4. OR, ser. 4, vol. 2, 192–93. Twelve million pounds provided only 30 pounds per man if the army contained 400,000 men.

5. OR, ser. 4, vol. 2, 574; ser 1, vol. 35, pt. 2, 395. Unfortunately, the *Official Records* do not contain an estimate of the depletion.

6. OR, ser. 4, vol. 2, 574; vol. 3, 1006–1007. See also OR, ser. 1, vol. 23, pt. 2, 658, 702, 769; vol. 35, pt. 2, 431.

7. OR, ser. 1, vol. 35, pt. 2, 431.

8. Taylor 1988, 31; Lash 1991, 123, 126–27; OR, ser. 1, vol. 32, pt. 2, 565; *Confederate Records of the State of Georgia* 1910, vol. 3, 454–58; Buker 1993, 52, 144–60; ORN, ser. 1, vol. 17, 562. General Lee commented on the poor quality of the beeves delivered to his troops: "In fact, those [beeves] which we are now using are very poor on account of the difficulty of procuring good grazing, and it would save great loss if these could be retained and fattened in the spring. I

will be glad, therefore, if you will cause arrangements to be made to supply us with salt meat, of which I hope the chief commissary has enough on hand to supply the army until we can again procure beeves in proper condition for use" (OR, ser. 1, vol. 51, pt. 2, 669). A Federal expedition invaded northern Florida primarily in order to establish a loyal government of Unionists, but also to curb the movement of Florida cattle to the armies (Johns 1963, 190). However, the expedition was defeated, and Florida continued to supply moderate numbers of beeves to the Confederate armies (Eaton 1954, 284).

9. Quotes from Lonn [1933] 1965, 39; OR, ser. 4, vol. 2, 574. See also Lonn [1933] 1965, 40; Lash 1991, 124–25; OR, ser. 1, vol. 32, pt. 2, 557.

10. OR, ser. 4, vol. 2, 414, 575; ser. 1, vol. 35, pt. 1, 614–16. The standard Confederate daily ration was based upon the existing U.S. Army ration. The individual soldier was to get 12 ounces of pork or bacon or 20 pounces of fresh and/or salt beef; 18 ounces of bread or flour or 12 ounces of hard bread (or 20 ounces of corn meal); and a share of his company's (perhaps 100 men) vegetables, coffee, sugar, vinegar, tallow, salt, and soap (Goff 1969, 17–18). The announced April 28, 1862, reduction to one half pound of pork or bacon or one pound of beef was a significant reduction in the rations, and, to compensate, an additional four ounces of bread and meal per day was granted (OR, ser. 4, vol. 2, 414). General Lee balked at the scanty rations and restored the daily rations, but his action merely speeded the depletion of the meat supply. During a three-month period in early 1863, only 400,000 pounds of meat reached Lee from the South (OR, ser. 4, vol. 2, 457). By January 1863, Lee's men were reduced to *one-quarter* pound of beef per day (OR, ser. 1, vol. 21, 1110–11).

11. Schwab [1901] 1913. Lerner's nominal beef and pork prices for Augusta and Wilmington are also interesting. Augusta was on the northeast fringe of the Georgia counties with surplus meat products. Although the south central portion of Georgia did not contain any railroads, Augusta was probably as well situated to receive meat as any city in the eastern Confederacy. Wilmington, too, was in a region producing modest surpluses of meat, as well as being the entrepot for meat products smuggled through the blockade. However, pork prices were generally higher in Wilmington than in Augusta from July 1863 on (even though this was the beginning of Wilmington's ascent as a blockade-running center). A similar, though not as pronounced, phenomenon occurred for beef and bacon prices.

12. OR, ser. 1, vol. 35, pt. 2, 394; Confederate States of America 1941, 151–52.

13. OR, ser. 1, vol. 46, pt. 2, 1211, 1216–20. Of course, the paucity of funds was indirectly a legacy of the blockade's constriction of revenue from the export of southern staples.

14. OR, ser. 1, vol. 52, pt. 2, 649.

15. New Orleans *Picayune,* June 10, 15, 29, 1861; New Orleans *Price Current.*

16. Confederate States of America 1925, vol. 7, 138; OR, ser. 1, vol. 46, pt. 2, 122. See also Davis 1923, vol. 8, 580.

17. OR, ser. 3, vol. 1, 1101. For example, in November 1863, the Confederate secretary of war urged the generals commanding the departments on both sides of the Mississippi to coordinate efforts in getting cattle across the Mississippi (OR, ser. 1, vol. 53, 914). A report in a Richmond newspaper stated that 20,000 Texas cattle had crossed the Mississippi in late 1862 (Coulter 1950, 246).

18. Gard 1954, 37–38; OR, ser. 1, vol. 23, pt. 2, 759, 771; McCoy [1874] 1940, 43–44.

19. McCoy [1874] 1940, 94.

Notes to Chapter 5

1. Black 1952, 294; Vandiver 1970, 246; Ramsdell 1917, 810.

2. OR, ser. 4, vol. 1, 859, 941, 1054, 1145; ser. 4, vol. 2, 881; Coulter 1950, 271.

3. OR, ser. 4, vol. 1, 1013–14, 1073; vol. 2, 107–8. The debate in the Confederate Senate revolved around whether the proposed railroad was really a "military necessity" or an assistance to "private speculations" (*Southern Historical Society Papers,* 1925, vol. 7, 158–60).

4. OR, ser. 4, vol. 3, 1095.

5. OR, ser. 4, vol. 3, 968–69, 1053–54.

6. OR, ser. 4, vol. 2, 139, 144, 198, 200; vol. 3, 312, 576, 742; vol. 1, 944–46.

7. OR, ser. 4, vol. 2, 882. Black cites the inability to obtain chilled tires (Black 1952, 125). See also OR, ser. 4, vol. 1, 881; Johnston 1957, 320.

8. Johnston 1961, 12; 1957, 321; OR, ser. 4, vol. 1, 881; Black 1952, 125.

9. OR, ser. 4, vol. 1, 646.

10. OR, ser. 4, vol. 2, 882; vol. 3, 227–28; Johnston 1961, 13.

11. Lash 1991, 116–17; OR, ser. 4, vol. 1, 617, 634, 646.

12. OR, ser. 4, vol. 2, 485–86 (Wadley's report of April 15, 1863); Black 1952, 88, 127. For shortages of wood fuel, see OR, ser. 4, vol. 2, 551; Johnston 1961, 124, 128.

13. U.S. Department of the Treasury 1860, 461; OR, ser. 4, vol. 2, 512–13; vol. 3, 1092; Johnston 1957, 317; Black 1952, 23; Dew 1966, 152, 175, 177, 268; *Southern Historical Society Papers* 1876b, vol. 2, 121; Johnston 1961, 10.

14. *Confederate Records of the State of Georgia* 1909, vol. 2, 270–71; Black 1947, 519; Lerner 1954, 183; Bulloch 1884, vol. 1, 20; OR, ser. 1, vol. 18, 766.

15. OR, ser. 4, vol. 1, 844, 868.

16. OR, ser. 4, vol. 2, 394–95, 409, 842, 852.

17. OR, ser. 4, vol. 3, 478, 508, 514. Historians Ramsdell, Diamond, Black, and Johnston characterize the results as "trifling" and "negligible" (Ramsdell 1917, 804; Diamond 1940, 487; Black 1952, 134; Johnston 1961, 225).

18. OR, ser. 4, vol. 1, 1091–92; vol. 2, 365–66.

19. OR, ser. 4, vol. 2, 648–50; vol. 3, 560–62, 570–71.

20. Black 1952, 133.

21. OR, ser. 4, vol. 3, 9–10, 442.

22. Ringold 1966, 55; OR, ser. 4, vol. 1, 842; vol. 2, 276–77; Turner 1946, 526. See also OR, ser. 4, vol. 1, 120, 132, 224, 228, 236, 267, 269, 538; Johnston 1961, 15.

23. OR, ser. 4, vol. 3, 617.

24. Lash 1991, 108–9.

25. All of these issues deal with the allocation mechanism: market or fiat. The Confederate government chose fiat and interference, thereby wasting the invaluable resource provided by a market economy: information. The prices would have provided better clues as to the judicious allocation of resources.

26. Johnston 1961, 34, 227; OR, ser. 4, vol. 3, 643–44, 1087; ser. 1, vol. 5, 857–77; Lash 1991, 112; *Confederate Records of the State of Georgia* 1909, vol. 2, 556.

27. Stover 1955, 15–17; Derrick 1930, 222–23.

Notes to Chapter 6

1. Gorgas 1947, 222, 235; Weller 1959, 158; OR, ser. 4, vol. 1, 292 (for initial stocks of arms and munitions); vol. 2, 957 (see also page 299 in the same volume as well as vol. 3, 987); Huston 1966, 178.

2. Dew 1966, 50, 277; Bruce 1968, 390; OR, ser. 4, vol. 2, 47–48; Vandiver 1952, 93, 196. Nevins estimated that the Confederates captured 100,000 weapons during 1862 (Nevins 1959, 359).

3. OR, ser. 4, vol. 2, 227.

4. Wise 1988, 226; Weller 1959, 164, 173, 180; OR, ser. 4, vol. 1, 958; vol. 2, 52, 956; vol. 3, 930, 954–55, 987; Huston 1966, 178; Vandiver 1952, 93.

5. Vandiver 1947, Part 2; Chandler 1977, 199–200; OR, ser. 2, vol. 1, 1108; Donnelly 1956.

6. ORN, ser. 1, vol. 21, 600; Still 1971, 44, 97–98, 144. Confederate naval officers tested armor plating (ORN, ser. 2, vol. 1, 785–86). The hope was to cover the vessels with two two-inch thick layers of iron (one layer perpendicular and the other horizontal). Indeed, Secretary of the Navy Mallory hoped to cover the vessels with three-inch plate, but the Southern mills were unable to roll this thickness.

7. ORN, ser. 2, vol. 2, 184. At least one expert on the Confederate navy believes that Bulloch's idea was feasible and astute (Wells 1971, 136). However, Raimondo Luraghi disagrees (Luraghi 1996, 203).

8. Spencer 1983, 67. Because the Laird rams and the warship under Commander North's administration needed to traverse the Atlantic, they were larger than the ironclads constructed in the South; however, their size made them inoperable in most of the shallow coastal waters.

9. Luraghi 1996, 189–90.

10. OR, ser. 2, vol. 3, 357; Hill 1926, 343.

Notes to Chapter 7

1. ORN, ser. 2, vol. 3, 884–85. Mobile imported only $208,000 worth of goods between May 1862 and April 1863 (Bergeron 1991, 121).

2. Corsan [1863] 1996, 65.

3. Wright 1981.

4. Lerner 1954. Schwab's price index for the entire Confederacy makes a similar point (Schwab [1901] 1913).

5. Corsan [1863] 1996, 63; Ekelund and Thornton 1992.

6. Lebergott 1983, 867, 873, 884.

7. Quote from Davis 1966, vol. 1, 143. Luraghi (1978) describes Southern industrialization; Massey [1952] 1993; Ball 1991, 113–19; Hill 1926, 339, 349, 375.

8. Power 1998, 217; Ramsdell 1944, 30–31, 50–56, 113; Beringer, et al. 1986, 20–34.

Notes to Chapter 8

1. Ramsdell 1944, 98–99, also 1930, 764; Gorgas 1947, 91–92; Moore 1996, 225–26.

2. OR, ser. 4, vol. 1, 885; Goff 1969, 154–55.

3. OR, ser. 4, vol. 2, 510.

4. Lash 1991, 27–31; Early [1960] 1989, 55.

5. OR, ser. 4, vol. 1, 859, 912.

6. OR, ser. 4, vol. 2, 175–76, 385–86; vol. 3, 392; Black 1952, 227; Price 1961, 305.

7. OR, ser. 4, vol. 1, 394, 405–6, 485–86.

8. OR, ser. 4, vol. 2, 486. James F. Rhodes believes that Wadley's estimates are too high (Rhodes [1904] 1920, 385). See also *Southern Historical Society Papers* 1877, vol. 3, 100.

9. OR, ser. 1, vol. 29, pt. 1, 227–28; ser. 4, vol. 2, 486; Johnston 1961, 181; Black 1952, 198.

10. Schwab [1901] 1913, 276.

11. OR, ser. 1, vol. 46, pt. 2, 1297; also vol. 29, pt. 2, 656; vol. 35, pt. 2, 395; vol. 46, pt. 2, 1297; Ramsdell 1944, 43–44; Bryan 1953, 122.

12. OR, ser. 4, vol. 2, 970; vol. 3, 941, 955. Apparently the Confederate Commissary Department was averse to wasting even rotten meat. One Confederate veteran reminisced that Commissary-General Northrop refused to discard "rotten, putrid bacon called 'Nassau (because it had spoiled on the docks there while awaiting blockade-runners),'" and supplied it to the troops. However, the veteran admitted that the soldiers eventually "so vitiated in our taste by eating it that at last we came to prefer it to good bacon, and like the strong rancid taste" (Johns 1866, 498). In fairness to Northrop, soldiers' complaints about food recur in almost every war. In the Spanish-American War, there was a congressional investigation into General Nelson Miles' complaints about the quality of meat shipped to his troops.

13. OR, ser. 4, vol. 2, 956–60.

14. OR, ser. 4, vol. 2, 457; vol. 3, 261–62; ser. 1, vol. 21, 1110; vol. 35, pt. 1, 614–16; vol. 42, pt. 1, 944–47; vol. 46, pt. 2, 1075–77; Goff 1969, 167; Lebergott 1983, 72; Lee 1915, 307–8; Davis 1923, vol. 6, 416–18.

15. See Jones [1866] 1935, vol. 1, 284–86; Davis 1890, vol. 2, 373–76; Chesson 1984, 131–75.

16. OR, ser. 1, vol. 29, pt. 2, 664–65; Ramsdell 1930, 773; Heth 1877, 153; McCrady 1885, 13; Goff 1969, 74, 196; Lee 1915, 246–47.

17. OR, ser. 1, vol. 33, 1114; vol. 46, pt. 2, 1143; Lee 1915, 72; Jones [1866] 1935, vol. 2, 187–90; Lee 1961, 616–17, 696–97.

18. *Southern Historical Society Papers* 1876a, vol. 2, 93–95, 100; OR, ser. 1, vol. 46, pt. 2, 1297–98.

19. New York *Price Current,* daily cargo manifests; Heyl 1953–54, various volumes for descriptions of the vessels.

Notes to Chapter 9

1. The elasticity of demand for American-grown raw cotton was more elastic than the world demand for *all* raw cotton (econometric evidence shows this to be 0.5 to 0.6); the greater elasticity of world demand for American-grown raw cotton than that for all raw cotton reflected the increased supply of non-American grown raw cotton in response to higher raw cotton prices (East Indian raw cotton could be diverted from domestic consumption or from exports to Japan and China to Europe).

2. The point of tangency will not occur at the maximum revenue. If it did occur there, the probability of victory isoquant would be at its "minimum," i.e. the slope would be horizontal (to correspond with the horizontal slope of the total revenue at the maximum). Therefore, the optimal mix will occur to the right of the maximum total revenue accruing to the South.

3. London *Times,* October 21, 1861, 6; H. Jones 1992; Vanauken 1989, 49.

4. It took 550,000 man-years to grow 5 million bales. Reducing the crop from 4,590,500 to 3,050,000 would free up (550,000/5,000,000) x (1,540,500) = 169,455 man-years (Fogel and Engerman 1992a, 301 ftn. 34). In addition, such a crop reduction would reduce the labor needed to process and transport raw cotton to southern ports. U.S. Senate, *Report of the Secretary of the Navy,* 1859–60, 19–20; U.S. Senate, *Report of the Secretary of War,* 1859–60, 213.

5. *DeBow's Review* 1849, vol. 7, 74; 1852, vol. 12, 276–77; 1852, vol. 13, 64, 294. During one debate, a delegate to the Montgomery commercial convention of 1858 took exception to another delegate's belief that the smaller the output of raw cotton, the greater the profit [revenue]. The disagreeing delegate claimed if reducing output raised profits, why not produce only one bale (Wender 1930, vol. 48, 642).

6. *DeBow's Review* 1851, vol. 11, 638–39. DeBow clearly thought that the slaves could easily be switched from raising cotton to other pursuits. For a discussion of prospective southern cotton textile mills, see *DeBow's Review* 1852, vol. 12, 279; 1852, vol. 13, 64–65; 1849, vol. 7, 50, 485; 1861, vol. 30, 558–60; vol. 31, 305–313; *Confederate Records of the State of Georgia* 1909–10, vol. 1, 52; Confederate States of America [1904] 1968, 915; Lee 1963, 182.

7. Todd 1954, 125–27; Cobb 1907, pt. 1, 184; pt. 2, 238, 244.

8. Ball 1991, 10–17; Davis 1994, 189, 198.

1. Davis 1992, vol. 7, 23; Phillips 1905, 273–75.
2. Jones, H. 1992, 45; Vanauken 1989, 49.
3. Arnold 1864, 42–44, 47, 80, 170.
4. Brady 1963, 162; Dunham 1928, 292–93; Owsley 1931, 153.
5. Farnie 1979, 140.
6. Wright 1978, 95–97.
7. Wright 1974, 632; Hanson 1979.
8. Mann 1860, 89. Suppose production followed a Cobb-Douglas equation with $Q=C^aL^bK^c$, where C=raw cotton, L=labor, and K=capital. If a=0.5, b=0.25, and c=0.25, then a doubling of the price of raw cotton raises costs by 41 percent in the short-run in a perfectly competitive market (see Fogel and Engerman 1971, 152). It would increase by 41 percent only if the proportions between the factors of production were *fixed,* and, of course, the proportions between the factors of production would not be fixed. First, producers could shift towards cheaper raw materials. Producers could also adulterate their product by "sizing"- mixing flour and other ingredients with the cotton (*Economist,* September 27, 1862). Second, with less raw cotton, the demand for labor would fall and wages would be depressed (or the least-efficient workers would be released, raising the marginal product of labor), offsetting part of the increase in raw cotton prices.
9. Hammond 1897, 291; *Economist,* January 4, 1862, 4.
10. *Economist,* June 14, September 6, 1862. Although the *Economist* lamented the loss of the German market (February 2, 1862), Sandberg's data shows only a modest falling off in cotton goods exports to Germany in 1861 and this may have been the result of growing German textile production (Sandberg 1974, 254–61). Clapham notes that German textile production was increasing rapidly during the 1850–75 period (Clapham [1921] 1961, 295). The rest of Europe increased its consumption of Lancashire goods between 1860 and 1861, but was also expanding its textile production. Henderson described the growing Russian textile industry (Henderson 1933, 198–203). See also Heywood 1977, 11.
11. Of course, we would need to examine the sales figures for other cotton textile-producing countries to definitively state that world demand was essentially stationary in 1861.
12. Forwood 1870, Table C; Dunham 1928, 303; Tyson 1968, 103. Wood (1910, 131) shows that the real wage of cotton textile workers slumped only slightly during the Civil War before rebounding in 1864 and 1865. However, since over half the workers were either unemployed or underemployed during the Civil War, the real income of these workers was probably reduced. In addition, British consumption of cotton textile products could be affected by the price of foodstuffs and the weather. Farnie blamed the downturn in the "fancy goods" sector on cold weather and famine (Farnie 1979, 138).

13. Great Britain *Statistical Abstract for the United Kingdom,* [1867] 1965, 64–67, 70–71, 74–75. Great Britain's imports of flax and wool increased during the Civil War. These increased imports helped suppress the price increases of flax and wool. Helm presented figures showing that while cotton prices averaged 158 percent higher during 1862–68 than 1855–61, flax and hemp prices rose only 10 percent and wool 25 percent between these periods (Helm 1869, 428–37). For per-capita domestic consumption of cotton goods, see Dunham 1928, 303; Tyson 1968, 103.

14. *Hunt's Merchants' Magazine* 1863, vol. 49, 360; Clark 1929, vol. 2, 31; Watkins 1908, 30.

15. Forwood 1870, Table C. Mulhall ([1898] 1903) listed 42.6 million English statute miles of cotton cloth production during the 1850s and 42.4 million miles during the 1860s. British production amounted to 41.1 percent of the total during the 1850s and 38.4 percent during the 1860s. The world's output during the 1870s increased to 70.1 million miles (Britain's share rose to 41.8 percent). For GDP changes, see Bairoch 1976, 279; Feinstein 1972, Table 1; Jostock 1955, 82; Maddison 1982, Table A4; Mitchell 1983, 898; Berry 1968; Gallman 1966; Saini 1969, 262.

16. Much of the world still awaited improvements in transportation that would enable it to consume cheap cotton manufactures. There was, indeed, a huge untapped reservoir of demand.

17. *Economist,* January 4, 1862, 4; Donnell 1872, 518–19; Brady 1963, 157.

18. Donnell 1872, Liverpool Reports for 1860, 1861.

19. Brady 1963, 157; Yang 1992, 270.

20. An alternative procedure giving similar results is to compare the ending stock with the long-term trend consumption path. Comparing this level of consumption to the actual stock yields similar estimates of the relative stock during the Civil War as that yielded by the three-year average consumption of raw cotton. The ending 1862 stock was good for just over ten and a half weeks of consumption at the long-term trend consumption level. The number of spindles in cotton factories increased between 1861 and 1865 (Great Britain Parliamentary Papers 1862; Forwood 1870, 372).

21. Donnell 1872. The general price trend during 1861 was downward, at a rate of 4–5 percent for the year. Thus, the nominal prices slightly understate the increase in real raw cotton prices.

22. Cassels 1862, 299; Hammond 1897, 274; Harnetty 1972, 44; Royle 1851, 24. A regression using the rate of change in consumption of American cotton as the independent variable and the rate of change in consumption of Indian cotton as the dependent variable yielded a coefficient of -1.376 (with an R^2 of .46).

23. Great Britain *Statistical Abstract for the United Kingdom,* [1867] 1965, 58–59; Wright 1974, 616–18; Hansen and Nashashibi 1975, 147–48.

24. Harnetty 1972, 54; *Times of India,* January 1868. One final surge in acreage occurred in 1864–65 when acreage totaled 7.8 million (from 4.5 million in

1860–61). Acreage diminished quickly after the war, although it rebounded in 1869–70.

25. Great Britain *Statistical Abstract for the United Kingdom,* [1867] 1965, 58–59.

26. All quotes from (London) *Times,* August 14, 1862, 12; see also Great Britain *India Office* 1863, 224.

27. Mulhall [1898] 1903, 156.

Notes to Chapter 11

1. Owsley claims that the official English trade records are biased downwards, as much American cotton arrived via Nassau or other Caribbean ports and that this cotton was counted as originating from "Other Countries" (Owsley 1931, 287; *Economist,* May 21, 1864). Owsley believes this caused an undercount of 170,000 bales of American cotton. Although this is true (one needs to add the Bermuda/Bahamas and Mexico cotton imports to the American imports to get the "true" level of imports of Southern cotton), when comparing Hammond, Ellison and Donnell's figures with the revised *Statistical Abstract of the United Kingdom,* there are only minor differences. It appears they were familiar with this quirk in the official data and adjusted for it; see also Owsley 1931, 289; Lebergott 1981, 880–82.

2. Lebergott 1983, 883.

3. Lebergott 1981, 869. The New Orleans/New York price differential was due partly to the increased shipping costs for Northern shippers in the face of Confederate commerce raiders, but also to the imposition of taxes at New Orleans (Futrell 1950, 446).

4. Douglas Ball has a good discussion of the Confederacy's inability to make cotton bonds popular (1991, 132–34). Daniel Hill discusses North Carolina's partially successful attempt in using cotton-based bonds as a form of credit (1926, 349).

5. Capers 1893, 349.

6. Goldin and Lewis 1975, 308.

Notes to Chapter 12

1. New Orleans *Price Current,* September 1, 1860.

2. *Hunt's Merchants' Magazine* 1861, vol. 45, 501.

3. Owsley 1931, 260; New Orleans *Price Current,* September 1, 1860, 1861; New Orleans *Daily Crescent,* August 1, October 1, 1861. The U.S.S. *Brooklyn* arrived at Pass a l'Outre on May 26, 1861, to blockade the Mississippi. The U.S.S. *Powhatan* arrived off Southwest Pass on May 30, 1861, to bolster the blockade (ORN, ser. 1, vol. 4, 187–89).

4. ORN, ser. 1, vol. 16, 629; Fleming [1905] 1949, 183, 191; OR, ser. 4, vol. 2, 21.

5. Lebergott estimated that the average sailing vessel carried 76 500–pound bales of cotton out of Charleston and 130 500–pound bales out of all other Southern ports. He estimated that the average steamer carried 590 500–pound bales out of Charleston and 554 500–pound bales out of all other Southern ports (Leber-

gott 1981, 880). Table 12.3 converts these into 400–pound bales to correspond with the data presented in Chapter 11. The trade, in terms of value, was export-dominated; customhouse statistics revealed that between May 1862 and April 1863, the value of exports was more than eight times that of imports (Bergeron 1991, 121).

6. Fleming [1905] 1949, 187, 286; Bergeron 1991, 196–97; Wise 1988, 181.

7. Price 1948, 1949, 1951, 1952, 1955. A statement of the commerce of the port of Charleston with foreign countries lends credence to this estimate. For the period October 1, 1861, through March 30, 1863, 14.5 million pounds of raw cotton (roughly 36,000 bales) were exported to foreign countries (OR, ser. 4, vol. 2, 562; ORN, ser. 2, vol. 3, 884–85). My estimates show 52,000 bales for this time period.

8. Futrell 1950, 179; Johnson 1985, 65; *Hunt's Merchants' Magazine* 1860, vol. 42, 480–82.

9. U.S. House of Representatives 1864–65c, 122, 126; see also the testimony of John R. Winslow (page 24).

10. Johnson 1985, 76–78; U.S. House of Representatives 1864–65c, 126, 132; see also testimony of Major L. L. Stackpole (144); OR, ser. 1, vol. 29, pt. 1, 478; Futrell 1950, 408–9.

11. U.S. House of Representatives 1864–65c, 59.

12. OR, ser. 1, vol. 17, pt. 2, 272–75, 861; Sherman 1875, 267. Echoing Sherman, Washburn more forcefully lamented the deleterious effects of the trade: "Memphis has been of more value to the Southern Confederacy since it fell into Federal hands than Nassau" (OR, ser. 1, vol. 39, pt. 2, 22). Nassau was a major staging point for European and New York contraband to be run through the blockade into Wilmington and Charleston. See also *Congressional Globe* 1864, 3324.

13. Irby 1977, 52. For wagon shortage, see OR, ser. 1, vol. 20, 741–42.

14. U.S. House of Representatives, 1864–65c, 79–80. Benjamin Camp was a New York farmer turned cotton trader. He originally opened a store in Memphis and then became involved in trading cotton (ibid., 74–75).

15. U.S. House of Representatives, 1864–65c, 79–80. In some ways the Texans' attitude mirrored that of the New Englanders in the War of 1812, who freely traded with the British and were lukewarm about United States policies. Tyler 1970, 463; Ellis 1973, 209–10; Lea 1957, 195, 222; Irby 1977, 44.

16. Stillman was discussed in the Congressional Investigation of New York Customs House (U.S. House of Representatives, 1864–65b). Although suspected of trading in contraband and investigated by a congressional committee, he was never convicted.

17. Great Britain *Statistical Abstract for the United Kingdom,* [1867] 1965, 58–59; Daddysman 1984, 160; Owsley 1931, 263. An estimated 1.6 to 1.9 million bales was shipped from the South during the war.

18. Watson 1892, 142; OR, ser. 1, vol. 9, 642–43; Daddysman 1984, 34; Chase 1903, 427–29.

19. OR, ser. 1, vol. 46, pt. 2, 1035, 1039–40, 1075; ser. 4, vol. 3, 955; Lamb 1884, vol. 4, 642.

20. ORN, ser. 1, vol. 6, 11–12; Gragg 1991, 12; *Hunt's Merchants' Magazine,* 1861, vol. 45, 18.

21. OR, ser. 4, vol. 2, 486–87; Trotter 1989, 301; Wise 1988, 218.

22. OR, ser. 1, vol. 52, pt. 2, 585–86, 593.

23. Yearns and Barrett 1980, 76–78; Drysdale 1977, 377; Gorgas 1947, 137; Hill 1926, 380; Wise 1988, 191–92; Wilmington *Journal,* various quarterly reports; *Hunt's Merchants' Magazine* 1858, vol. 39, 603; 1859, vol. 41, 469; 1860, vol. 43, 507; 1861, vol. 45, 498.

24. Two prominent Confederate political leaders, Vice President Alexander Stephens and Robert Toombs, discussed the possibility of the government purchasing raw cotton early in 1861 (Davis 1994, 301, 348). Jefferson Davis received letters from planters throughout the Confederacy urging government purchase of cotton (Davis 1992, vol. 7, 230, 236, 312, 367). The Confederate government launched a produce loan early in the war. Planters were able to obtain bonds by pledging raw cotton (*DeBow's Review,* 1862, vol. 7, 328). Bettersworth discusses Mississippians' support for government purchase of cotton (Bettersworth 1943, 96, 109).

25. Jefferson Davis had personal reason to lament the disruptions in the valley. His plantation, Brierfield, was on the Mississippi River near Vicksburg. He left the plantation in the hands of a trusted slave, Ben Montgomery. His older brother, Joseph, had a larger plantation on the Mississippi. Agreeing not to export raw cotton in late 1861, Joseph Davis attempted to ship part of his large inventory of raw cotton up the Big Black River when he was forced to flee after the fall of New Orleans and the first attack against Vicksburg, but all of his efforts were in vain. Davis lost over 840 bales of cotton. Jefferson Davis's bales were burned, too. The elder Davis had appealed to Jefferson to intervene with the local military authorities and prevent them from burning his cotton. Naturally, such attempts attracted the ire of neighbors who saw their own cotton being burned. Jefferson Davis was unable to intervene in time to save the cotton (Hermann 1990, 105).

26. Bettersworth 1943, 15; Dougan 1976, 33–34, 55–56, 72–73.

27. OR, ser. 1, vol. 32, pt. 3, 625; vol. 52, pt. 2, 387–88, 493; vol. 53, 836–37; ser. 4, vol. 3, 709; Tatum 1934, 25–26, 35; Dougan 1976, 73–74, 83–86, 106–7, 110; Bettersworth 1943, 207.

28. OR, ser. 1, vol. 48, pt. 1, 1316, vol. 39, pt. 3, 860.

29. OR, ser. 1, vol. 31, pt. 3, 833–34.

30. OR, ser. 1, vol. 39, pt. 2, 725–26.

Notes to Chapter 13

1. The burden of the export duty also depends upon the elasticities of demand and supply. Usually, if supply is less elastic than demand (in absolute value),

suppliers of raw cotton bear a greater share of the burden. From the Federal government's viewpoint, it was desirable that the growers bear more of the burden of the export duty. However, if the Confederate government was levying the duty (as suggested in previous chapters), that government could mitigate the burden by giving growers rebates.

2. U.S. House of Representatives 1864–65c, 73–74. For other descriptions of taxes on raw cotton, see 87, 118; Futrell 1950, 425–26.
3. Schuckers 1874, 319.
4. OR, ser. 1, vol. 17, pt. 2, 272–75, 861.
5. OR, ser. 1, vol. 45, pt. 2, 639.
6. OR, ser. 1, vol. 46, pt. 2, 1075.
7. OR, ser. 1, vol. 46, pt. 2, 1075; Lee 1915, 328–29.
8. OR, ser. 4, vol. 3, 588–89; see 525–29 in the same volume for the contract. Of course, Trenholm is ignoring the fact that the Confederate government would face high transportation costs in smuggling its 5,000 bales overseas. See Davis's thoughts in OR, ser. 4, vol. 2, 151.
9. OR, ser. 1, vol. 39, pt. 2, 584; vol. 46, pt. 2, 1075.
10. Powell and Wayne 1983, 35. E. Merton Coulter expresses similar views regarding interbelligerent trade (Coulter 1919, 387–93).
11. Lincoln 1953, vol. 8, 163–64. Atkinson's argument implicitly assumed close to unitary elasticity of demand; of course, in such a case, reducing the price would do little to reduce Confederate revenues. For Atkinson's influence on Lincoln, see Futrell 1950, 417; Welles 1911, vol. 2, 66–67. Lincoln expressed different thoughts on the trade to individuals seeking permits to trade; he emphasized that trade would resume when residents accepted "the national authority" (Lincoln 1953, vol. 5, 345–46; vol. 6, 307). Lincoln occasionally intervened to have permits issued to associates (Lincoln 1953, vol. 8, 35). Jefferson Davis thought that the Federals were partially motivated by the need to defend their currency (see New York *Times,* July 29, 1865; Pollard 1866, 482; Davis 1923, vol. 8, 183, 432; Johnson 1970, 314). See also Futrell 1950, 133, 458; OR, ser. 1, vol. 17, pt. 2, 186.
12. Futrell 1950, 458; Hammond 1897, 264; Atkinson 1863, 1; Watkins 1908, 30.
13. U.S. House of Representatives 1865–66, Appendix 3; Watkins 1908, 30; Donnell 1872.
14. OR, ser. 1, vol. 52, pt. 1, 331. Chase also unveiled his new policy on April 13, 1864, while further explaining why the previous system had failed (U.S. House of Representatives 1864–65a, 2).
15. Jordan 1958, 21; Adams 1915, 214; London *Times,* March 22, 1861, 9; Ferris 1976.
16. London *Quarterly Review* 1865, vol. 23, 334–35.
17. *Economist,* August 10, 1861.
18. Jefferson Davis, too, believed that the North needed to insure that Europeans received enough cotton to deter them from intervening (Davis 1881, vol. 2, 344–45). Other Cabinet members hoped for a port seizure (see Bates 1933, 195).

For discussion of Seward's policies, see Welles 1911, vol. 1, 79–80, 167, 283, 304, 334–35, 339–40; Crook 1974, 97, 197; Bates 1933, 414, 427.

19. Schmidt 1918; Adams 1925; Owsley 1931; Ginzburg 1936; Ferris 1976; Blumenthal 1966; Crook 1974; Henderson 1969; Lester 1975.

20. Bates 1933, 264–66. Although the Union army occupied Norfolk in 1862, Lincoln lifted the blockade against Norfolk only in November 1864 (Lincoln 1953, vol. 8, 115). He announced the lifting of the blockade with the following hopes: "It is hoped that foreign manufacturers will now consider whether it is not safer and more profitable to themselves, as well as just to the United States, to resort to these and other open ports, than it is to pursue, through many hazards, and at vast cost, a contraband trade with other ports which are closed, if not by actual military occupation, at least by a lawful and effective blockade" (ibid., 140).

21. Lincoln [1946] 1969, 617.

22. Lincoln 1953, vol. 4, 290, 292, 293.

23. Winters 1963, 325; Johnson 1958. Porter, himself, disliked the interbelligerent trade, claiming that the treasury agents were easily bribed. However, he, too, had a plan for regulating the cotton trade (OR, ser. 1, vol. 31, pt. 1, 780–81).

24. Futrell 1950, 272–73.

25. U.S. House of Representatives 1866–67, 5–6.

26. Futrell 1950, 83–85; Chase 1954, 143–44; OR, ser. 1, vol. 17, pt. 2, 140–41; ser. 3, vol. 2, 349.

27. Bates 1933, 404–5. Treasury agent George Denison recommended a different plan to Chase (see Chase 1903, vol. 2, 401–2). Chase 1954, 164; Futrell 1950, 87, 93, 421–25; Johnson 1963, 636; U.S. House of Representatives 1864–65c, 164–65; Lincoln 1953, vol. 8, 20.

28. OR, ser. 1, vol. 41, pt. 4, 1025–26, 1093; Futrell 1950, 422–23. See also Abraham Lincoln 1953, vol. 8, 20–21, for one-third rule. For the results of the purchasing acts, see U.S. House of Representatives 1866–67, 6. Lincoln's thoughts are in Futrell 1950, 421–22. There was a slight difference between the Treasury Department's rules for government purchasing agents (paying one-fourth of the proceeds at the time of purchase) and Lincoln's executive order (paying one-third of the proceeds); both sets of rules were issued on September 24, 1864 (U.S. House of Representatives 1864–65c, 164, 167).

29. Beringer et al. 1986, 201.

30. O'Conner 1961, 35; Nicolay and Hay [1886] 1890, vol. 4, 76.

31. U.S. House of Representatives 1864–65c, 1–2.

32. Rhodes [1904] 1920, 420.

33. Lincoln [1946] 1969, 617.

Notes to Chapter 14

1. Silverstone 1989, ix; "List of Union Ships" in ORN, ser. 2, vol. 1, 15–23; U.S. Senate 1879–80, 2; Fox [1889] 1893, 537; Livermore 1900, 1. The expenditures

on the navy "growing out of the war" were $411 million, while there was an additional $156 million in "expenditures on the navy other than for the war." The bulk of the latter expenditures were on pay of naval personnel.

2. Turner (1988) and Willoughby (1993) discuss the Apalachicola region and its potential for supplying the Confederate armies.

Notes to Appendix 1

1. OR, ser. 4, vol. 1, 875. Moore describes the fifth quarter as including hides and hooves (Moore 1996, 89). In addition, Ruffin estimated that these hogs would supply 53 percent of their live weight as bacon (OR, ser. 4, vol. 2, 192–93). See also Genovese [1961] 1965, 109–115; Battalio and Kagel 1970, 29, 36–37; Gallman 1970, 12–16; U.S. Department of Agriculture 1862, 332; Dobie 1941, 34; Allen [1868] 1875, 177; McCoy [1874] 1940, 147; New Orleans *Price Current,* "Jefferson City Livestock Market" (weekly report); *Hunt's Merchants' Magazine* 1862, vol. 46, 542–43; OR, ser. 4, vol. 1, 875.

2. U.S. Patent Office 1850, vol. 2, 138; Gallman 1970, 15, footnote 24; U.S. Department of Agriculture 1864, 265; Jordan 1903, 97; Morrison [1898] 1943, 807, 810.

Notes to Appendix 2

1. Using the demand function $Q^D = 12,000 - 143.86714P + 0.5111959P^2$ generates TR(South)$=-72,000 + 12,863.20284P - 146.93432P^2 - (P - 6)BS$, where BS = Beginning Stock. If another intercept, "a," is chosen for the demand function, the TR(South) is altered slightly. For a = 12,500, TR(South) is greater for any given price under the demand function listed above; for a = 11,000, TR(South) is smaller for any given price under the demand function listed above. The differences are relatively small for prices less than $65; for prices greater than $65, the differences begin to widen dramatically.

2. The actual beginning 1861–62 stock was just over 800,000 bales. The 900,000–bale figure used in the discussion was chosen to provide a conservative estimate of the revenue accruing to the South.

Notes to Appendix 3

1. Lebergott 1981, 869. The transportation costs between blockaded Southern ports and New York also escalated rapidly. The transportation costs between Federal-controlled New Orleans and Northern ports increased, but not as rapidly as the costs between blockaded ports and European ports or New York.

2. Wright 1974, 630–32; Hanson 1979, 1019.

Notes to Appendix 4

1. Cassels 1862, 34; Silver 1966, 163.

Notes to Appendix 5

1. Hanson 1979, 1017.
2. Wright 1974, 628–30. Wright's estimate of price elasticity of world demand for American-grown raw cotton was based on running the regression with quantity first as an independent variable and then as a dependent variable. The 0.8 elasticity estimate fell between the estimates found with quantity as the dependent variable (roughly 0.3) and with quantity as the independent variable (roughly 1.1). Wright believes that measurement errors in the quantity variable probably biased both of the above estimates and felt that the actual elasticity was between 0.75 and 1.0 (Wright 1971, 117; 1974, 628–30; 1978, 92–93).
3. The t-ratios are in parentheses. The equation using Liverpool prices had slightly different coefficients (-0.939 for the quantity and 0.049 for the trend). The adjusted R^2 is calculated as follows:

Adjusted $R^2 = 1 - [(N - 1)/(N - k)](1 - R^2)$

where N = number of observations and k = number of independent variables.
4. The equation using Liverpool prices:

Liverpool Price = 345.65 - 22.813Ln(US Total Bales) + 1.176(Trend)
           (3.723) (-3.445)   (3.149)

with an adjusted R^2 of 0.2830.

Bibliography

Primary Sources

Adams, Charles Francis Jr. 1920. *A Cycle of Adams Letters, 1861–1865.* 2 vols. Edited by W. C. Ford. Boston: Houghton Mifflin.

Bates, Edward. 1933. "Diary of Edward Bates, 1859–1866." In *The Annual Report of the American Historical Association for the Year 1930.* Vol. 4. Edited by Howard K. Beale. Washington, D.C.: GPO.

Butler, General Benjamin F. 1917. *Private and Official Correspondence of Gen. Benjamin F. Butler.* 5 vols. Norwood, Mass.: Plimpton Press,

Chase, Salmon P. 1903. "Diary and Correspondence of Salmon P. Chase—Letters from George S. Denison to Chase, 1862–1865," In *Annual Report of the American Historical Association for the Year 1902.* Vol. 2. Washington: GPO.

———. 1954. *Inside Lincoln's Cabinet: The Civil War Diaries of Salmon P. Chase.* Edited by David Donald. New York: Longmans, Green.

Cobb, Thomas R. R. 1907. "The Correspondence of Thomas Reade Rootes Cobb, 1860–62," *Publications of the Southern History Association* 11:147–85, 233–60, 312–28.

Davis, Jefferson. 1923. *Jefferson Davis, Constitutionalist: His Letters, Papers and Speeches.* 10 vols. Edited by Dunbar Rowland. Jackson: Mississippi Department of Archives and History.

———. 1966. *Messages and Papers of Jefferson Davis and the Confederacy.* 2 vols. Edited by James D. Richardson. New York: Chelsea House-Robert Hector.

———. 1992. *The Papers of Jefferson Davis.* Vol. 7, 1861. Edited by Lynda Lasswell Crist and Mary Seaton Dix. Baton Rouge: Louisiana State University Press.

Gorgas, General Josiah. 1947. *The Civil War Diary of General Josiah Gorgas.* Edited by Frank E. Vandiver. Tuscaloosa: University of Alabama Press.

Jones, John B. [1866] 1935. *A Rebel War Clerk's Diary at the Confederate States Capital.* 2 vols. New York: Old Hickory Bookshop.

Lee, Robert E. 1915. *Lee's Dispatches—Unpublished Letters of General Robert E. Lee.* Edited by Douglas S. Freeman. New York: G.P. Putnam's & Sons.

———. 1961. *The Wartime Papers of Robert E. Lee.* Edited by Clifford Dowdey and Louis Manarin. Boston: Little, Brown.

Lincoln, Abraham. [1946] 1969. *Abraham Lincoln: His Speeches and Writings.* Edited by Roy P. Basler. New York: Kraus Reprint.

———. 1953. *The Collected Works of Abraham Lincoln.* Edited by Roy P. Basler. 8 vols. New Brunswick: Rutgers University Press.

Sherman, General William T. 1875. *Memoirs of General William Tecumseh Sherman.* 2 vols. New York: D. Appleton.

Welles, Gideon. 1911. *Diary of Gideon Welles, Secretary of the Navy under Lincoln and Johnson.* 3 vols. Boston: Houghton Mifflin.

Government Documents

Confederate Records of the State of Georgia. 1909–11. 6 vols. Edited by Allen D. Candler. Atlanta: Chas. P. Byrd.

Confederate States of America. [1904] 1968. *Journal of the Congress of the Confederate States of America, 1861–1865.* New York: Kraus Reprint.

Confederate States of America. 1925. "Proceedings of the First Confederate Congress." In *Southern Historical Society Papers.* New Series 7.

Confederate States of America. 1941. *Laws and Joint Resolutions of the Last Session of the Confederate Congress.* Edited by Charles W. Ramsdell. Durham: Duke University Press.

Congressional Globe. 1858. 35th Cong., 1st Sess., pt. 1.

Congressional Globe. 1864. 38th Cong., 1st Sess., pt. 4.

Congressional Globe. 1865. 38th Cong., 2nd Sess., pt. 2.

Great Britain. *Parliamentary Papers.* "Factory Reports." 1862 Session (House of Commons), Vol. 55, 69.

Great Britain. *India Office.* East India (Cotton). "Return to an Address of the Honourable, the House of Commons, Dated 10 Feb. 1863."

Great Britain. [1867] 1965. *Statistical Abstract for the United Kingdom.* Vol. 18 (1856–70). Reprint. London: Kraus Reprint.

U.S. Bureau of the Census. 1862. *Preliminary Report on the Eighth Census.* Washington: GPO.

U.S. Bureau of the Census. 1864. *Eighth Census—Agriculture.* Washington D.C.: GPO.

U.S. Bureau of the Census. 1865. *Eighth Census—Manufacturing.* Washington D.C.: GPO.

U.S. Bureau of the Census. 1883. *Tenth Census—Agriculture.* "Report on Cattle, Sheep, and Swine." Prepared by Clarence W. Gordon. Washington D.C.: GPO.

U.S. Bureau of Statistics (Treasury Department). 1886. "Internal Commerce of the United States." Washington, D.C.: GPO.

U.S. Bureau of Statistics (Treasury Department). 1900. "Cotton Trade of the United States and the World's Cotton Supply and Trade." *Monthly Summary of Commerce and Finance.* No. 9 Ser. 1899–1900 (March 1900).

U.S. Bureau of Statistics (Treasury Department). 1900. "The Grain Trade of the United States." *Monthly Summary of Commerce and Finance.* No. 7, Ser. 1899–1900. Washington D.C.: GPO.

U.S. Congress. 1865. *Light-Draught Monitors. Report of the Joint Committee on the Conduct of the War.* Vol. 3. 38th Congress, 2nd Sess. Washington D.C.: GPO.

U.S. Department of Agriculture. 1907. *Bureau of Statistics—Bulletin.* "Costs of Hauling Crops from Farms to Shipping Points." Frank Andrews. 49. Washington D.C.: GPO.

United States. Department of the Navy. 1894–1922. *Official Records of the Union and Confederate Navies in the War of Rebellion.* 30 vols. Washington D.C.: GPO. Denoted as ORN.

U.S. Department of State. 1934. *Policy of the United States towards Maritime Commerce in War.* Prepared by Carlton Savage. Washington D.C.: GPO.

U.S. Department of the Treasury. 1859. *Report of the Secretary of the Treasury— Commerce and Navigation, for the Year ending June 30, 1859.* 36th Cong., 1st Sess.

U.S. Department of the Treasury. 1860. *Report of the Secretary of the Treasury— Commerce and Navigation, for the Year ending June 30, 1860.* 36th Cong., 2nd Sess., Sen. Exec. Doc. 8. Washington D.C.: GPO.

U.S. Department of the Treasury. 1862. *Report of the Secretary of the Treasury— Commerce and Navigation, for the Year ending June 30, 1861.* 37th Cong., 2nd Sess.

U.S. House of Representatives. 1864–65a. *Captured and Abandoned Property in Insurrectionary States.* House Miscellaneous Document No. 78. 38th Cong., 1st Sess. Washington, D.C.: GPO.

U.S. House of Representatives. 1864–65b. *New York Custom-House.* House Report No. 25. 38th Cong., 2nd Sess..

U.S. House of Representatives. 1864–65c. *Trade with Rebellious States.* House Report No. 24, 38th Cong., 2nd Sess.

U.S. House of Representatives. 1865–66. *Revenue System of the United States.* House Executive Doc. No. 34, pt. 2 (Appendix 3), 39th Cong., 1st Sess. Washington, D.C.: GPO.

U.S. House of Representatives. 1866–67. *Captured and Forfeited Cotton.* House Executive Docs. No. 97, 39th Cong., 2nd Sess.

U.S. Naval Academy. Department of History. 1974. *Project Cheesebox: A Journey into History.* 3 vols. Edited by Edward M. Miller. Annapolis.

U.S. Naval History Division. 1971. *Civil War Naval Chronology.* Washington D.C.

U.S. Department of Agriculture. 1862. *Report of the Commissioner of Agriculture, 1862.* "Beef and Beef-Cattle of the West." Prepared by W. W. Corbett. Washington D.C.: GPO. 326–35.

U.S. Department of Agriculture. 1864. *Report of the Commissioner of Agriculture, 1864.* "Raising and Feeding Cattle and Sheep." Prepared by Charles W. Taylor. Washington D.C.: GPO. 249–88.

U.S. Department of Agriculture. 1870. *Report of the Commissioner of Agriculture, 1870.* "The Texas Cattle Trade." Edited by J. R. Dodge. Washington D.C.: GPO. 346–51.

U.S. Patent Office. 1850. "Letter of Charles Yancey to Commissioner of Patents," vol. 2: 136–39. (*Report of the Commissioner of Patents, 1849.* 2 vols.) Washington D.C.: GPO.

U.S. Patent Office. 1851. *Report of the Commissioner of Patents, 1850.* 2 vols. Washington D.C.: GPO.

U.S. Senate. 1859–60. *Report of the Secretary of the Navy.* Senate Exec. Doc. No. 1, 36th Cong., 2nd Sess.

U.S. Senate. 1859–60. *Report of the Secretary of War.* Senate Exec. Doc. No. 1, 36th Cong., 2nd Sess.

U.S. Senate. 1864. *Report of the Secretary of the Treasury on the value and present condition of our foreign and domestic commerce.* 38th Cong., 1st Sess. Exec. Doc. 55.

U.S. Senate. 1879–80. *Letter from the Secretary of the Treasury.* "Showing the expenditures of the government on account of the war of the rebellion." Senate Exec. Doc. No. 206, 46th Cong., 2nd Sess. Washington, D.C.: GPO.

U.S. War Department. 1880–1901. *The War of the Rebellion: A Compilation of the Official Records of the Union and Confederate Armies in the War of Rebellion.* 70 vols. in 128 parts. Washington D.C.: GPO. Denoted as OR.

Newspapers, Periodicals, and Annual Reports

Baltimore *American and Commercial Advertiser.* 1858–60. Annual Statements.

Boston. Board of Trade. 1857–62. *Review of the Boston Market.*

Charleston (South Carolina) *Daily Courier.*

Chicago. Board of Trade. 1856–62. *Annual Reports.*

DeBow's Review. 1848–64.

Economist (London). 1856–62.

Galveston (Texas) *Tri-Weekly News.* 1860–61.

Galveston (Texas) *Weekly News.* 1860–61.

Hunt's Merchants' Magazine and Commercial Review (New York). 1848–66.

Imperial Gazetteer of India. 1909. Vol. I. Oxford: Clarendon Press.

London *Quarterly Review.* January 1865. "The History of the Cotton Famine, from the Fall of Sumter to the Passing of the Public Works Act by R. Arthur Arnold." 23:313–55.

London Times. May 1 and October 21, 1861; and August 14, 1862.

Memphis (Tennessee) *Appeal.* 1861.

Mobile (Alabama) *Daily Register.* 1858–61.

New Orleans (Louisiana) *Daily Crescent.* Various issues, 1858–62.

New Orleans (Louisiana) *Picayune.* 1858–62.

New Orleans (Louisiana) *Price Current.* Various years, 1858–65.

New Orleans (Louisiana) *Price Current.* 1855–61. "Annual Reports."

New York. Chamber of Commerce. 1858–63. *Annual Report of the Chamber of Commerce of the State of New York.* Vols. 1–5. New York: John W. Amerman.

New York *Shipping and Commercial List, and Price Current.* 1858–61.

New York *Times*. July 29, 1865.

Philadelphia. Board of Trade. 1859–62. *Annual Report*. 26th, 27th, 29th reports.

Philadelphia. *Price Current*. 1860.

Richmond (Virginia) *Daily Whig*. 1860–1.

Savannah (Georgia) *Daily Morning News*. 1860.

Texas Almanac (Galveston). 1859.

The Times of India (Bombay). 1860–68.

Wilmington (North Carolina) *Journal*. 1857–60.

General References

Adams, Charles Francis Jr. 1915. "The British Proclamation of May, 1861." *Massachusetts Historical Society Proceedings* (October 1914–June 1915). Boston. 48: 190–242.

Adams, E. D. 1925. *Great Britain and the American Civil War*. 2 vols. New York: Longmans, Green.

Allen, Lewis F. [1868] 1875. *American Cattle: Their History, Breeding, and Management*. Reprint. New York: Orange Judd.

Anderson, Bern. 1962. *By Sea and By River: The Naval History of the Civil War*. New York: Alfred A. Knopf.

Arnold, Arthur R. 1864. *The History of the Cotton Famine: From the Fall of Sumter to the Passing of the Public Works Act*. London: Saunders, Otley.

Atkinson, Edward. 1863. *Report to the Boston Board of Trade on the Cotton Manufacture of 1862*. Boston: n.p.

Bairoch, Paul. 1976. "Europe's Gross National Product: 1800–1975." *Journal of European Economic History* 5:273–340.

Ball, Douglas. 1991. *Financial Failure and Confederate Defeat*. Urbana: University of Illinois Press.

Battalio, Raymond C. and John Kagel. 1970. "The Structure of Antebellum Southern Agriculture: South Carolina, a Case Study." *Agricultural History* 44:25–37.

Bergeron, Arthur W. Jr. 1991. *Confederate Mobile*. Jackson: University Press of Mississippi.

Beringer, Richard E., Herman Hattaway, Archer Jones, and William Still Jr. 1986. *Why the South Lost the Civil War*. Athens: University of Georgia Press.

Berry, Thomas S. 1968. *Estimated Annual Variations in Gross National Product, 1789 to 1909*. Richmond: Bostwick Press.

Bettersworth, John K. 1943. *Confederate Mississippi: The People and Policies in a Cotton State in Wartime*. Baton Rouge: Louisiana State University Press.

Black, Robert C. III. 1947. "The Railroads of Georgia in the Confederate War Effort." *Journal of Southern History* 13:511–34.

———. 1952. *The Railroads of the Confederacy*. Chapel Hill: University of North Carolina Press.

Blumenthal, Henry. 1966. "Confederate Diplomacy: Popular Notions and International Realities." *Journal of Southern History* 32:151–71.

Boritt, Gabor. [1978] 1994. *Lincoln and the Economics of The American Dream.* Urbana: University of Illinois Press (Reprint from Memphis State University Press).

Brady, Eugene. 1963. "A Reconsideration of the Lancashire 'Cotton Famine.'" *Agricultural History* 37:156–62.

Brayer, Garnet M. and Herbert O. 1952. *American Cattle Trails, 1540–1900.* Denver: Smith-Brooks. Bayside, N.Y.: American Pioneer Trails Association.

Browning, Robert M. Jr. 1993. *From Cape Charles to Cape Fear: The North Atlantic Blockading Squadron during the Civil War.* Tuscaloosa: University of Alabama Press.

Bruce, Kathleen. 1968. *Virginia Iron Manufacture in the Slave Era.* New York: Augustus M. Kelley.

Bryan, T. Conn. 1953. *Confederate Georgia.* Athens: University of Georgia Press.

Buker, George E. 1993. *Blockaders, Refugees, and Contrabands: Civil War on Florida's Gulf Coast, 1861–1865.* Tuscaloosa: University of Alabama Press.

Bulloch, James. 1884. *The Secret Service of the Confederate States in Europe.* 2 vols. New York: G. P. Putnam's Sons.

Capers, Gerald M., Jr. [1939] 1966. *The Biography of a River Town, Memphis: Its Heroic Age.* New Orleans: Tulane University. (Reprint, Chapel Hill: University of North Carolina Press.)

Capers, Henry D. 1893. *The Life and Times of C. G. Memminger.* Richmond: Everett Waddey Co.

Cassels, Walter R. 1862. *Cotton: An Account of its Culture in the Bombay Presidency.* Cornhill: Smith, Elder.

Cauley, T. J. 1927. "The Cost of Marketing Texas Cattle in the Old Trail Days." *Journal of Farm Economics* 9:356–60.

Chandler, Alfred D., Jr. 1977. "Du Pont, Dahlgren, and the Civil War Nitre Shortage." *Military Analysis of the Civil War: An Anthology by the Editors of Military Affairs.* Millwood, N.Y.: KTO Press. 199–206.

Chesson, Michael B. 1984. "Harlots or Heroines? A New Look at the Richmond Bread Riots." *Virginia Magazine of History and Biography.* 92:131–75.

Clapham, J. H. [1921] 1961. *The Economic Development of France and Germany, 1815–1914.* Reprint. Cambridge: University Press.

Clark, Victor. 1929. *History of Manufactures in the United States.* 3 vols. Carnegie Institution of Washington. New York: McGraw-Hill.

Coddington, Edwin B. 1949. "The Civil War Blockade Reconsidered." *Essays in History and International Relations in Honor of George Hubbard Blakeslee.* Edited by D. L. Lee and G. E. McReynolds. Worcester, Mass.: Clark University. 284–305.

Connelly, Thomas L. 1970. "Vicksburg: Strategic Point or Propaganda Device?" *Military Affairs* 34:49–53.

Corsan, W. C. [1863] 1996. *Two Months in the Confederate States: An Englishman's Travels through the South.* Baton Rouge: Louisiana State University Press.

Coulter, E. Merton. 1919. "Commercial Intercourse with the Confederacy in the Mississippi Valley, 1861–65." *Mississippi Valley Historical Review* 5:377–95.

———. 1926. *The Civil War and Readjustment in Kentucky*. Chapel Hill: University of North Carolina Press.

———. 1950. *The Confederate States of America, 1861–65*. Baton Rouge, La.: Baton Rouge Press.

Crook, D. P. 1974. *The North, the South, and the Powers, 1861–65*. New York: John Wiley and Sons.

Dabney, Thomas E. 1944. "The Butler Regime in Louisiana." *Louisiana Historical Quarterly* 27:487–526.

Daddysman, James W. 1984. *The Matamoros Trade: Confederate Commerce, Diplomacy and Intrigue*. Newark: University of Delaware Press.

Davis, Jefferson. 1881. *The Rise and Fall of the Confederate Government*. 2 vols. New York: D. Appleton.

Davis, Varina. 1890. *Jefferson Davis, Ex-President of the Confederate States of America: A Memoir by His Wife*. 2 vols. New York: Belford Co.

Davis, William C. 1994. *A Government of Our Own: The Making of the Confederacy*. New York: Free Press.

———. 1991. *Jefferson Davis: The Man and His Hour*. New York: HarperCollins.

Derrick, Samuel M. 1930. *Centennial History of South Carolina Railroad*. Columbia: The State Company.

Dew, C. B. 1966. *Ironmaker to the Confederacy—Joseph R. Anderson and the Tredegar Iron Works*. New Haven: Yale University Press.

Diamond, William. 1940. "Imports of the Confederate Government from Europe and Mexico. *Journal of Southern History* 6:470–503.

Dobie, J. Frank. 1941. *The Longhorns*. New York: Bramhall House.

Donnell, E. J. 1872. *Chronological and Statistical History of Cotton*. New York: James Sutton.

Donnelly, Ralph. 1956. "Scientists of the Confederate Nitre and Mining Bureau." *Civil War History* 2:69–92.

Dougan, Michael B. 1976. *Confederate Arkansas: The People and Politics of a Frontier State in Wartime*. Tuscaloosa: University of Alabama Press.

Drysdale, Richard. 1977. "Blockade Running from Nassau." *History Today* 27:332–37.

Dunham, Arthur. 1928. "The Development of the Cotton Industry in France and the Anglo-French Treaty of Commerce of 1860." *Economic History Review* 1:281–307.

Early, General Jubal A. [1960] 1989. *War Memoirs: Autobiographical Sketch and Narrative of the War Between the States*. Baltimore: Nautical & Aviation Publishing.

Eaton, Clement. 1954. *A History of the Southern Confederacy*. New York: Macmillan.

Ekelund, Robert B. and Mark Thornton. 1992. "The Union Blockade and Demoralization of the South: Relative Prices in the Confederacy." *Social Science Quarterly* 73:890–902.

Ellis, Tuffy L. 1973. "Maritime Commerce on the Far Western Gulf, 1861–65." *Southwestern Historical Quarterly* 77:167–226.

Ellison, Thomas. [1886] 1968. *The Cotton Trade of Great Britain*. Reprint. New York: A.M. Kelley.

Engels, Donald. 1978. *Alexander the Great and the Logistics of the Macedonian Army*. Berkeley: University of California Press.

Farnie, D. A. 1979. *The English Cotton Industry and the World Market, 1815– 1896*. Oxford, U.K.: Clarendon Press.

Feinstein, C. H. 1972. "National Income, Expenditure and Output of the United Kingdom, 1855–1965." *Studies in the National Income and Expenditure of the United Kingdom*. Cambridge, U.K.: University Press.

Ferris, Norman. 1976. *Desperate Diplomacy: William H. Seward's Foreign Policy, 1861*. Knoxville: The University of Tennessee Press.

Fishlow, Albert. 1964. "Antebellum Interregional Trade Reconsidered." *American Economic Review: Proceedings* 54:352–64.

Fishlow, Albert. 1965. "Postscript to Fogel's 'A Provisional View of the New Economic History.'" *New Views on American Economic Development*. Edited by Ralph Andreano. Cambridge: Schenkman Publishing. 209–12.

Fleming, Walter L. [1905] 1949. *Civil War and Reconstruction in Alabama*. New York: Peter Smith.

Fogel, Robert W. 1964. "Discussion of Douglass C. North's March 1963 Note in the *American Economic Review*." *American Economic Review: Proceedings* 54:377–89.

———. 1965a. "American Interregional Trade in the Nineteenth Century." *New Views on American Economic Development*. Edited by Ralph Andreano. Cambridge: Schenkman Publishing. 213–24.

———. 1965b. "A Provisional View of the 'New Economic History.'" *New Views on American Economic Development*. Edited by Ralph Andreano. Cambridge: Schenkman Publishing. 201–8.

Fogel, Robert W. and Stanley L. Engerman. 1971. "The Economics of Slavery." *The Reinterpretation of American Economic History*. New York: Harper & Row. 311–41.

———. 1974a. *Time on the Cross—The Economics of American Negro Slavery*. Boston: Little, Brown.

———. 1974b. *Time on the Cross—The Economics of American Negro Slavery. Evidence and Methods: A Supplement*. Boston: Little, Brown.

———. 1992a. "Explaining the Relative Efficiency of Slave Agriculture in the Antebellum South: Reply." *Without Consent or Contract. Technical Papers*. Vol. 1, New York: Norton. 266–303.

———. 1992b. "The Slave Diet on Large Plantations in 1860." *Without Consent or Contract: The Rise and Fall of American Slavery. Evidence and Methods*. Edited by Robert W. Fogel, Ralph A. Galantine, and Richard L. Manning. New York: Norton. 291–304.

Forwood, William B. 1870. "The Influence of Price upon the Cultivation and Consumption of Cotton during the Ten Years 1860–70." *Journal of the Royal Statistical Society* 33:366–83.

Fox, William F. [1889] 1893. *Regimental Losses in the American Civil War.* Albany, N.Y.: Albany Publishing.

Fremantle, Arthur. 1864. *Three Months in the Southern States.* New York: John Bradburn.

Friedman, Gerald and Donghyu Yang. 1992. "The Debate on the Elasticity of the Cotton Supply." Edited by Robert W. Fogel, Ralph A. Galantine, and Richard L. Manning, *Without Consent or Contract: The Rise and Fall of American Slavery. Evidence and Methods.* New York: W. W. Norton. 264–69.

Friedman, Milton. 1952. "Economic Development, the Role of War in America: Price, Income, and Monetary Changes in Three Wartime Periods." *American Economic Review* 42:612–25.

Futrell, Robert F. 1950. *Federal Trade with the Confederate States.* Ph.D. dissertation. Nashville: Vanderbilt University.

Galenson, David. 1977. "The Profitability of the Long Drive." *Agricultural History* 51: 737–58.

Gallman, Robert E. 1966. "Gross National Product in the United States, 1834–1909." *Output, Employment and Productivity in the United States after 1800. Studies in Income and Wealth.* New York: NBER. 30:3–76.

———. 1970. "Self-Sufficiency in the Cotton Economy of the Antebellum South." *Agricultural History* 44:5–23.

Gard, Wayne 1954. *The Chisholm Trail.* Norman: University of Oklahoma Press.

Genovese, Eugene D. [1961] 1965. *The Political Economy of Slavery.* Reprint. New York: Pantheon Books.

Ginzberg, Eli. 1936. "The Economics of British Neutrality during the American Civil War." *Agricultural History* 10:147–56.

Goff, Richard D. 1969. *Confederate Supply.* Durham: Duke University Press.

Goldin, Claudia and F. Lewis. 1975. "The Economic Cost of the American Civil War: Estimates and Implications." *Journal of Economic History* 35:299–326.

Gragg, Rod. 1991. *Confederate Goliath: The Battle of Fort Fisher.* New York: HarperCollins.

Gray, Lewis C. [1933] 1958. *History of Agriculture in the Southern United States to 1860.* 2 vols. Gloucester: Carnegie Institution of Washington.

Grossman, Randall. 1992. "An Alternative Approach to the Valuation of Farm Output." *Without Consent or Contract: The Rise and Fall of American Slavery. Evidence and Methods.* Edited by Robert W. Fogel, Ralph A. Galantine, and Richard L. Manning. New York: Norton. 223–28.

Hammond, M. B. 1897. *The Cotton Industry.* New York: Macmillan.

Haney, Lewis. 1910. "A Congressional History of Railroads in the United States, 1850–1887." *Bulletin of the University of Wisconsin.* 6. Madison: Economics and Political Science Studies.

Hansen, B. and K. Nashashibi, 1975. *Foreign Trade Regimes and Economic Development: Egypt*. New York: National Bureau of Economic Research.

Hanson, John R., II. 1979. "World Demand for Cotton During the Nineteenth Century: Wright's Estimates Re-examined." *Journal of Economic History* 39:1015–21.

Harnetty, Peter. 1972. *Imperialism and Free Trade: Lancashire and India in Mid-Nineteenth Century*. Vancouver: University of British Columbia Press.

Hayes, Charles W. [1879] 1974. *Galveston: History of the Island and the City*. Austin: Jenkins Garret Press.

Helm, Elijah. 1869. "The Cotton Trade of the United Kingdom, during the Seven Years, 1862–68 as compared with the Seven Years, 1855–61." *Journal of the Royal Statistical Society* 32:428–37.

Henderson, Conway W. 1969. "The Anglo-American Treaty of 1862 in Civil War Diplomacy." *Civil War History* 15:308–19.

Henderson, W. O. 1933. "The Cotton Famine on the Continent, 1861–1865." *Economic History Review* 4:195–207.

Hermann, Janet. 1990. *Joseph E. Davis: Pioneer Patriarch*. Jackson: University Press of Mississippi.

Heth, Major-General Henry. 1877. "Letter from Major-General Henry Heth, of A. P. Hill's Corps, A.N.V." *Southern Historical Society Papers* 4:151–60.

Heyl, Erik. 1953–1964. *Early American Steamers*. 6 vols. Self-published.

Heywood, Colin. 1977. *The Cotton Industry in France, 1750–1850*. Loughborough, U.K.: Loughborough University.

Hill, Daniel H. 1926. *History of North Carolina in the Civil War: Bethel to Sharpsburg*. Raleigh: Edwards and Broughton.

Hilliard, Sam B. 1972. *Hog Meat and Hoecake: Food Supply in the Old South, 1840–1860*. Carbondale: Southern Illinois University Press.

Hunter, Louis C. 1949. *Steamboats on the Western Rivers: An Economic and Technological History*. Cambridge: Harvard University Press.

Huston, James. 1966. *The Sinews of War: Army Logistics, 1775–1953*. Washington D.C.: U.S. Army.

Hutchison, William and Samuel Williamson. 1971. "The Self-Sufficiency of the Antebellum South: Estimates of the Food Supply." *Journal of Economic History* 31:591–612.

Irby, James A. 1977. "Backdoor at Bagdad—The Civil War on the Rio Grande." *Southwestern Studies*. Monograph #53. El Paso: Texas Western Press.

Johns, John. 1866. "Wilmington during the Blockade." *Harper's New Monthly Magazine* 33:497–503.

———. 1963. *Florida during the Civil War*. Gainesville: University of Florida Press.

Johnson, Ludwell H. 1958. *Red River Campaign: Politics and Cotton in the Civil War*. Baltimore: Johns Hopkins University Press.

———. 1963. "Contraband Trade During the Last Year of the Civil War." *Mississippi Valley Historical Review* 49:635–52.

————. 1970. "Trading with the Union: The Evolution of Confederate Policy." *Virginia Magazine of History and Biography* 78:308–25.

————. 1985. "Blockade or Trade Monopoly: John A. Dix and the Union Occupation of Norfolk." *Virginia Magazine of History and Biography* 93:54–78.

Johnston, Angus J., II. 1957. "Virginia Railroads in April, 1861." *Journal of Southern History* 23:307–30.

———— 1961. *Virginia Railroads in the Civil War.* Chapel Hill: University of North Carolina Press.

Jones, Archer. 1992. *Civil War Command and Strategy: The Process of Victory and Defeat.* New York: The Free Press.

Jones, Howard. 1992. *Union in Peril: The Crisis Over British Intervention in the Civil War.* Chapel Hill: University of North Carolina Press.

Jordan, Weymouth T. 1958. "Rebels in the Making—Planters' Conventions and Southern Propaganda." *Confederate Centennial Studies.* Vol. 7. Tuscaloosa: Confederate Publishing.

Jostock, Paul. 1955. "The Long-Term Growth of National Income in Germany." *Income and Wealth.* 5. London: Bowes and Bowes.

Kerby, Robert L. 1972. *Kirby Smith's Confederacy: The Trans-Mississippi South, 1863–1865.* New York: Columbia University Press.

Kohlmeier, Albert L. 1938. *The Old Northwest as the Keystone of the Arch of American Federal Union: A Study in Commerce and Politics.* Bloomington: Principia Press.

Lamb, Colonel William. 1884–88. "The Defense of Fort Fisher." *Battles and Leaders of the Civil War.* New York: The Century Co. 4 vols. 4:642–54.

Lash, Jeffrey N. 1991. *Destroyer of the Iron Horse—General Joseph E. Johnston and Confederate Rail Transport, 1861–65.* Kent, Ohio: Kent State University Press.

Lea, Tom. 1957. *The King Ranch.* 2 vols. Boston: Little, Brown.

Lebergott, Stanley. 1981. "Through the Blockade—The Profitability and Extent of Cotton Smuggling, 1861–1865." *Journal of Economic History* 41:867–88.

————. 1983. "Why the South Lost—Commercial Purpose in the Confederacy, 1861–1865." *Journal of American History* 70:58–74.

Lee, Charles Robert. 1963. *The Confederate Constitutions.* Chapel Hill: University of North Carolina Press.

Lerner, Eugene. 1954. "Money, Prices, and Wages in the Confederacy, 1861–65." Ph.D. dissertation. Chicago: University of Chicago.

————. 1955. "Money, Prices, and Wages in the Confederacy, 1861– 65." *Journal of Political Economy* 63:20–40.

Lester, Richard. 1975. *Confederate Finance and Purchasing in Great Britain.* Charlottesville: University of Virginia Press.

Lindstrom, Diane. 1970. "Southern Dependence upon Inter-regional Grain Supplies: A Review of the Trade Flows, 1840–1860." *Agricultural History* 44:101–13.

Livermore, Thomas L. 1900. *Numbers and Losses in the Civil War in America, 1861–65.* Boston: Houghton, Mifflin.

Lonn, Ella. [1933] 1965. *Salt as a Factor in the Confederacy.* Reprint. Tuscaloosa: University of Alabama Press.

Luraghi, Raimondo. 1978. *The Rise and Fall of the Plantation South.* New York: New Viewpoints.

———. 1996. *A History of the Confederate Navy.* Annapolis: Naval Institute Press.

Maddison, Angus. 1982. *Phases of Capitalist Development.* Oxford: Oxford University Press.

Mann, James A. 1860. *The Cotton Trade of Great Britain: Its Rise, Progress, & Present Extent.* London: Simpkin, Marshall.

Massey, Mary E. [1952] 1993. *Ersatz in the Confederacy: Shortages and Substitutes on the Southern Homefront.* Columbia: University of South Carolina Press.

McCoy, Joseph G. [1874] 1940. *Historical Sketches of the West and Southwest.* Edited by Ralph P. Bieber. Reprint. Glendale: Arthur H. Clark.

McCrady, Edward Jr. 1885. "Gregg's Brigade of South Carolinians in the Second Battle of Manassas." *Southern Historical Society Papers* 8:3–40.

Mitchell, B. R. 1983. *International Historical Statistics: The Americas and Australasia.* Detroit: Gale Research.

Mitchell, B. R., and Phyllis Deane. 1962. *Abstract of British Historical Statistics.* Cambridge: University Press.

Mitchell, Wesley C. 1908. "Gold, Prices, and Wages Under the Greenback Standard." *University of California Publications in Economics.* 1. Berkeley: University Press.

Moneyhon, Carl H. 1994. *The Impact of the Civil War and Reconstruction on Arkansas: Persistence in the Midst of Ruin.* Baton Rouge: Louisiana State University Press.

Moore, Frank D., editor. 1861–68. *Rebellion Record.* 11 vols. New York: D. Van Nostrand and G. P. Putnam.

Moore, Jerrold Northrop. 1996. *Confederate Commissary General: Lucius Bellinger Northrop and the Subsistence Bureau of the Southern Army.* Shippensburg, Penn.: White Mane Publishing.

Morrison, Frank B. [1898] 1943. *Feeds and Feeding.* 20th edition. Ithaca, N.Y.: Morrison Publishing.

Mulhall, Michael G. [1898] 1903. *Dictionary of Statistics.* Reprint. Fourth edition. London: George Routledge and Sons.

Nevins, Allan. 1959. *War for the Union.* 4 vols. New York: Charles Schribner's Sons.

Nicolay, John G. and John Hay. [1886] 1890. *Abraham Lincoln: A History.* 10 vols. New York: Century.

O'Conner, Thomas H. 1961. "Lincoln and the Cotton Trade." *Civil War History* 7:20–35.

Owens, Harry P. 1990. *Steamboats and the Cotton Economy: River Trade in the Yazoo-Mississippi Delta.* Jackson: University Press of Mississippi.

Owsley, Frank L. 1931. *King Cotton Diplomacy—Foreign Relations of the Confederate States of America.* Chicago: University of Chicago Press.

Phillips, Ulrich B. 1905. "The Economic Cost of Slaveholding in the Cotton Belt." *Political Science Quarterly* 20:257–75.

Pollard, Edward A. 1866. *The Lost Cause: A New Southern History of the War of the Confederates.* New York: E. B. Treat.

Porter, Admiral David D. 1886. *Naval History of the Civil War.* New York: Sherman Publishing.

Powell, Lawrence N. and Michael S. Wayne. 1983. "Self-Interest and the Decline of Confederate Nationalism." *The Old South in the Crucible of War.* Edited by Harry P. Owens and James J. Cooke. Jackson: University Press of Mississippi. 29–45.

Power, J. Tracy. 1998. *Lee's Miserables: Life in the Army of Northern Virginia from the Wilderness to Appomattox.* Chapel Hill: University of North Carolina.

Prest, A. R. 1954. "Consumers' Expenditure in the United Kingdom, 1900–1919." Studies in the National Income and Expenditure of the United Kingdom. No. 3. Cambridge: University Press.

Price, Charles L. 1961. "North Carolina Railroads During the Civil War." *Civil War History* 7:298–309.

Price, Marcus W. 1948. "Ships That Tested the Blockade of the Carolina Ports, 1861–1865." *American Neptune* 8:196–241.

Price, Marcus W. 1949. "Blockade Running as a Business in South Carolina during the War Between the States, 1861–65." *American Neptune* 9:31–62.

———. 1951–52. "Ships That Tested the Blockade of the Gulf Ports, 1861–1865." *American Neptune* 11:262–90; 12:52–59, 154–61, 229–38.

———. 1955. "Ships That Tested the Blockade of the Georgia and East Florida Ports, 1861–1865." *American Neptune* 15:97–132.

Ramsdell, Charles W. 1917. "The Confederate Government and the Railroads." *American Historical Review* 22:794–810.

———. 1930. "General Robert E. Lee's Horse Supply, 1862–65." *American Historical Review* 35:758–77.

———. 1944. *Behind the Lines in the Southern Confederacy.* Baton Rouge: Louisiana State University Press.

Reed, S. G. 1941. *A History of Texas Railroads.* Houston: St. Clair Publishing Company.

Rhodes, James Ford. [1904] 1920. *History of the United States. Vol. 5, 1861–1865.* 9 vols. New York: Macmillan.

Ringold, May Spencer. 1966. *The Role of the State Legislatures in the Confederacy.* Athens: University of Georgia Press.

Royle, John F. 1851. *On the Culture and Commerce of Cotton in India and Elsewhere.* London: Smith, Elder.

Saini, Krishan. 1969. "The Growth of the Indian Economy, 1860–1960." *Review of Income and Wealth.* Ser. 15: 247–63.

Sandberg, Lars. 1974. *Lancashire in Decline: A Study in Entrepreneurship, Technology, and International Trade.* Columbus: Ohio State University Press.

Scharf, J. Thomas. 1887. *History of the Confederate States Navy.* New York: Rogers and Sherwood.

Schmidt, Louis B. 1918. "The Influence of Wheat and Cotton on Anglo-American Relations during the Civil War." *Iowa Journal of History and Politics* 16:400–439.

———. 1920. "The Internal Grain Trade of the United States, 1850–1860." *Iowa Journal of History and Politics* 18:94–124.

Schwab, John Christopher. [1901] 1913. *The Confederate States of America, 1861–1865: A Financial and Industrial History of the South During the Civil War.* New Haven: Yale University Press.

Schuckers, J. W. 1874. *The Life and Public Services of Salmon Portland Chase.* New York: D. Appleton.

Sharpe, Henry G. 1899. "The Art of Supplying Armies in the Field as Exemplified During the Civil War." *Notes on the Supply of an Army.* Edited by O. Espanet. Kansas City: Hudson-Kimberly.

Shirras, George F. 1923. "Report on an Enquiry into Working Class Budgets in Bombay." *Bombay (Presidency).* Bombay: Government Central Press.

Showalter, Dennis. 1975. *Railroads and Rifles: Soldiers, Technology and the Reunification of Germany.* Hamden, Conn.: Archon Books.

Silver, Arthur W. 1966. *Manchester Men and Indian Cotton, 1847–72.* Manchester, U.K.: Manchester University Press.

Silverstone, Paul H. 1989. *Warships of the Civil War Navies.* Annapolis: Naval Institute Press.

Southern Historical Society Papers. 1876a. "Resources of the Confederacy in February, 1865: Report of Commissary General Northrop." 2:85–105.

———. 1876b. "Resources of the Confederacy in February, 1865. 2:113–28.

———. 1877. "Resources of the Confederacy in 1865: Report of General I. M. St. John, Commissary-General." 3:97–111.

Spencer, Warren. 1983. *The Confederate Navy in Europe.* Tuscaloosa: University of Alabama Press.

Still, William N., Jr. 1971. *Iron Afloat: The Story of the Confederate Armorclads.* Nashville, Tenn.: Vanderbilt University Press.

Stover, John F. 1955. *The Railroads of the South, 1865–1900: A Study in Finance and Control.* Chapel Hill: University of North Carolina Press.

Tatum, Georgia Lee. 1934. *Disloyalty in the Confederacy.* Chapel Hill: University of North Carolina Press.

Taylor, Robert A. 1988. "Rebel Beef: Florida Cattle and the Confederate Army, 1862–64." *Florida Historical Quarterly* 67:15–31.

Todd, Richard C. 1954. *Confederate Finance.* Athens: University of Georgia Press.

Towne, Marvin W. and Wayne D. Rasmussen. 1960. "Farms Gross Product and Gross Investment in the Nineteenth Century." *Trends in the American Economy in the Nineteenth Century; Studies in Income and Wealth.* 24: 255–315. National Bureau of Economic Research. Princeton, N. J.: Princeton University Press.

Trotter, William R. 1989. *Ironclads and Columbiads: The Civil War in North Carolina—The Coast*. Winston-Salem: John F. Blair.

Turner, Charles W. 1946. "The Virginia Central Railroad at War, 1861–1865." *Journal of Southern History* 12:510–33.

Turner, Maxine. 1988. *Navy Gray: A Story of the Confederate Navy on the Chattahoochee and Apalachicola Rivers*. Tuscaloosa: University of Alabama Press.

Tyler, Ronnie C. 1970. "Cotton on the Border." *Southwestern Historical Quarterly* 73:456–77.

Tyson, R. E. 1968. "The Cotton Industry." *The Development of British Industry and Foreign Competition, 1875–1914*. Edited by Derek H. Aldcroft. London: George Allen & Unwin Ltd. 100–127.

Ure, Andrew. [1836] 1861. *The Cotton Manufacture of Great Britain*. Reprint. London: E. G. Bohn.

Vandiver, Frank E. 1944. "Texas and the Confederate Army's Meat Problem." *Southwestern Historical Quarterly* 47:225–33.

———. 1947. *Confederate Blockade Running Through Bermuda, 1861–1865*. Austin: University of Texas Press.

———. 1952. *Ploughshares into Swords—Josiah Gorgas and Confederate Ordnance*. Austin: University of Texas Press.

———. 1970. *Their Tattered Flags: The Epic of the Confederacy*. New York: Harper's Magazine Press Book.

Warren, G. F., and F. A. Pearson. 1932. "Wholesale Prices for 213 Years, 1720 to 1932, Part 1." *Cornell University Agricultural Experimental Station Memoirs*. 142. Ithaca, N.Y.: Cornell University Press.

Watkins, James L. 1908. *King Cotton—A Historical and Statistical Review, 1790 to 1908*. New York: James L. Watkins & Sons.

Watson, William. 1892. *The Adventures of a Blockade Runner; Or, Trade in Time of War*. London: T. Fisher Unwin.

Weller, Jac. 1959. "Imported Confederate Shoulder Weapons." *Civil War History* 5:157–81.

Wells, Tom Henderson. 1971. *The Confederate Navy: A Study in Organization*. Tuscaloosa: University of Alabama Press.

Wender, Herbert. 1930. "Southern Commercial Conventions, 1837–59." *Johns Hopkins University Studies in Historical and Political Science* 48: 423–662.

Williams, T. Harry. [1941] 1969. *Lincoln and the Radicals*. Madison: University of Wisconsin Press.

Willoughby, Lynn. 1993. *Fair to Middlin': The Antebellum Cotton Trade of the Apalachicola/Chattahooche River Valley*. Tuscaloosa: University of Alabama Press.

Winters, John D. 1963. *The Civil War in Louisiana*. Baton Rouge: Louisiana State University Press.

Wise, Stephen R. 1988. *Lifeline of the Confederacy—Blockade Running during the Civil War*. Columbia: University of South Carolina Press.

Wood, George Henry. 1910. *History of Wages in the Cotton Trade during the Past Hundred Years.* London: Sherratt and Hughes.

Wright, Gavin. 1971. "An Econometric Study of Cotton Production and Trade, 1830–60." *Review of Economics and Statistics* 53:111–20.

———. 1974. "Cotton Competition and the Post-Bellum Recovery of the American South." *Journal of Economic History* 34: 610–35.

———. 1978. *The Political Economy of the Cotton South: Households, Markets, and Wealth in the Nineteenth Century.* New York: W. W. Norton.

———. 1986. *Old South, New South: Revolutions in the Southern Economy Since the Civil War.* New York: Basic Books.

Wright, Michael F. 1981. "Vicksburg and the Trans-Mississippi Supply Line (1861–1863)." *Journal of Mississippi History* 43:210–25.

Yang, Donghyu. 1992. "The Debate Over the Growth in the Demand for Cotton." In *Without Consent or Contract: The Rise and Fall of American Slavery. Evidence and Methods.* Edited by Robert W. Fogel, Ralph A. Galatine, and Richard L. Manning. New York: W. W. Norton. 269–73.

Yearns, W. Buck and John G. Barrett, editors. 1980. *North Carolina: Civil War Documentary.* Chapel Hill: University of North Carolina Press.

INDEX

Numbers in italics denote entries in tables and figures.

Boston Board of Trade's *Review of the Market,* 23

Brady, Eugene, 120, *127,* 138, 139, 141

Bragg, Braxton, Gen., 62, 63, 81

brandy, 12, 94. *See also* luxury items, imported

Brazil, 121, 138, *143, 144, 145,* 147. *See also* cotton, rival producers; Great Britain, cotton consumption

Brazos Santiago, Tex., 28

"bread riots," 104

Breckinridge, John C. (Secretary of War), 74–75, 183

Britain. *See* Great Britain

Brown, Joseph E. (Georgia governor), 76, 82, 96, 115–16

Brownsville, Tex., 6, 163, 167, 170, 176, 178, 204

Bruce, Kathleen, 86

Brunswick, Ga., 208

Bulloch, James, Capt., 78, 89

Butler, Benjamin, Gen., 170, 171, 174, 192

Calcasieu River, 27

Camp, Benjamin, 176

Canada, 66, 199

Canby, Edward, Gen., 195–96

cannons, 86. *See also* arms, small; ordnance

Capers, Henry D., 162

carts, 33. *See also* wagons

Cassels, Walter R., 226

cattle, 1, 14, 18, *19,* 24–26, 31, *32,* 64–65; from Arkansas, 26, 27, 31, 33, 63, 68, 211; from Florida, 19, 26, 31–33, 63–64, 68, 100, 211; overland driving, 27, 33, 64, 68, 69, 70; from Texas, 26–28, *29*–31, 32–33, 48, 61, 65, 67, 68, 69, 70–71, 73, 100, 208,

211–13; "Western," 23, 24, 27, *29,* 55, 69, 212. *See also* meat; pork supplies; swine

Cedar Keys, Fla., 32, 68, 208

Central of Georgia Railroad, 77. *See also* railroads

Central Railroad, 67. *See also* railroads

Chandler, Zachariah, 175

Charleston, S.C., 11, *12,* 24, 26, 100, 202, 207–8; and blockade-running activity, 92–93, *171, 172*–73, 209; as a cotton port, 39, 164–66, 169, 181, 187, 188; flour exports, 43, 44, *45,* 46–47; meat shortages, 68; railroad connections, 38

Charleston *Daily Courier,* 23, 47, *166*

Charlotte, N.C., 63

Chase, Salmon P. (Treasury Secretary), 192, 197, 200–201, 202

Chattahoochee River, 38, 169

Chattanooga, Tenn., 40

Chesapeake Bay, 46, 50, 67, 69, 84

China, 134, 135, 146. *See also* cotton, rival producers

cholera, hog, 62, 63, 102. *See also* bacon; pork

Chowan River, 173–74

cigars, 12. *See also* luxury items, imported

civilian discontent, Southern, 6, 96–97, 104, 116, 183–85, 194. *See also* morale, Southern; unionism

Clark, Victor, 136

Clarksville, Va., 101

clothing, manufactured, 33–*34,* 96

Cobb, Thomas R.R., 116

Cockrill, S., 115

Coddington, Edwin B., 2

coffee, 12, 93, 96, 174, 178. *See also* luxury items, imported; tea

Collie Company, 90–91

Columbia, S.C., 74, 75

Columbus, Ga., 38, 84, 85, 208

Confederacy, the: and consumption of goods, 13, 18, 19; exports, 1, 7, 109, 146–47, 154–57, 159, 160, 163, 165–69, 170–80; imports, 1, 11–12, 90, 95; and inadequate railroads, 2, 17, 37–39, 40–41, 49–50, 63–64, 67, 72, 83–84, 88, 99, 100–101, 104, 105–6, 181, 187, 208; manufacturing, 1, 33–*34,* 36–37, 41, 50, 72, 76, 85–86, 88, 97. *See also* Army, Confederate; Confederate Congress; Confederate government; Navy, Confederate

Confederate Congress, 36, 67, 70, 71, 102; and railroad legislation, 73–74, 79, 80. *See also* Confederate government

Confederate government: assistance to railroads, 78–79; and cotton price-setting power, 7–8, 109, 111–14, 115, 117, 118, 154, 161, 185–86, 198; currency, 82, 95–96; loans, 161; purchasing power, 5–6, 90–91; and railroad freight rates, 80–82; setting of meat prices, 70–71

Confederate states. *See* Confederacy, the

Congress, Confederate. *See* Confederate Congress

cordials, 12. *See also* luxury items, imported

Corinth, Miss., 27–28, 37, 38, 168; capture of, 73

corn, 1, *14, 15, 16,* 17, 44–46, 48–49, 106; prices, 47, 55–*57,* 104. *See also* agriculture, Southern; grain; hay; oats; wheat

Corsan, W. C., 92–93, 95

costs, shipping. *See* shipping costs

cotton: "abandoned," 201; antebellum trade movements of, 164–69; burning of, 172, 175, 185; embargo, 57, 59–60, 80, 109, 112, 116, 120, 137, 159–60, 161, 170, 171; "famine," 112, 121; output restriction, 114, 136; overproduction theories, 120–21, 125, 138; Pernambuco, 145; price increases, 120, 124–25, 128–30, 141–42, 147–50, 152, 155, 158, 160, 222, 229–32; prices, 3, 7–8, 93, 112–13, 115–17, 118, 123–24, 126–27, *128–29,* 130–*31,* 136, 141, 146, 155, 159, 160, 163, 177, 182, 187–89, 190–91, 195–96, 220–24, 229–32; purchasing power of, 93–94; "reservation" prices, 189, 190; rival producers of, 121, 138–41, 142–44, 145–46, 147, 148–49, 152, 155, 219–20, 226–27; shipping, 7–8, 38–39, 113, 124, 158–59, 160, 164–67, 168, 177, 190, 221, 226; shortages, in Europe, 124, 135, 137; smuggling, 154, 155, 158–59, 171–72, 202; Southern export of, 1, 7–8, 109, 137–41, 145–47, 154–62, 163–*65,* 166–69, 170–80, 184, 187–88, 195–96, 204, 224; and the South's price-setting power, 7–8, 109, 111–12, 115, 118, 154, 161, 198; stocks, 112, 119, 120, 125–26, *127,* 133, 138–39, *140*–41, 147, 148, 150, 159, 160, 161–62, 172, 196, 217, 229, 231, 233; Surat, 130, 142; trading for iron, 78–79; trading for meat, 103, 193; trading with individuals, 177; Union exploitation of, 187–88, 194–95, 197, 200–201, 203–5;

engines, steam, 33–*34,* 36–37. *See also* machinery; manufacturing, Southern

England. *See* Great Britain

Etowah Iron Works, 77. *See also* iron; Shelby County Iron Manufacturing Company; Tredegar Iron Works

Europe: exports to the Confederacy, 86–87, 89–90, 92

export duties, cotton, 114, 115–17, 187, 188–91, 195, 197, 198, 200, 204. *See also* Confederate government; cotton

exports, Confederacy, 1, 7–8, 109, 146–47, 154–57, 159, 160, 163, 165–69, 170–80

Farnie, D. A., 120

Farragut, David Glasgow, Adm., 57, 60, 89

Fayetteville, N.C., 85, 94, 104, 182

Fernandina, Fla., 32, 80, 208

Ferris, Norman, 199

Fessenden, William, 191, 202

Fishlow, Albert, 19, 43

Florida, 48, 56, 69; and blockade-running activity, *171;* cattle, 19, 26, 31–33, 63–64, 68, 100, 211; cotton shipping, 163–*65,* 168–69, 171, 181; grain production, *15, 16;* livestock, *19, 20, 21;* meat supplies, 24, *25,* 65, 67, 103; railroads, 16, 32, 38, 75, 80

flour, 15, *16*–17, 33–*34,* 43–*45,* 46–47, 55, 178; prices, 56–*57,* 93–94, 104, 171. *See also* foodstuffs; meal

fodder, 42, 43, 98, 104, 105

Fogel, Robert W., 18, *20, 21,* 43, 213

foodstuffs: production of, 47, 181–83; regional redistribution of, 53, 98–99, 100–101, 182; shipment from North to South, 19, 46, 55, 117

forks, 33–34. *See also* implements, agricultural

Fort Jackson, La., 60

Fort Macon, N.C., capture of, 187

Fort St. Phillip, La., 60

Fort Sumter, S.C., 59, 85, 86, 112, 196

Forwood, William B., 126, 136

Fox, William F., 206

France: cotton consumption, 142, *143;* intervention of, 112, 199–200; textile industry of, 134, 142, 197. *See also* Great Britain; intervention, European

Freeman, Douglas, 105

freight rates, railroad, 80–81. *See also* railroads

Friedman, Milton, 65–66

fruit, 12, 96

furniture, 47. *See also* luxury items, imported

Galenson, David, 31

Gallman, Robert E., 18, *20, 21,* 213

Galveston, Tex., 28, 71, 163, 207; as a cattle port, 31, 69, 71, 208; as a cotton port, 166–67, 168, 178–79, 187

Galveston Island, 28

Galveston *Tri-Weekly News,* 28

Galveston *Weekly News,* 28

Gaston, N.C., 101

gauge, railroad, 37, 38, 39. *See also* railroads

Genovese, Eugene, 23

Georgia, 36, 47, 64, 68, 100–101, 172; cotton, 168, 169, 190; grain production, *15, 16;* livestock, *19, 20, 21;* meat supplies, 24–25, 67, 103; railroad connections, 37–38, 63, 75, 80–82, 102, 169, 208; wheat production, 43

Mitchell, Wesley C., *151*

Mobile, Ala., 11, *12,* 17, 24, 56, 92, 185, 194; and blockade-running activity, *171;* as a cattle port, *32,* 69, 71; as a cotton port, 160, 163, 164–66, 167, 168, 169, 170–72, 181, 183, 187–88, 207; meat supplies, 26, 48, 68; railroad connections, 27–28, 37, 38, 73–74

Mobile & Ohio Railroad, 168. *See also* railroads

Mobile Bay, 27, 73, 169

Mobile *Daily Register, 32*

molasses, 12, 17, 56, *58,* 59, 60, 93

Moneyhon, Carl H., 167

Monroe, La., 37, 73

Montgomery, Ala., 40, 41, 62; railroad connections, 28, 37–38, 73–74, 75

Montgomery and West Point Railroad, 75. *See also* railroads

Moore, Thomas, 59

Monitor, the, 35

morale, Southern, 2, 96, 97, 104, 182–84, 185–86, 194, 197. *See also* civilian discontent, Southern; unionism

Morrill Tariff, 119–20, 124, 133, 137, 226. *See also* Great Britain, cotton textiles industry

Morrison, Frank B., 213

mules, *14,* 17, 39–40, 48, 49. *See also* asses; horses

Mulhall, Michael G., 137

munitions, 33, 42. *See also* arms, small; ordnance

musical instruments, 12. *See also* luxury items, imported

nails, 94

Nashashibi, Karim, 144

Nashville, Tenn., 24

Nashville, the, 106

Nassau, Bahamas, 172, 180

Natchitoches, La., 27

Navy, Confederate, 34, 36, 37, 78, 88–90, 162, 185

Navy, Union, 34–35, 36, 70, 72, 114, 153, 185, 190, 206–8. *See also* blockade, Union Navy's

Neches River, 27

New Granada, West Indies, 145–46

New Iberia, La., 27, 73, 74

New Orleans, Jackson & Great Northern Railroad, 164. *See also* railroads

New Orleans, La., 15–*16, 29, 30,* 49, *58,* 59, 182, 185; capture of, 60, 70, 73, 89, 109, 160, 170, 183, 186–88, 194; as a cotton port, 155, 157, 158, 163–67, 171, 181, 183, 184, 190, 197, 199; and the interbelligerent trade, 192, 204; meat supplies, *22,* 26–27, 28–29, 48, 69–70; prices in, 57, 217; shipbuilding facilities at, 36–37, 84, 89; shortages in, 55–57, 68; value as export port, 11, 12, 17, 60, 164, 169–70

New Orleans and Texas Railroad, 74

New Orleans *Daily Crescent,* 55, 56, *57,* 59

New Orleans-Mobile Mail Company, 69

New Orleans *Picayune, 30,* 69

New Orleans *Price Current, 16, 22, 26, 29, 30, 57, 58, 156–57,* 183

New York, N.Y., 11, 12, 13, 43, 44–45, 47, 66, 71, 92; as a cotton port, 154, *156,* 178, 191; cotton prices, 3, 7, *149,* 150–*51,* 155, 158–60, 163, 177, 196, 217, 229, 232; meat supplies, 23, 24

New York Chamber of Commerce *Annual Reports,* 23

New York *Price Current,* 43, *45,* 57, 58, 69, 157

New York *Shipping and Commercial List,* 43

niter, 1, 87, 97

Niter Corps, 87

Norfolk, Va., *12,* 26, 43, 44, *45,* 46, 92, 106, 200, 207; capture of, 187, 188, 192–93; as a cotton port, 163, 169, 170, 173–74, 173–75, 181, 199, 204–5; and the interbelligerent trade, 100, 173–75, 192–93, 204; railroad connections, 101; ship-building facilities at, 36

North Carolina, 43, 44, *45,* 46, 47, 100, 103, 179–80; and blockade-running activity, *171;* cotton, 96, 164–*65;* grain production, *15, 16;* and the interbelligerent trade, 193; live-stock, *19, 20, 21;* meat supplies, *25,* 103; railroads, 73; shortages in, 75, 93, 163–64; troops in, 103, 179–80; wheat production, 43, 103

North Carolina Railroad, 101. *See also* railroads

Northrop, Lucius B. (Commissary General), 61–62, 63, 64, 65, 68, 70, 212

oats, *14, 15,* 48–49. *See also* agriculture, Southern; corn; grain; hay; wheat

O'Conner, Thomas H., 203

Official Records, 194

Ogeechee River, 169

Ohio, 14–15, *16*

Oklahoma Territory, 27

Opelousas Railroad, 69. *See also* railroads

Orange, Tex., 27, 38, 73, 74

Orange & Alexandria Railroad, 102. *See also* railroads

ordnance, 33, 36, 72, 78, 85, 86, 101. *See also* arms, small

Ordnance Department, 76

Owsley, Frank L., 1, 2, 120, 154, *156–57,* 160, 199

oxen, *14,* 17, 48. *See also* asses; horses; mules

paper, 96

peanuts, 94

Pearson, F. A., *158*

peas, 94

Pennsylvania, 105

Petersburg, Va., 37, 38, 49, 100–102; Lee's army in, 104, 105, 193

Petersburg Railroad, 101. *See also* railroads

Phelan, James, 184

Philadelphia, Pa., 11, 23, 24, 43–44, 47, 92

Philadelphia Board of Trade's *Twenty-Ninth Annual Report,* 23

Philadelphia Board of Trade's *Twenty-Seventh Annual Report,* 44, 47

Philadelphia Board of Trade's *Twenty-Sixth Annual Report,* 44, 47

Phillips, Ulrich B., 118

Piedmont Railroad, 73, 101. *See also* railroads

political discord, 183–84. *See also* Confederate government; unionism

Polk, Leonidas, Gen., 194

Pope, John, Gen., 105

porcelain, 12. *See also* luxury items, imported

pork. *See* meat

pork supplies, 18–21, *22,* 23, 25–26, 61–63, 65, 66–67, 102–3, 211–13. *See also* beef supplies; meat; swine

Port Hudson, La., 60, 200

Port Lavaca, Tex., 28, 38

porter, 12

Porter, David, Rear Adm., 201

ports, Northern. *See* individual names

ports, Southern. *See* individual names

potatoes, *14, 15*

Powell, Lawrence N., 194

Prest, A. R., 125

Price, Marcus W., 3, *4,* 5, *171*–72, 173

price-setting power, the Confederate
government's, 7–8, 109, 111–14,
115, 117, 118, 154, 161, 185–86, 198.
See also cotton

prices: cotton, 3, 7–8, 112–13, 115–17,
118, 123–24, 126–27, *128–29,*
130–*31,* 136, 141, 146, 155, 159, 177,
182, 187–89, 190–91, 220–24,
229–32; cotton textiles, 133–35, 137,
144–45; food, 56–57, 104; meat, 23,
64–67, 69–70, 71, 94; "relative,"
94–95

prisoners of war, 86, 98, 105. *See also*
labor

Providence, R.I., 46, 47

railroad cars, production of, 76, 77

railroad gauge, 37–38

railroads, 1, 6, *16,* 28, 53; civilian rates,
81; construction of, in the South,
27, 73–75, 79–80, 101, 116; and cotton shipping, 163–66; deterioration
of Southern, 76–77, 80, 82, 101–2,
179; and dividends paid, 82–83;
freight rates, 80–82; gaps in Southern, 37–38, 39, 73–75; inadequacies
of Southern, 2, 37–39, 40–41,
49–50, 63–64, 67, 72, 83–84, 88, 99,
100–101, 104, 105–6, 181, 187, 208;
lack of, in the South, 14, 16, 38; legislation, 73–74, 79, 80; and livestock

shipping, 31–32, 64, 68; in the
North, 14–15; overreliance upon,
207; and rail shortages, 76–78;
shortage of building materials for,
75–80; single-tracked, 39

railway system, Confederate. *See* railroads

Raleigh, N.C., 101

Ramsdell, Charles W., 72, 99, 102

Randolph, George, 56, 74, 193

Rasmussen, Wayne D., 18, *20, 21,* 213

rations: animal, 48–49; troop, 65, 105

Red River, 27, 31, 57, 60, 166, 167, 201

Reed, S. G., 166–67

*Report of the Commisioner of Agricul-
ture,* 27

*Report of the Secretary of the Treasury
for the year ending June 30, 1860,* 77

*Report of the Secretary of the Treasury
on the Commerce and Navigation of
the United States,* 44

revenues: Federal tax, from cotton,
187–90, 191, 195, 197, 201, 202, 204;
Southern, from cotton, 7–8,
111–12, 113–14, 115, 116, 117,
152–53, 154, 155–56, 158–59,
160–62, 207, 215–17

Rhodes, James Ford, 204

rice, *45,* 94

Richmond, Fredericksburg & Potomac
Railroad, 79. *See also* railroads

Richmond, Va., 11, *12,* 25, 26, 43–44,
45, 56, 84, 92, 96; armories at, 85;
flour, 46; during Grant's siege, 66;
Lee's army in, 42, 73, 100, 104–5,
192–93, 207; meat supplies, 48, 49,
68–69; population, 83, 106; prices,
57, 66, 182; railroad connections,
37, 38, 67, 101–2, 179; rolling mills,
88; supply shortages, 68–69, 93, 98,

Slidell, John, 92

Smith, H., 115

Smith, Kirby, Gen., 177

smuggling, 3, *4,* 5, 95, 97, 154, 155, *157,* 158–59, *171–72,* 202. *See also* blockade, Union Navy's

South Carolina, 24, 47; and blockade-running activity, *171;* cotton, 169; grain production, *15, 16;* livestock, *19, 20, 21;* meat supplies, 18, *25,* 64; railroads, 63; shortages in, 75, 100; troops in, 103; wheat production, 43

South Carolina Railroad, 24, 75, 169. *See also* railroads

South Side Railroad, 102. *See also* railroads

Southern Historical Society Papers, 67

spades, 33–*34. See also* implements, agricultural

Spartanburg and Union Railroad, 75. *See also* railroads

Springfield Armory, 85

St. Marks, Fla., 208

St. Petersburg, Fla., 31

Stanton, Edwin, 175–76, 197

Statistical Abstract for the United Kingdom (1867), *140, 143, 144, 145, 156,* 178

steam engines, 33–*34,* 36–37. *See also* machinery; manufacturing, Southern

steamboats. *See* steamers, river

steamers, coastal, 5, 69, 106. *See also* shipping

steamers, river, 39, *58,* 59. *See also* shipping

steel, 12, 76

Stillman, Charles, 178

stone wares, 12

sugar, 17, 56, *58,* 59, 60, 93, 94, 96, 206

swine, 13, *14,* 18–19, 23, *29,* 53, 62, 103, 211–13. *See also* beef supplies; meat; pork supplies

Talladega, Ala., 75

Tampa, Fla., 32

Tampa Bay, 33

taxes. *See* export duties, cotton

Taylor, Richard, Gen., 184

Taylor, Robert A., 64

tea, 12, 96. *See also* coffee

technology, naval, 35

Tennessee, 17, 18, 23, 24, 26, 47, 69, 70, 119; capture of, 102; corn production, 44; cotton, 164; grain production, 14, *15, 16;* horses, 40; livestock, *19, 20, 21;* manufacturing in, 36–37, 40; meat supplies, *25,* 61–63, 65, 67, 100; occupation of, 56, 200; railroads in, 181; shortages in, 75; troops in, 60, 72, 98, 172, 180; Unionists in, 176; wheat production, 43

Tennessee River, 38

Tensas, Ala., 28, 73, 169

Tenth Census, 68

Texas, 11, *12,* 17, 18, 24, 25, 38, 57, 60; blockade of, 176–79; and blockade-running activity, *171;* cattle, 1, 26–28, *29*–31, 32–33, 48, 61, 65, 67, 68, 69, 70–71, 73, 100, 208, 211–13; cotton, 160, 163, 164–65, *165,* 166–67, 167, 171, 176–78, 181; grain production, *15, 16;* horses, 40; livestock, *19, 20, 21;* trade, 40; trade with North in, 162; Unionists in, 177, 183

textiles, cotton, 12; demand for, 121–25, *132,* 134–38, 225–27, *228,* 230, 233;